3. Understanding users, groups, and
4. `suid`

G. Unix system administration

    1. `/etc/skel/...` and home director...

    2. Daemons

    3. Cron

    4. Superuser

    5. Syslogd and logging

    6. Backup and restore tasks

    7. Control of network services and daemons

    8. System crontab

    9. Using and managing the system log files

    10. Basic system backup and restore operations

H. Basic TCP/IP Networking

    1. IP numbers and classes

    2. The network address, broadcast address, and subnet mask

    3. Tools and commands

        a) `ping`

        b) `ifconfig`

        c) `netstat`

        d) Name resolution configuration

            (1) `/etc/hosts`

            (2) `/etc/resolv.conf`

            (3) `/etc/host.conf`

            (4) `/etc/nsswitch.conf`

        e) Familiarity with Standard Networking Services

            (1) NFS and remote file systems

            (2) Sendmail

            (3) POP, IMAP

            (4) FTP

            (5) DNS

            (6) DHCP

            (7) SMB

            (8) httpd

            (9) YP, NIS

            (10) `inetd`

        f) Basic network security

RHCE:
Red Hat Certified Engineer
Exam Notes

RHCE:
Red Hat Certified Engineer

Exam Notes™

Bill McCarty

San Francisco • Paris • Düsseldorf • Soest • London

SYBEX®

Associate Publisher: Richard J. Staron
Contracts and Licensing Manager: Kristine O'Callaghan
Acquisitions and Developmental Editor: Ellen Dendy
Editor: Donna Crossman
Production Editor: Mae Lum
Technical Editor: Util_Man
Graphic Illustrator: Tony Jonick
Electronic Publishing Specialist: Judy Fung
Proofreader: Mae Lum
Indexer: Nancy Guenther
Book Designer: Bill Gibson
Cover Designer: Archer Design
Cover Illustrator/Photographer: Tony Stone

Library of Congress Card Number: 00-109118
ISBN: 0-7821-2812-2

*This book is dedicated to the faculty and staff of
the School of Business and Management of
Azusa Pacific University, the most effective—
and fun—team of colleagues I've had or could
ever hope to have. God bless you all!*

Acknowledgments

Having written more than 10 books, I've worked with more editors than I can recall. So, I believe that it means something significant when I say that Sybex's editors are tops. My heartfelt thanks go to Ellen Dendy, Mae Lum, Donna Crossman, and the other members of the Sybex crew.

My agent, Margot Maley-Hutchison of Waterside Productions Inc., introduced me to Sybex. Thanks, Margot, for the good match!

Thanks also to Util_Man, who reviewed the manuscript for technical accuracy. He found many errors and suggested many improvements. Whatever errors remain are attributable to me.

My family—Jennifer, Patrick, and Sara—paid the bills, made dinner, and washed the car while I worked on this book. Consequently, the book is as much their accomplishment as mine: I couldn't—and wouldn't—have completed it without them. Thanks, guys!

My special thanks go to Jesus Christ, the God-man who gave His life that we might break free of the bondage of sin and live abundantly now and forever.

Sybex would like to thank electronic publishing specialist Judy Fung and indexer Nancy Guenther for their valuable contributions to this book.

Contents

Introduction

Like many in the Linux community, you've probably heard of the Red Hat Certified Engineer (RHCE) program and the related RHCE exam, both of which were created by Red Hat. You may have heard that the RHCE exam is challenging, or you may have heard that it is not. You may have heard that the exam is focused on Red Hat Linux and that knowledge of Unix or a Linux distribution other than Red Hat Linux will not help you to pass the exam. I wrote this book to answer these and similar questions and to provide brief but comprehensive material designed to prepare you to pass the RHCE exam.

Is This Book for You?

If you want to learn how to administer a Red Hat Linux system, this is the book for you. In it, you'll find brief, yet clear, explanations of the concepts you need to understand and procedures you need to be able to perform. This book is a succinct, portable exam review guide that you can use either in conjunction with a more complete study program (study guide, CBT courseware, classroom environment) or—if you don't feel the need for more extensive test preparation—as an exam refresher or preview. This book doesn't "give away the answers," but instead identifies the topics on which you can expect to be tested and provides adequate but not in-depth discussions of those topics. If you need a book that is a handy reference guide that provides succinct, quick-hitting, easily memorized coverage of the information you need to know, this book is for you.

If you plan to take the RHCE exam, you will find this book to be even more valuable, because it focuses on the topics identified by Red Hat as central to the RHCE exam. It contains many practice questions that help you prepare for, and assess your readiness to take, the RHCE exam. However, the RHCE exam and this book are not for everyone. The RHCE exam is mostly a hands-on exam that attempts to assess your system administration skills. This book will help you learn and refine these skills, but unless you've had some experience with Unix or Linux, you probably won't make much sense of this book or the RHCE exam. To succeed, you don't need to be a Unix or Linux expert—although it certainly won't hurt if you are—but you should be at least a Unix or Linux power user, who has some experience in system installation and administration. If you've installed Linux on several systems and spent some time figuring out some system administration commands such as mount and umount, you can expect to understand the material in this book.

The RHCE Exam

The RHCE exam tests your conceptual understanding of, and skill in performing, Red Hat Linux system administration tasks. The exam takes about seven hours, including a one-hour break for lunch. The exam is challenging: Currently, about one of every three examinees fails the exam. However, proper preparation for the exam can significantly increase your likelihood of success.

Red Hat offers the RHCE exam about once a month at its Durham, North Carolina, headquarters and less frequently at its Santa Clara, California, facility. At the time of writing, Red Hat has just announced that it will soon offer the RHCE exam in Europe and East Asia. The RHCE exam is also offered in several additional cities by Red Hat's training partners, including Global Knowledge and IBM Global Services.

You can take just the RHCE exam, or you can take a special four-day RHCE exam preparation course, the price of which includes the exam, which is taken the following day. The Red Hat course numbers and the cost at the time of writing are as follows:

RHCE exam only   RH302 ($749)

RHCE exam and preparation course   RH300 ($2,498)

To register for an RHCE exam or RHCE exam preparation course to be offered by Red Hat at a U.S. location, contact Red Hat at 800-454-5502 ext. 241 or e-mail training@redhat.com.

Getting More Information

Check the following Web sites for up-to-the-minute details and additional registration information:

Red Hat www.redhat.com/training

Global Knowledge www.globalknowledge.com

IBM Global Services www.ibm.com/services/learning/spotlight/linux.html

Exam Tips

The RHCE exam has three parts:

- the multiple-choice exam (1 hour)
- the Server Install and Network Services Setup exam (2½ hours)
- the Debug exam (2½ hours)

Each of the three parts of the RHCE exam is scored on a 100-point scale. To pass the exam, you must score a total of 240 points, an average of 80 points on each part of the exam. Moreover, you must score at least 50 points on each part of the exam.

The multiple-choice exam resembles exams you had in high school or college. You have one hour to answer 40–50 technical questions. Some of the questions may require a true/false response; others may require you to identify which responses in a set are correct or to choose the best response from among a set of responses.

The remaining two parts of the exam are performance-based, requiring you to install, configure, or troubleshoot an actual system. If you've never taken a performance exam, you may be anxious. However, your anxiety is unwarranted. Unlike a written exam, a performance exam includes no trick questions. You'll be asked to perform the same sort of system administration tasks that system administrators perform on the job. If you have the requisite experience and expertise, you can master the performance exam.

Red Hat states that many examinees score well on the multiple-choice exam but do poorly on the performance-based exams, thereby failing the test. This leads some to believe that the performance-based exams are more difficult than the multiple-choice exam. This may be so. But, it's possible that the unfamiliar format of performance-based exams and apprehension arising from a significant failure rate hamper student performance. By learning more about the RHCE exam and its performance-based exams in particular, you can minimize test anxiety and increase your likelihood of passing the exam.

WARNING   Because the RHCE exam includes performance-based units, it's important that your exam preparation includes practice in installing, configuring, administering, and troubleshooting Red Hat Linux. You'd likely find the exercises in my book *RHCE: Red Hat Certified Engineer Study Guide* (Sybex, 2000) helpful in this regard. However, you can use this book with or without the *RHCE Study Guide*, according to your preference.

Exam Protocol

The RHCE exam requires about seven hours. The three parts of the exam require a total of six hours. Another hour is allocated as a lunch break.

You should plan to arrive early. Bring at least two forms of identification, including a photo ID. Otherwise, bring a minimum of belongings: During the exam, you're not allowed to use materials other than those provided by the exam proctor. You can expect to receive such items as these:

- pen or pencil
- blank paper
- non-disclosure agreement

Immediately prior to the relevant part of the exam, you can expect to receive such items as these:

- task assignments for the performance-based exams
- rescue disk for the Debug exam
- installation media for the Server Install and Network Services Setup exam

You must sign the non-disclosure agreement, in which you agree not to divulge information about the RHCE exam; if you don't, you will not be permitted to take the exam.

TIP The non-disclosure agreement is intended to safeguard the integrity of the examination process. Because the value of RHCE certification rests on accurately assessing the knowledge and skills of examinees, it is in your interest, as well as that of Red Hat, to comply with the terms of the non-disclosure agreement.

The examination room will be equipped with PCs. The proctor will assign you to a PC, which you will use to take the exam.

The exams are timed; as the proctor will announce, you are not to open materials or begin the exam until the proctor instructs you to do so.

The three parts of the exam will be given in an order chosen by the proctor. For example, the proctor might choose the following schedule:

10:00AM–12:30PM: Server Install and Network Services Setup exam

12:30–1:30PM: Lunch

1:30–2:30PM: Multiple-choice exam

2:30–5:00PM: Debug exam

Do not communicate—or attempt to communicate—with another examinee during the exam. If you breach this, or other protocols explained by the exam proctor, you will immediately fail the exam.

The Multiple-Choice Exam

The multiple-choice exam tests your knowledge of Red Hat Linux, Linux, and Unix. Items address topics such as Linux commands, command redirection, and system administration. You cannot consult computer-based documentation or other resources, such as notes or books, during the exam.

You're allowed a maximum of one hour to complete this exam, which consists of about 50 items. An item may require you to respond by

- classifying the item as true or false

- identifying correct responses among a set of responses

- identifying the best response from among a set of responses

Be sure you clearly understand the sort of response appropriate for each item.

TIP   In taking the exam, you'll probably notice items that were not addressed in this book or in the RH300 course, if you took it. Bear in mind that the purpose of the exam is to certify readiness to function as a Red Hat Linux system administrator. Red Hat's description of the exam is intentionally general and vague, in order to avoid certifying as RHCEs persons who are knowledgeable of the exam but not knowledgeable of system administration. Contrary to statements by a few, the exam is not littered with trick questions. Rather, it is a good faith effort by Red Hat to identify and certify examinees who possess Red Hat Linux system administration skills. If you have the proper experience and have prepared diligently, you should expect to pass the exam.

Here are some hints that can improve your score on the multiple-choice exam:

- Review any information you find difficult before taking the test. When you're allowed to begin, immediately write as much of the information as you can recall on the blank paper provided by the proctor. Then, you can refer to your notes during the exam.

TIP In order to avoid a mistaken accusation of cheating, you should put the proctor on notice that you intend to use the blank paper in this fashion. Make sure it's clear that you haven't smuggled a crib sheet into the exam room.

- Be sure to read each question carefully; you may find it worthwhile to read each question twice.

- Be sure to read each response. Don't mark the first response that seems correct, because another response may be better. This is perhaps the most important exam hint of all.

- Read the responses carefully. Little words such as *not* are easily overlooked but significantly change the meaning of a response.

- Quickly eliminate any responses that are obviously incorrect and focus on the remaining responses, seeking the best response.

- If you can't confidently identify the best response, make a note of the question number and move on. Don't waste too much time pondering a single question until you've answered the straightforward questions.

- After completing the straightforward questions, return to those you noted as problems. With luck, some other question has jogged your memory and questions that initially seemed difficult are now clear. If, however, you're still unable to eliminate all the distractor responses, make your best guess.

The Server Install and Network Services Setup Exam

The 2½-hour Server Install and Network Services Setup exam requires you to install and configure a Red Hat Linux system that satisfies a provided set of requirements. Many of the exercises in this book resemble requirements you may find on the Server Install and Network Services Setup exam. For example, you can expect to be asked to do the following:

- install Red Hat Linux

- compile and install a kernel that is configured to support specified options

- set up user accounts

- install and configure network services, such as Apache, NFS, and Samba

- configure the user environment

- establish security measures that restrict access to files or services

The proctor will use an automated script to verify your work, so completeness and accuracy are important to scoring well. You shouldn't expect curveballs or odd requirements on the Server Install and Network Services Setup exam. Your score will depend largely on your use of time and careful checking of your work.

If you plan your work well, you can anticipate a surplus of time. Before starting work, spend a few minutes carefully reading the requirements. Then decide the following:

- which requirements you expect will be easy to satisfy and which requirements you expect will be hard to satisfy

- the sequence in which you'll complete the requirements

Chances are, you'll find some requirements that must be completed before you begin work on others. For example, you must establish user accounts before you can give users specified file-access privileges.

You may find that some requirements involve tasks that take significant time, such as compiling a kernel; you may be able to work toward completing other requirements while these are ongoing.

TIP While reading the requirements, you may find it useful to jot down reminders that keep you on track when implementing the requirements.

Once you begin work, don't get bogged down attempting to meet a difficult requirement unless completing it is prerequisite to meeting other requirements. Instead, make a note of the problem and move on to satisfy the remaining requirements. Later, time permitting, you can return to the problem requirement, resolve the problem, and complete the requirement.

TIP You'll be allowed free access to man (manual) pages and other online documents during the Server Install and Network Services Setup exam, so be sure to install any documentation packages that you expect you may find useful.

Check off requirements as you complete them so that you don't inadvertently fail to complete a requirement. When you've satisfied all the requirements, spend the remainder of the allotted time checking and rechecking your work. Don't cease work until you're confident that you've correctly completed each requirement.

The Debug Exam

Like the Server Install and Network Services Setup exam, the Debug exam is a 2½-hour performance-based exam. You're given a series of 2–4 exercises that cannot be completed unless you first identify and resolve one or more system configuration problems. For example, you may be asked to configure the system to boot to runlevel 5, but the system may not boot at all or the /usr file system may not mount.

When you complete an exercise, the exam proctor will verify your work and provide you with the next exercise. You're required to keep a log of the steps you took in solving the exercise and should be prepared to explain your procedure in case it's unclear that you've properly completed the exercise.

You're allowed to consult documentation installed on the system but, as on other parts of the exam, you cannot refer to books or notes. And you won't be allowed to fix problems by reinstalling packages. For some exercises, you'll be provided with a system rescue disk.

The Debug exam is potentially the most stressful of the three exams, because you can't map out your procedure in advance. Instead, you must follow a problem-solving process that distinguishes symptoms and problems:

- Identify the symptoms.

- Discover the problem or problems causing the symptoms.

- Fix the problem or problems.

- Perform any requested configuration changes.

Here is a general procedure that you can tailor to fit the demands of specific exercises, especially those that involve boot-related problems:

1. Boot the system. If the system will not boot normally, you may have to boot it either in single-user mode or by using a rescue disk.

2. Mount the required file systems. You may need to inspect /etc/fstab or use fdisk to check the partition table in order to identify the partitions and file systems. You may need to run fsck to check or repair file systems.

3. Perform repairs and make configuration changes as needed.

4. Prepare the system for rebooting. You may need to reinstall the lilo boot map or unmount file systems before rebooting. Under some circumstances, you may need to use the sync command to flush output buffers to disk.

5. Reboot the system and check your work.

It's especially important to remain calm during this exam. With the permission of the proctor, use hard candy or other relaxation aids. If the system doesn't perform as you expect, consider the resources available to you and use your imagination to devise a way of working around the problem.

How Is This Book Organized?

This book is organized according to the official study points for the RHCE exam published by Red Hat. Within each chapter, the study points are covered in turn. Each study point section is further divided according to the nature of the material it presents.

You can also find additional RHCE preparation information and help on the Sybex Web site, www.sybex.com. For instance, the site includes a review of basic information of the sort you should know before beginning your preparation for the RHCE exam. You may find it helpful to peruse this material before beginning your study of this book.

Critical Information

This section presents the conceptual information pertaining to one or more RHCE study points. This is the place to start unless you're quite familiar with the study point topic.

Necessary Procedures

Here you'll find step-by-step procedures that you should be able to perform before sitting for the RHCE exam. Not every study point has associated procedures. For such study points, the Necessary Procedures section has been omitted.

Exam Essentials

Here you'll find a quick summary of the facts, concepts, and skills you should possess in order to perform well on the RHCE exam. This section can help you identify areas that require additional study.

Key Terms and Concepts

This section presents a handy glossary of terms and concepts related to the study points. You should thoroughly understand these terms and concepts before sitting for the RHCE exam.

Sample Questions

Sample questions resemble the questions you're likely to find on the multiple-choice portion of the RHCE exam. The questions include answers and explanations that give you some insight into the test-taking process.

How to Contact the Author

Bill McCarty can be reached at bmccarty@apu.edu.

How to Contact the Publisher

Sybex welcomes reader feedback on all of their titles. Visit the Sybex Web site at www.sybex.com for book updates and additional certification information. You'll also find online forms to submit comments or suggestions regarding this or any other Sybex book.

Chapter

1

Installation

RHCE PREPARATION TOPICS COVERED IN THIS CHAPTER:

▶ **Preparing for Installation** *(pages 2 – 8)*

- Determine System Needs
- Know What Information May Be Required during Installation
- Know How to Select and Prepare Installation Media

▶ **Working with Partitions** *(pages 9 – 12)*

- Know How to Design a Partition Structure
- Know How to Use Fips to Split an MS-DOS Partition

▶ **Performing the Installation** *(pages 13 – 26)*

- Know How to Select the Installation User Interface
- Know How to Select the Installation Class and Type
- Know How to Select Components and Packages

▶ **Configuring Options after Installation** *(pages 26 – 34)*

This chapter summarizes what you need to know to be able to install and initially configure Red Hat Linux. One of the two performance-based parts of the RHCE exam requires you to install and configure Red Hat Linux to satisfy a list of requirements, so you'll find this chapter important in preparing for that part of the exam. This chapter is also a handy reference whenever you're planning or performing a Red Hat Linux installation.

Preparing for Installation

- **Determine System Needs**
- **Know What Information May Be Required during Installation**
- **Know How to Select and Prepare Installation Media**

Preparation is important to effective and efficient execution, no less in system administration than in other endeavors. This section describes the tasks you should perform and the decisions you should make before installing Red Hat Linux. If you follow the instructions given here, you can expect the installation of Red Hat Linux to go smoothly, with only an occasional exception.

Critical Information

The first step in installation planning is to determine the needs that the system must satisfy. For example, a worker who will use the system as a workstation for preparing graphics will have a different set of needs than a system administrator who plans to use the system primarily as an FTP server. Once you know what the system must do, you're ready to decide what hardware is needed and how Red Hat Linux should be installed and configured.

Gathering Information

Installation will go more smoothly if you've collected information about the hardware on the target system. If you have the flexibility to choose the hardware, choose hardware listed in the Red Hat Hardware Compatibility List (HCL) over other hardware. Be wary of devices, such as CD-ROM drives, that have proprietary interfaces. Also be wary of WinModems and WinPrinters.

Before beginning the installation, have the following information handy:

- CPU: type and speed.

- Motherboard: bus type (ISA, EISA, VESA, PCI, MCA, and so on).

- Drive controllers: the type of interface and the chipset used.

- Drives: the make and model of each drive and its drive number or SCSI ID on the controller.

- System RAM: size.

- Network adapters: the make and model. For non-PCI cards, know the IRQ, DMA, and I/O ports used.

- Modems: the IRQ, DMA, and I/O ports used by an internal modem or the number of the serial port to which an external modem is connected.

- Sound cards: the IRQs, DMAs, and I/O ports used.

- Serial and parallel ports: the IRQs and I/O ports used.

- Mouse: type (serial, PS2, or bus) and number of buttons. For a serial mouse, know the number of the serial port to which it's connected.

- Video card: make, model, chipset, amount of RAM, and color depths supported.

- Monitor: make, model, horizontal sync range, and vertical sync range.

You should have similar information for any other hardware devices installed in the system.

If your system will be attached to a network, you should also have the following information available:

- Method of IP address assignment: static, DHCP, BOOTP

For statically defined hosts, you should have the following information available:

- IP address

- Network IP address or network mask

- Gateway IP address

- Fully qualified domain name (FQDN)

In some circumstances, additional information will be needed. But, generally, this information will be enough to let you complete the installation procedure. Once the installation procedure is complete, you can configure special options as needed.

In addition to information on the hardware of the target system, you should have available *The Red Hat Linux Installation Guide* and other Linux documentation, particularly the HOWTOs. If necessary, you can use another Linux system or a Microsoft Windows system to read documentation stored on the installation CD-ROM or to access Web sites and newsgroups providing pertinent information. Having this information available will help you complete the installation procedure; otherwise, you may find it necessary to terminate the installation procedure, obtain the needed information, and then restart the installation.

Selecting and Preparing Boot Media

In order to install Red Hat Linux, you must boot the target system using a special Linux kernel. You can boot the system from the installation CD-ROM or from a floppy disk you create from files on the CD-ROM. You can also boot the system from MS-DOS.

Booting from CD-ROM

Most recently manufactured PCs can boot from a CD-ROM that contains appropriate boot information, such as that contained on the Red Hat Linux installation CD-ROM. To boot from a CD-ROM, the system BIOS must specify that the system will attempt to boot from the CD-ROM before attempting to boot from a hard-disk drive or a floppy-disk drive. Generally, this BIOS setting is labeled Boot Sequence or something similar.

Booting from MS-DOS

If the system is set up to boot DOS, you may be able to boot by using the files on the CD-ROM, even if the system cannot boot from its CD-ROM. The file `dosutils/autoboot.bat` invokes the Linux Loadlin program, which uses DOS-system calls to boot a Linux kernel residing on a hard disk or CD-ROM drive.

To use `autoboot.bat`, boot the system into DOS, not Microsoft Windows. If the system runs Microsoft Windows, restart the system in MS-DOS mode by using the Shut Down dialog box. When the system enters DOS, move to the drive associated with the CD-ROM. Then, launch the boot sequence by issuing the command

```
dosutils/autoboot.bat
```

The system should load and execute the Linux kernel.

Booting from a Floppy Disk

If you can't boot the system from a CD-ROM, and the system isn't set up to boot DOS, you must prepare a boot floppy disk from which to boot the system. This is most easily done using a Linux system to copy the image file on the CD-ROM to a floppy disk. An image file contains an exact replica of a floppy disk. By copying the image file to a disk, you create a duplicate of the disk that was used to make the image file.

Mount the Red Hat Linux installation CD-ROM by issuing the command

```
mount -t iso9660 /dev/cdrom /mnt/cdrom -o ro
```

Place a formatted floppy disk in the floppy drive and issue the command

```
dd if=/mnt/cdrom/images/boot.img of=/dev/fd0H1440
↳obs=18k
```

It may take a minute or so to write the image to the floppy disk. When activity ceases, remove the disk, which can now be used to boot the target system.

NOTE   If you plan to install Linux via the network rather than from a CD-ROM, copy the image file bootnet.img, rather than boot.img.

If you need to access PCMCIA devices during installation, you'll need a second floppy disk. Use a similar command to copy the file pcmcia.img to a second floppy disk.

If you don't have handy access to a Linux system, you can make a floppy from an image file by using the DOS program Rawrite, which resides in the dosutils directory of the CD-ROM. The Rawrite program can be run from DOS or from a Microsoft Windows MS-DOS Prompt window. The program prompts for the letter of the drive containing the floppy disk (usually drive A) and for the path of the image file (usually d:\images\boot.img).

Selecting Installation Media

Most users install Red Hat Linux from an installation CD-ROM. However, if you frequently install Linux, you may prefer to set up a server that makes the installation files available via a network. You can access Red Hat Linux installation files

- via FTP
- via NFS
- via HTTP
- on a local hard drive

TIP   Red Hat Linux does not currently support installation via files shared by a Samba server.

Exam Essentials

Be thoroughly familiar with, and capable of, Red Hat installation, particularly network installations   This section explained installation planning, ways of booting the installation procedure, and the preparation of installation media. You should be familiar with these topics.

Understand different approaches to multiple-boot installations and be familiar with installation-related tools (such as Rawrite) sometimes used during multiple-boot installations   This section explained the use of Rawrite and the dd command to prepare installation media. You should be able to prepare installation media using either method.

Key Terms and Concepts

Image file   A file that can be used to create a floppy disk that's used to boot a system or as a device driver.

Loadlin   A program that can be used to boot Linux from MS-DOS.

Rawrite   A program that can create a floppy disk from an image file.

Sample Questions

1. What is the name of the MS-DOS batch file that can be used to boot Red Hat Linux?

A. dosutils/autoboot.bat

B. dosutils/boot.bat

C. dosutils/linux.bat

D. dosutils/loadlin.bat

Answer: A. You can boot Linux from MS-DOS by invoking the batch file dosutils/autoboot.bat on the Red Hat Linux installation CD-ROM.

2. Which of the following should you know if you're installing Red Hat Linux on a PC that has a static network configuration (choose all that apply)?

A. Fully qualified domain name

B. Gateway IP address

C. IP address

D. Network IP address

Answer: A, B, C, D. All this information is needed if the host has a static network configuration. Little information is needed if the host uses DHCP or BOOTP to obtain its network configuration.

Working with Partitions

- **Know How to Design a Partition Structure**
- **Know How to Use Fips to Split an MS-DOS Partition**

When installing Red Hat Linux, if you select the workstation or Server installation class, the installation procedure partitions your hard-disk drive automatically. However, if you select the Custom installation class, you must partition the hard disk. This section summarizes what you need to know about partitions and the related procedures you should be able to perform.

Critical Information

Partitions improve system data integrity and can improve system data security. If a hard disk suffers damage, the damage is often confined to a single partition. Recovery of a single partition may be simpler and quicker than recovery of an entire drive. It's also possible to mount partitions as read-only. By organizing data that need not be changed into a partition and mounting the partition as read-only, data integrity and security can be improved. A partition that cannot be written is less vulnerable to corruption than one mounted for reading and writing. And, it's more difficult for a hacker to surreptitiously modify data on a read-only partition than on a read-write partition.

In designing a partition structure, the following directories should be kept in a single partition:

- /
- /etc
- /lib
- /bin
- /sbin
- /dev

These directories—and their subdirectories—contain programs and files essential to proper system operation. They should always be present and, therefore, should be part of the so-called root partition, mounted as /.

The non-Custom installation classes create a 16MB boot partition, mounted as /boot. Generally, your design should include such a partition. By locating a boot partition within the 1024-cylinder region addressable by the system's BIOS, you ensure that the kernel will be accessible at boot time.

Generally, you should include one or more swap partitions. As a rule of thumb, the swap partitions should have a total size 2–3 times that of the installed RAM. For example, a system having 16MB of RAM should have 32–48MB of swap space. No more than eight swap partitions can be defined; the total swap space cannot exceed 4GB.

Directories that are often used as mount points include

- /home
- /opt
- /tmp
- /usr
- /usr/local
- /var

Necessary Procedures

This section describes how to use Fips to split an MS-DOS partition.

Using Fips

Often, a target system has insufficient free disk space for installing Linux. If an MS-DOS (FAT or FAT32) partition contains unused space, you can use Fips to split the partition, creating an empty partition into which you can install Linux.

To use Fips, follow these steps:

1. Use Microsoft ScanDisk to check the partition for errors.

2. Use Microsoft Defrag to move the files to the low end of the partition.

3. Disable virtual memory using the System Control Panel applet.

4. Create an MS-DOS boot floppy by using the Add/Remove Programs Control Panel applet.

5. Copy the following files from the installation CD-ROM to the floppy disk:

   - `\dosutils\fips20\restorrb.exe`

   - `\dosutils\fips20\fips.exe`

   - `\dosutils\fips20\errors.txt`

6. Rename `autoxec.bat` and `config.sys` to `autoexec.fips` and `config.fips` so that no startup programs will write to the hard disk.

7. Boot from the floppy, and run Fips.

8. Let Fips create a backup of the partition table on the floppy.

9. Specify the number of the partition you want to split and the number of the cylinder on which the new partition should begin.

10. Type y to save changes, and then exit.

11. Boot MS-DOS, and run ScanDisk to make sure the disk is okay.

12. Re-enable virtual memory, and restore your `autoexec.bat` and `config.sys` files to their original names.

Exam Essentials

Understand different approaches to multiple-boot installations and be familiar with installation-related tools (Rawrite, Fips) sometimes used during multiple-boot installations   This section explained the use of Fips to split an MS-DOS partition. Be sure you know how to use Fips.

Understand disk partitioning and know how to use Red Hat's install-time partitioning tools This section explained how to design a partition structure for Red Hat Linux. Be sure you can design a partition structure.

Key Term and Concept

Root partition The Linux partition that hosts a file system that contains all essential system files, except those required to boot the system.

Sample Questions

1. How many times more swap space than RAM should a Red Hat Linux system generally have?

   A. 1–2

   B. 2–3

   C. 3–4

   D. 4–8

   Answer: B. The system should generally have an amount of swap space 2–3 times its amount of RAM.

2. What is the maximum amount of swap space a Red Hat Linux system can use?

   A. 1 GB

   B. 2 GB

   C. 4 GB

   D. 8 GB

   Answer: C. A Red Hat Linux system can have as much as 4GB of swap space.

◗ Performing the Installatio

- **Know How to Select the Installa**
- **Know How to Select the Installation c**
- **Know How to Select Components and Pac**

Red Hat Linux is designed to be easy to install. But, that does mean that you should approach installation naively. This section summarizes what you need to know to be able to install Red Hat Linux efficiently and effectively.

Critical Information

Red Hat Linux supports two installation types: Install and Upgrade. You should choose Install when installing Linux on a target system that doesn't currently host Linux. Choose Upgrade when the target system already hosts an earlier version of Red Hat Linux. The Upgrade procedure generally saves the existing configuration files rather than overwriting them. The existing files are renamed with the extension .rpmsave. Some updated packages may require replacement of the existing configuration files; in such cases, the existing configuration file is renamed with the extension .rpmorig.

Red Hat Linux 6.1 introduced a graphical mode installation procedure based on X. The initial screen of the installation procedure lets you choose the new graphical mode installation procedure or a text mode installation procedure.

Beginners generally find the graphical mode installation procedure easier to use. However, you may prefer the text mode installation for the following reasons:

- The graphical mode installation procedure may fail if the target system has unusual video characteristics, such as an old or uncommon video adapter.

- The text mode installation procedure can recover from some errors—such as running out of disk space—that cause the graphical mode installation procedure to fail.

- The text mode installation will run better and faster than the graphical mode installation on computers having a slow processor or a small amount of RAM.

- The graphical mode installation supports only media mounted as a file system, such as an existing hard-drive partition, a CD-ROM, or media made available via NFS.

The operation of the graphical mode user interface resembles that of familiar point-and-click interfaces in the following ways:

- You use the mouse to select a control, such as a button or text field, and to manipulate check boxes and radio buttons.

- If you prefer, you can use the Tab key to move from control to control.

- You use the keyboard to enter text.

The text mode user interface is not a command-line interface, but a mouse-less, low-resolution graphical user interface. It includes familiar controls such as text boxes, check boxes, scroll bars, and buttons. Since the text mode interface is mouse-less, you use it somewhat differently from more familiar graphical user interfaces. This interface works in the following ways:

- You use Tab and Alt+Tab to move from control to control.

- You press the spacebar to select or deselect check boxes.

- You use the Left, Right, Up, and Down keys to move the cursor.

- You press Enter or the spacebar to click a highlighted button.

- You press Enter to select an item from a list.

Installation Consoles and Message Logs

The installation program uses the Linux virtual consoles to display a variety of information. Virtual consoles let you associate the keyboard and monitor with any of several tasks, performing in text mode a function that's analogous to using Windows in graphical mode. Virtual consoles are handier than having several physical consoles, because they don't require extra desk space and it's easy to switch from one to the other. Table 1.1 summarizes the virtual consoles used during installation.

TABLE 1.1: Virtual Consoles Used during Installation

Console	Keystrokes	Contents
1	Ctrl+Alt+F1	Text-based installation procedure
2	Ctrl+Alt+F2	Shell prompt
3	Ctrl+Alt+F3	Messages from the installation program
4	Ctrl+Alt+F4	Kernel messages
5	Ctrl+Alt+F5	Other messages, including file system creation messages
7	Ctrl+Alt+F7	Graphical installation procedure

The indicated keystrokes let you switch to a given console. By switching to a console, you can view messages that can help you diagnose and troubleshoot installation problems. Console 2 provides a shell prompt that you can use to issue commands to resolve problems.

The Installation Process

To start the installation process, you must boot the target system using a special Red Hat Linux installation kernel. You can boot the system in any of several ways, as described earlier in this chapter. In order to boot the system, you must provide the proper boot medium (for example, a boot floppy disk).

You must also configure the target system's BIOS to boot from the boot medium. Often, the BIOS is set to boot the system from its internal hard drive and must be reconfigured to boot from a floppy or CD-ROM.

Installation Mode

When the system boots, it displays the Welcome to Red Hat Linux screen. This screen lets you select the installation mode: graphical, text, or expert. The graphical mode installation is the easiest to use. The text mode installation is more robust, but somewhat clumsier to use. The expert mode installation suppresses automatic device probes and gives you almost complete control over the installation process. Expert mode is useful primarily when automatic device probes hang a system. Otherwise, it's generally more convenient to use graphical or text mode.

Language

If you selected the graphical mode installation and the installation program detects a Red Hat Linux CD-ROM, it immediately enters graphical mode. Otherwise, the next several screens are presented in text mode even if you selected graphical mode. The Language Selection screen lets you specify the language in which the installation program displays instructions.

The selected language also becomes the default language used by the target system. Most installation options, including the language, can be changed after the installation is complete.

Keyboard

The Keyboard Configuration screen lets you select the system's keyboard type. The graphical mode screen lets you test your choice by typing characters in the text box at the bottom of the screen.

Mouse

The Mouse Configuration screen lets you specify the system's mouse type. The Port and Device options are required only for a serial mouse; do not specify them for a PS/2 or bus mouse. If the mouse has two buttons, you should generally specify the Emulate 3 Buttons option. The three-button mouse emulation lets you simultaneously press both mouse buttons of a two-button mouse to emulate the pressing of the missing middle mouse button. Use the Generic mouse type if you find no closer match.

Installation Media

If you selected an installation mode other than graphical or the installation program failed to detect a Red Hat Linux CD-ROM, the Installation Method screen appears. This screen lets you specify the installation media, which can be a CD-ROM or files on a local hard drive. You can also install Red Hat Linux via FTP, HTTP, or NFS. However, you must use a special boot floppy that supports network installation. Chapter 2, "Advanced Installation," explains network installations.

If you selected the graphical mode installation, a second welcome screen appears. This screen contains no options; it merely explains where to find documentation that explains the installation procedure and how to register Red Hat Linux.

Installation Path

Next, you're prompted to select the installation path, which defines the type—Install or Upgrade—and class—GNOME Workstation, KDE Workstation, Server, or Custom—of the installation.

WARNING   If you specify Install rather than Upgrade as the installation type, the installation program will erase all Linux partitions present on the system.

WARNING   If you specify Server as the installation class, the installation program will erase all partitions present on the system, including non-Linux partitions.

TIP   Neither the GNOME Workstation nor KDE Workstation class will overwrite existing non-Linux partitions, unless there is insufficient free disk space available.

The Red Hat Linux installation procedure provides three default installation classes, or configurations:

- GNOME Workstation
- KDE Workstation
- Server

The workstation classes are a quick way to get a Red Hat Linux system up and running. Both workstation classes install the most commonly used packages. In addition, the GNOME Workstation class installs the GNOME desktop manager and the KDE Workstation class installs the KDE desktop manager.

The workstation classes are particularly useful for building a dual-boot system, because they don't disturb non-Linux partitions as long as sufficient unallocated disk space is available. They do, however, delete all existing Linux (ext2) partitions. They establish three standard partitions:

- a 64MB swap partition
- a 16MB boot partition (/boot)
- a root partition (/) that uses the remaining free disk space

Both workstation installation classes require about 600MB of free disk space.

In contrast to the workstation classes, the Server installation class deletes all existing partitions, including DOS/Windows partitions. The Server installation class requires about 1.6GB of disk space. A Server installation also includes a different set of default packages than a workstation installation. Moreover, a Server installation creates a more elaborate partition structure, including

- a 64MB swap partition
- a 16MB boot partition (/boot)
- a 256MB root partition (/)
- a 256MB /var partition

Two further partitions split the remaining free disk space equally:

- /home
- /usr

If neither the workstation classes nor the Server installation class meets your needs, you can specify a Custom installation. The Custom installation class has no predefined characteristics. You can partition hard-disk drives and install components and packages as you choose.

Partitioning Hard Disks

If you selected the GNOME Workstation, KDE Workstation, or Server installation class, the installation procedure offers to perform automatic partitioning of the system's hard disks.

If you prefer to partition the disks manually, check the Manually Partition check box. If you do so, the installation program displays the Partitions screen, which lets you access Disk Druid, Red Hat Linux's partitioning program, or Fdisk, the standard Linux partitioning program.

The Partitions screen displays the existing partitions, if any, giving the following information:

Mount Point   The directory name at which the device will be mounted. Use the Edit button to specify the mount point. Swap partitions have no mount point.

Device   The name of the device on which the partition resides.

Requested The partition's original size. You cannot change the size of a partition; you must delete the partition and add a new one.

Actual The amount of space allocated to the partition.

Type The type of partition.

The Partitions screen also summarizes the status of each hard-disk drive, giving the drive's geometry, total space, free space, and allocated space.

Buttons let you add, edit, and delete partitions. Clicking the Reset button returns Disk Druid to its original state. You can use the Make RAID Device button to create a software RAID device.

Clicking the Add button opens a dialog box that lets you add a new partition. The dialog box contains the following fields:

Mount Point Lets you specify the directory at which the partition will be mounted. You shouldn't specify a mount point for a swap partition.

Size The size of the partition, in MB.

Grow to Fill Specifies that the partition size should be increased until all available free space is allocated.

Allowable Type The partition type.

Allowable Drives The drive or drives from which you're willing to let Disk Druid choose in placing the partition.

Once the partitions have been automatically or manually established, the installation program displays the Choose Partitions to Format screen, which lets you specify which partitions should be formatted.

WARNING Formatting a partition destroys all the data on the partition. Be sure not to format partitions that contain useful data or programs.

Configuring LILO

If you specified the Custom installation class, the installation program displays the LILO Configuration screen. You can use the LILO Configuration screen to specify that the installation program should skip the creation of a boot disk or the installation of LILO. You can also specify whether LILO should be installed on the master boot record (MBR) or on the first sector of the boot partition. Unless the system has a boot manager installed, such as the Windows NT loader or OS/2 boot manager, and you wish to use the boot manager to boot Linux, you should install LILO on the MBR.

The LILO Configuration screen lets you disable use of linear block addressing (LBA); to do so, uncheck the Use Linear Mode check box. The screen also lets you specify parameters to be passed to LILO or the kernel. You might use this capability, for example, if you know that one or more system devices cannot be automatically probed and, therefore, require kernel parameters.

The LILO Configuration screen lists bootable partitions and lets you associate a boot label with a partition so that you can boot the partition by using LILO. You can also specify a default partition that is booted if no partition is specified at boot time.

Network Configuration

If the installation program determines that the system has a network adapter, the installation program displays the Network Configuration screen.

If the system has multiple network adapters, the Network Configuration screen includes tabs that let you choose each adapter. The screen lets you specify the following network configuration information:

Configure Using DHCP Specifies that network configuration will be obtained from a DHCP server at system startup. If you enable this option, you don't need to specify other network configuration options or parameters.

Activate on Boot Specifies that networking is enabled on system startup.

IP Address   The static IP address of the system.

Netmask   The static IP network mask of the system.

Network Address   The static network IP address of the system.

Broadcast Address   The static broadcast IP address of the system.

Hostname   The fully qualified domain name (FQDN) of the system.

Gateway   The IP address of the default gateway used by the system.

Primary, Secondary, and Ternary DNS Servers   The IP addresses of one or more DNS servers to be used to resolve host names to IP addresses and IP addresses to host names.

Setting the Time Zone

The Time Zone Selection screen lets you specify the time zone associated with the system's location. You can specify the time zone by using a world map or by specifying an offset from Universal Time (UTC). You can specify that the system's clock is set to UTC. However, other operating systems may not support this capability, so be careful about specifying this option if the system is to be configured for dual-booting.

Creating User Accounts

The Account Configuration screen lets you specify the password for the root user. This screen also lets you add other user accounts. For each account, you specify the user ID, password, and full name.

Specifying Authentication Options

If you specified the Custom installation class, the Authentication Configuration screen appears. Unless you plan to use network passwords, you can take the default values proposed by the installation program. Otherwise, you must enter an NIS domain. You may also enter an NIS server. You should generally enable MD5 and shadow passwords, as these options improve system security.

Selecting Packages

Red Hat Linux combines related programs, configuration files, and data files into a unit known as a *package* , which is contained in a single file. By treating a package as a unit, Red Hat Linux makes it relatively simple to install, update, or uninstall programs. Packages contain dependency information that identifies programs or libraries needed for proper operation. In general, Red Hat Linux will not let you install a package unless the package's dependencies are satisfied. This helps ensure that installed programs operate correctly.

If you selected the Server or Custom installation class, the Package Group Selection screen appears. This screen lets you select package groups (also known as components) for installation. You can also deselect package groups that you don't want to install. To gain greater control over package selection, you can specify the Select Individual Packages option. This causes the Individual Package Selection screen to appear.

The Individual Package Selection screen lets you select packages to be installed. You can also deselect specific packages. Clicking a package icon causes the installation program to display information about the selected package. The installation program uses the Red Hat Package Manager (RPM) to determine whether the selected packages require support provided by unselected packages. If so, the installation program displays the Unresolved Dependencies screen. The Unresolved Dependencies screen lets you specify whether the installation program will automatically install the required packages, even though you did not select it.

TIP   The RPM program makes it easy to install packages after installation is complete, so it's not crucial to select exactly the right components or packages during installation.

Configuring the X Window System

If you selected packages that are part of the X Window system, the installation program displays the X Configuration screen, which lets you configure X. The installation program uses Xconfigurator to probe and determine the type of video card and monitor on the system. If Xconfigurator cannot identify your card or monitor, it displays a list of hardware from which you can choose. Hundreds of cards and monitors are listed; scroll down the list to find your card and monitor. If your hardware is not listed, you may nevertheless be able to configure X. Select Unlisted Card and specify the characteristics of your video card. Alternatively, select Custom Monitor and specify the horizontal and vertical sync ranges of your monitor.

You can test the configuration to see that it works. To do so, click Test This Configuration. You can also select a custom resolution or color depth. To do so, click Customize X Configuration. Enable the Use Graphical Login check box to cause Linux to display an X login when the system starts. If you prefer a text-based login, disable the Use Graphical Login check box.

If you cannot configure X or you prefer not to try, you can postpone configuration by selecting Skip X Configuration.

Installing Packages

Finally, the installation program presents the About to Install screen. Up to this point, the configuration changes that you've specified have been stored in RAM memory. You can reboot at this point without affecting the configuration of the target system. However, clicking Next commits the changes.

When you click Next, the installation program displays the Installing Packages screen. The Installing Packages screen lets you monitor the progress of package installation. The Next button is disabled until the package installation is complete.

Creating a Boot Disk

Unless you specified that no boot disk is needed, the installation program displays the Boot Disk Creation screen. You can skip creation of the boot floppy disk by clicking Skip Boot Disk Creation and then clicking Next. However, in most cases, you should not do this; the boot disk is useful if you find that you're unable to boot Linux from the hard drive. To create the boot disk, place a blank floppy disk in the floppy drive and click Next.

Completing the Installation

Next, the installation program displays the Congratulations screen, which signals the completion of installation. You should remove the boot disk—if you created one—from the floppy drive, and click Exit. The computer will automatically restart. However, you may need to set the system's BIOS so that the system will boot from its hard disk.

Exam Essentials

Be thoroughly familiar with, and capable of, Red Hat installation, particularly network installations This section explained the procedure for non-network installation of Red Hat Linux. Be sure you're able to install and upgrade Red Hat Linux using both the graphical and text-based installation procedures.

Understand disk partitioning and know how to use Red Hat's install-time partitioning tools This section explained the use of Red Hat's install-time partitioning tools, Fdisk and Disk Druid. Be sure you're able to use them.

Understand install-time configuration elements (LILO, authentication, networking, system initialization, packages, etc.) This section explained the install-time configuration element. Be sure you're able to configure all install-time configuration elements, including X.

Key Terms and Concepts

Component A set of related packages that can be installed as a unit.

Dependency information Information on the files that are not stored in the same package as an application, but which are needed for proper operation of the application.

Installation class Red Hat Linux provides several installation classes, including GNOME Workstation, KDE Workstation, and Server.

Installation type   When installing Red Hat Linux, you can choose to either upgrade existing Red Hat Linux packages or perform a fresh install.

Package   An application and its associated files, which can be stored and installed as a unit.

Sample Questions

1. What program is generally used to manage the booting of Linux?

A. Fips

B. The NT loader

C. LILO

D. Loadlin

Answer: C. LILO is the LInux LOader.

2. What is the default swap partition size associated with the Server installation class?

A. 16MB

B. 32MB

C. 64MB

D. 128MB

Answer: C. The Server installation class has a 64MB swap partition.

▶ Configuring Options after Installation

The Red Hat Linux installation program presents a series of dialog boxes that make it easy to configure many devices and options. From time to time, you may need to reconfigure a device or option. You could reinstall Red Hat Linux, but that's unnecessarily difficult and time-consuming. Instead, you can use the appropriate configuration program or tool that enables you to reconfigure the device or option without otherwise disturbing the system configuration.

Critical Information

Table 1.2 describes some tools used to configure system options after installation. Each of these tools has a user interface that resembles that of the text-based installation procedure. However, you can perform many other configuration tasks by using the Linuxconf system administration tool, which Red Hat Linux installs by default.

TABLE 1.2: Tools for Configuring System Options

Program	Function
kbdconfig	Configures the keyboard
mouseconfig	Configures the mouse
timeconfig	Configures the time zone
sndconfig	Configures sound

Linuxconf

To launch Linuxconf, issue the command linuxconf. Linuxconf has several user interfaces; the appearance of the Linuxconf screen will vary depending upon whether you're running a text-mode virtual console or an X window. You can also access Linuxconf via a browser-based interface, but to enable this facility, you must configure /etc/inetd.conf.

In Linuxconf's text-mode and graphical-mode screens, the left half of the screen presents a collapsible menu tree. The right half of the screen presents a dialog box.

When you change a configuration option using Linuxconf, the change may occur immediately, or it may remain pending until the change is activated. Although configuration files are updated immediately, most system services will not detect changes in their configuration until the services are restarted. When you instruct Linuxconf to activate pending changes, it restarts those services whose configurations you've changed.

To activate pending changes, click Act/Changes. The Status of the System screen appears. If you want to know what changes are pending, click Preview What Has to Be Done. Linuxconf displays the pending changes. To activate pending changes, click Activate the Changes. To exit the Status of the System screen without activating any pending changes, click Quit.

You should generally activate pending changes before exiting Linuxconf. If you neglect to do so, Linuxconf will prompt you to confirm that you want to exit without activating the changes you specified.

Necessary Procedures

You can configure any install-time configuration after installation. This section gives the procedures for post-installation configuration of each install-time configuration element.

Configuring Authentication

The installation program lets you configure several authentication options. You can

- Enable or disable shadow passwords

- Set a password for the root user

- Enable or disable creation of MD5 passwords

After installation, you can easily enable or disable shadow passwords, set a new password for root, or enable or disable creation of MD5 passwords.

Shadow Passwords

You can convert to and from using shadow passwords after installation is completed. Recall that when shadow passwords are enabled, encrypted passwords are stored in a file (/etc/shadow) that is readable only by root. The /etc/shadow file contains several fields in addition to the encrypted password, including the following:

- the date that the account was disabled, given as the number of elapsed days since January 1, 1970

- the date that password was last changed, given as the number of elapsed days since January 1, 1970

- the number of days after which the password must be changed

- the number of days before the password may be changed

- the number of days before password expiration that the user is warned

- the number of days after password expiration that the account is disabled

Enabling shadow passwords improves system security. However, a handful of old Unix programs may not function correctly if shadow passwords are enabled.

To enable shadow passwords, issue the command

    pwconv

To disable shadow passwords, issue the command

    pwunconv

Changing the *root* Password

You can easily change the root password using linuxconf. To do so, select Config ➤ Users Accounts ➤ Normal ➤ Change root Password. The Changing Password screen appears.

You must first enter the current root password and click Accept. If you enter the correct password, the program prompts you for the new password. Type the new password and click Accept. The program confirms your choice for the new password by asking you to enter the new password again. Do so, and click Accept to set the new password.

TIP If you prefer using the command line, you can change the root password by issuing the passwd command, which will prompt you twice for the new password.

Configuring LILO

Rather than edit the /etc/lilo.conf file, you can use Linuxconf to configure LILO. To edit LILO defaults, select Config ➢ Boot Mode ➢ LILO ➢ Configure LILO Defaults from Linuxconf's menu tree. The LILO Defaults screen appears.

The LILO Defaults screen provides access to configuration options that correspond to LILO's global options, affecting every boot image. For example, you can use this screen to specify the location to which LILO is installed, the boot delay, and the prompt time-out. The screen does not include a control that lets you specify the default boot image. Another screen, described later in this subsection, provides access to this option.

Configuring Linux Boot Images

To add, change, or delete a Linux boot image, select Config ➢ Boot Mode ➢ LILO ➢ Configure LILO Linux Configurations from Linuxconf's menu tree. The LILO Linux Configurations screen appears.

You can add a new Linux boot image by clicking Add. To edit or delete an existing Linux boot image, select the image and press Enter. The Linux Boot Configuration screen appears. To delete the boot image, click the Del button. To edit the boot image, make the desired changes and click Accept. The screen provides access to LILO boot image options and several less commonly used options.

NOTE   You can find more information about the LILO boot image options in the online chapter at www.sybex.com.

Configuring Non-Linux Boot Images

To add, change, or delete a non-Linux partition, select Config ➢ Boot Mode ➢ LILO ➢ Configure LILO Other OSs Configurations from Linuxconf's menu tree. The LILO Other OSs Configurations Screen appears.

You can add a new non-Linux boot image by clicking Add. To edit or delete an existing non-Linux boot image, select the image and press Enter. The Other Operating System Setup screen appears. To delete the boot image, click the Del button. To edit the boot image, make the desired changes and click Accept. The Other Operating Systems Setup screen provides access to the label and other options. The text field labeled Partition to Boot corresponds to the other option.

Configuring the Default Boot Image

To specify the default boot image, select Config ➢ Boot Mode ➢ LILO ➢ Change Default Boot Configuration from Linuxconf's menu tree. The Default Boot Configuration screen appears.

To specify a different default boot image, click the radio button corresponding to the desired default boot image and click Accept.

Configuring Boot Options

You can use Linuxconf to configure boot options. To do so, select Config ➢ Boot Mode ➢ Mode ➢ Default Boot Mode from Linuxconf's menu tree. The Boot Mode Configuration screen appears.

You can use this screen to enable or disable LILO's boot menu and to specify the boot delay and prompt time-out. The latter two options are also available on the LILO Defaults screen. You can also use the Boot Mode Configuration screen to specify whether the system starts in text mode (runlevel 3) or graphical mode (runlevel 5).

Configuring Networking

You can use Linuxconf to configure basic and advanced networking options. This subsection explains how to configure basic options; subsequent chapters—especially Chapter 6, "System Initialization and Configuration"—explain how to configure advanced options.

Configuring the Host Name

To configure the host name, select Config ➤ Networking ➤ Client Tasks ➤ Basic Host Information from Linuxconf's menu tree. The This Host Basic Configuration screen appears.

The graphical This Host Basic Configuration screen includes several tabs that let you select from among various windows. If the Host Name screen is not visible in the graphical screen, click the Host Name tab. To specify the host name, type it into the text box and click Accept.

Configuring Network Adapters

To configure a network adapter, select Config ➤ Networking ➤ Client Tasks ➤ Basic Host Information from Linuxconf's menu tree. The This Host Basic Configuration screen appears. The graphical screen includes several tabs that let you select from among various windows. If the Adapter 1 screen is not visible in the graphical screen, click the Adapter 1 tab so that the Adapter 1 screen appears.

If you're using the text version of Linuxconf, simply scroll to view the portion of the This Host Basic Configuration screen that pertains to Adapter 1. The Linuxconf program provides access to configuration options for as many as five network adapters.

Using the Adapter 1 screen, or one of the other adapter screens, you can enable or disable the adapter, and you can specify whether its configuration is static or obtained via DHCP or BOOTP. If the configuration is static, you can specify the fully qualified domain name (FQDN) using the text box labeled Primary Name + Domain. You can also specify the IP address, netmask, and several other options, including device options. Click Accept to save your changes.

Configuring Nameservers

To configure nameservers, select Config ➤ Networking ➤ Client Tasks ➤ Name Server Specification from Linuxconf's menu tree. The Resolver Configuration screen appears.

If DNS is not required for normal operation, disable DNS Is Required for Normal Operation. Otherwise, specify the default domain and the IP address (number) of the primary nameserver associated with the system. You can specify as many as two additional nameservers and as many as six additional search domains. Click Accept to save your changes.

Configuring the Default Gateway

To configure the default gateway, select Config ➤ Networking ➤ Client Tasks ➤ Routing and Gateways ➤ Set Defaults from Linuxconf's menu tree. The Defaults screen appears.

Specify the IP address of the default gateway. If you want this system to act as a router, turn on Enable Routing. For more information on configuring routing, see Chapter 13, "Routing."

Exam Essentials

Understand and be able to implement post-installation configuration of install-time options This section gave procedures for post-installation configuration of install-time configuration elements. Be sure you're able to configure each such element.

Sample Questions

1. Which of the following is the program used to configure the keyboard?

   A. kbdconfig

   B. kboardconfig

   C. keyboardconfig

D. keyconfig

Answer: A. The kbdconfig program lets you configure the keyboard after system installation is complete.

2. Which of the following is the command to enable shadow passwords?

A. pwconv

B. pwenable

C. pwshadow

D. pwunconv

Answer: A. The pwconv program enables shadow passwords.

Chapter

2

Advanced Installation

RHCE PREPARATION TOPICS COVERED IN THIS CHAPTER:

This chapter covers some advanced odds and ends related to installation. It explains how to cope with several unusual types of installations, how to configure and troubleshoot several Linux facilities, and how to perform installations by using network servers. Although some of these topics may seem to be of minor importance, facilities such as kickstart installs can be major time-savers for busy system administrators. Moreover, examination questions are apt to address these topics. Be sure you invest sufficient time to master this chapter, paying special attention to unfamiliar topics.

Configuring and Troubleshooting LILO

Most Linux PCs boot by using the Linux loader, LILO. So, it's important that you know how to configure and troubleshoot LILO.

Critical Information

LILO can act as a primary bootloader or a secondary bootloader. When used as a primary bootloader, LILO is installed on the master boot record (MBR) of a hard disk so that the system's BIOS loads LILO when the system is booted. LILO then controls the booting of Linux and other installed operating systems.

Some operating systems have an associated bootloader. For example, Windows NT has a bootloader known as the NT Loader, and IBM's OS/2 has a bootloader known as the Boot Manager. Often, it's easier to boot an operating system by using its associated bootloader. Common bootloaders can also be configured to boot Linux. To do so, you install LILO on the boot sector of the /boot partition and create a bootloader entry for Linux that points to the /boot partition. In this configuration, LILO acts as a secondary bootloader: It provides the means to boot Linux, but it does not boot any other operating system.

When configured as a primary bootloader, LILO generally displays a LILO: prompt as soon as it's loaded. This prompt is called a boot prompt, and it provides an opportunity to choose the boot image to boot or to enter Linux boot parameters that control the boot and start-up process. If LILO has been configured to display no prompt, pressing Shift or Caps Lock will force the LILO: prompt to be displayed.

If you press Tab in response to LILO's prompt, LILO displays the boot images it is configured to boot. To boot an image, type the label displayed by LILO and press Enter. Typically, the label "dos" refers to Microsoft Windows and the label "linux" refers to Linux. However, you can configure LILO to display a label you choose, as described in the next subsection. For example, you may prefer to associate the label "Win95" with the Microsoft Windows 95 operating system.

Often, LILO is configured to automatically boot a default boot image if the user fails to choose one within a defined time period. The default boot image, if any, is the one listed first when you press Tab in response to the prompt. You can disable the automatic boot feature by pressing Shift or Caps Lock. If you want to boot the default boot image immediately, press Enter in response to LILO's prompt. However, you can configure LILO to ignore these Shift and Caps Lock functions, if you prefer.

Boot arguments let you control the boot and startup process. Many boot arguments have a *name=value* form. LILO recognizes and processes several such arguments. If LILO doesn't recognize a *name=value* argument, or if an argument has some other form, LILO passes the argument to the kernel. In turn, the kernel recognizes and processes some arguments. If the kernel doesn't recognize an argument, it passes the argument to the first process, usually init. The kernel passes *name=value* arguments as environment variables; it uses arguments to invoke the first process.

The most common use of a boot argument is to start the system in single-user mode. When booted in single-user mode, the system mounts only the root file system and starts only those system processes associated with runlevel 1. Booting a system in single-user mode may facilitate troubleshooting and repair.

To start a system in single-user mode, type **S**, **single**, or **1** after the name of the boot image. For example, you might start Linux in single-user mode as follows:

```
LILO: linux S
```

Configuring LILO

The installation program generally configures LILO correctly on your behalf. However, when configuring a system for multi-boot operation, you may find it necessary to tweak the LILO configuration after installation. To do so, you can use the Linuxconf program. However, the RHCE exam is likely to include questions or exercises that test your ability to configure LILO manually. This subsection explains LILO's configuration file and how to use it.

LILO's configuration file is /etc/lilo.conf. To install a new LILO configuration, you modify the configuration file using a text editor, and then run the LILO map installer, /sbin/lilo. Here's a sample LILO configuration file that illustrates the most important configuration options:

```
boot=/dev/hda
map=/boot/map
install=/boot/boot.b
prompt
delay=50
timeout=3000
default=dos

image=/boot/vmlinuz-2.2.12-20
    label=old
```

```
        root=/dev/hda4
        read-only

    image=/boot/vmlinuz-2.2.12-20b1
        label=linux
        root=/dev/hda4
        read-only

    other=/dev/hda1
        label=dos
```

This configuration file includes four stanzas. The first, consisting of the first six lines, specifies global parameters. Table 2.1 describes the global parameters that appear in the same configuration. Each remaining stanza describes a boot image that LILO should offer for booting. The first two boot images are associated with Linux, and the final boot image is associated with Microsoft Windows. Table 2.2 describes the parameters used to specify a boot image.

Note that both Linux boot images refer to the same partition. This arrangement lets you choose the kernel used to boot the system and is helpful when installing a new kernel. If the new kernel fails to work properly, you can use the LILO prompt to load the old kernel.

TABLE 2.1: LILO Global Parameters

LILO Global Parameter	Description
boot	Specifies the device or partition to which boot information will be written. Specify a device (for example, /dev/hda) to install LILO to the MBR, where it will act as the primary bootloader. Specify a partition (for example, /dev/hda3) to install Linux to the boot sector of the partition, where it will act as a secondary bootloader.
default	Specifies the default boot image.

TABLE 2.1: LILO Global Parameters *(continued)*

LILO Global Parameter	Description
delay	Specifies the amount of time (in tenths of a second) that LILO will wait before booting the default boot image.
install	Specifies the file installed as the new boot sector.
map	Specifies the name of the map file, which contains the names and locations of boot images.
prompt	Specifies that LILO will display a boot prompt.
timeout	Specifies the amount of time (in tenths of a second) that LILO will wait for keyboard input before booting the default boot image.

TABLE 2.2: LILO Boot Image Parameters

LILO Global Parameter	Description
image	Specifies the Linux kernel associated with the boot image (required for Linux boot images).
label	Specifies the label associated with the boot image.
other	Specifies the partition that contains the bootable non-Linux image (required for non-Linux boot images).
read-only	Specifies that the root partition is initially to be mounted as read-only.
root	Specifies the root partition associated with the Linux boot image (required for Linux boot images).

LILO Error Messages

LILO actually loads in two stages. LILO's first stage resides in the MBR or boot sector of a partition, depending on whether LILO is installed as the primary or a secondary bootloader. LILO's second stage resides in the file /boot/boot.b. LILO displays its prompt letter by letter as it loads. So, an incomplete LILO prompt provides useful information about what went wrong. LILO sometimes displays a modified prompt that indicates an error condition. Table 2.3 describes the LILO error messages.

TABLE 2.3: LILO Error Messages

Prompt	Meaning
nothing	LILO did not load.
L	First stage loaded.
LI	Second stage loaded.
LIL	Second stage started.
LIL?	Second stage loaded at incorrect address.
LIL-	Descriptor table is corrupt.
LILO	LILO loaded correctly.

Exam Essentials

Be able to configure, build, and install the Linux kernel and modules from source and understand LILO configuration and the elements—first stage, second stage, and installer—that make up LILO   This section explained LILO and LILO's configuration elements. Be sure you know how to configure LILO, update the LILO boot map, and troubleshoot LILO.

Key Terms and Concepts

Boot argument   A boot argument is a value passed to LILO or an operating system hosted by LILO.

Bootloader   A bootloader is a program that loads an operating system into memory.

Boot prompt   The LILO boot prompt provides you the opportunity to specify a boot image and boot arguments.

Primary bootloader   The primary bootloader provides a boot prompt, letting you specify the boot image and boot arguments.

Secondary bootloader   The secondary bootloader loads a specified operating system into memory.

Sample Questions

1. Which LILO option is used to specify the duration of the interval that LILO will wait before booting the default image?

    A. interval

    B. pause

    C. timeout

    D. wait

    Answer: C. After the timeout interval expires, LILO boots the default image.

2. Which LILO option is used to specify the location of a non-Linux boot image?

    A. boot

    B. dos

    C. image

    D. other

Answer: D. The other option specifies the location of a non-Linux boot image.

Setting Up Multi-boot Configurations

Many Linux users want to use a single computer to host multiple operating systems in what is called a multi-boot configuration. A computer configured for multi-boot operation does not generally boot an operating system. Instead, it boots a special program called a bootloader that lets the user choose an installed operating system and loads the user's choice. Desktop users often configure their systems to boot Microsoft Windows or Linux. However, it's possible to configure multi-boot configurations that support Windows NT and other operating systems, such as IBM's OS/2.

Critical Information

In a multi-boot configuration, each time you start the system, you choose the operating system you want to boot. However, instead of configuring a system for multi-boot operation, you can install special software that lets you use Windows programs and Linux at the same time. For example, the Wine project (www.winehq.com) is implementing the Win32 API under Linux. Already, you can use Wine to run many common Windows programs under Linux.

Another approach to running Windows programs under Linux is VMware Inc.'s product called VMware, which lets you run the Windows 9x or the Windows NT operating system under Linux. Alternatively, a Windows NT version of VMware lets you run Linux under Windows NT. The company's Web site is www.vmware.com. One of the most useful features of VMware is the ability to simultaneously run multiple versions of Linux on a single computer. By doing so, you can install, configure, and test new versions of Linux and Linux software without disturbing a running server.

Windows 9x

Configuring a multi-boot system that boots Microsoft Windows 9x and Linux is straightforward. If possible, you should install Microsoft Windows before installing Linux. If you then perform a Workstation or Custom installation of Red Hat Linux, the installation program can automatically configure the system to boot both operating systems. Simply ensure that the installation program's LILO Configuration dialog box lists the partition containing Microsoft Windows.

If you must install Linux first and then install Microsoft Windows, be sure to leave room for the Windows partition, which must be located in a bootable region of the hard disk (generally, below cylinder 1024). Also, be sure to create a Linux boot disk, because the Windows installation procedure overwrites the MBR, destroying LILO. After the Windows installation is complete, use the boot disk to boot Linux, revise the LILO configuration to include the Windows boot image, and run /sbin/lilo to reinstall LILO.

TIP You may find it helpful to use the BIOS to turn off plug-and-play for ISA slots. Otherwise, Windows may use plug-and-play to change the system resources associated with a device, rendering it unusable in Linux until you reconfigure the device.

Windows NT

Configuring a multi-boot system that boots Windows NT and Linux is somewhat more difficult than configuring a multi-boot system that boots Windows 9x and Linux. Again, you'll find the task easier if you install Windows NT before installing Linux. However, the Linux installation program will not automatically configure the system to boot Windows NT.

You can boot Linux using the Windows NT loader. The Windows NT loader configuration is stored in the hidden file c:\boot.ini. Here's a sample NT loader configuration file:

```
[boot loader]
```

```
timeout=60
default=multi(0)disk(0)rdisk(1)partition(1)\WINNT
[operating systems]
multi(0)disk(0)rdisk(1)partition(1)\WINNT="Windows NT
Workstation Version 4.00"
multi(0)disk(0)rdisk(1)partition(1)\WINNT="Windows NT
Workstation Version 4.00 [VGA mode]" /basevideo /sos
c:\="Microsoft Windows 95"
```

This configuration file contains two stanzas, set off by titles enclosed in square brackets. The first stanza is titled [boot loader]. It contains two lines: one that specifies a timeout and one that specifies a default boot image. The timeout works much like LILO's timeout. NT automatically boots a default image if it finds no response to its prompt within the specified time period. The default boot image is specified by the number of its disk (rdisk) and partition (partition), both of which are numbered relative to 0. The default boot image in the sample configuration is located in the \WINNT directory of the file system on the specified partition.

NOTE The multi and disk parameters of the boot.ini file are used with SCSI disks. You shouldn't need to learn these NT-related details in order to prepare for the RHCE exam.

The second stanza is titled [operating systems]. Each line of the second stanza specifies a boot image and an associated label, which is enclosed in double quotes. Two forms of specification appear: One is used to specify an NT boot image, and the other is used to specify a non-NT boot image. In the sample configuration, the first two lines specify NT boot images, and the third line specifies a non-NT boot image.

To configure NT to boot Linux, install Linux using LILO as a secondary bootloader. Be sure to create a boot disk so that you can boot Linux before reconfiguring the NT loader.

Suppose the /dev/hda3 partition is the one Linux mounts as /boot. Boot Linux and issue the following command:

```
dd if=/dev/hda3 of=/boot/linux.ldr bs=512 count=1
```

This command copies the Linux boot sector from the /boot partition to the file /boot/linux.ldr.

Insert an MS-DOS–formatted floppy disk into the floppy drive and issue the commands

```
mount -t msdos /dev/fd0 /mnt/floppy
cp /boot/linux.ldr /mnt/floppy
umount /dev/fd0
```

Remove the floppy disk and boot NT. Insert the floppy disk and copy the file linux.ldr from the floppy disk to the c:\ directory. Use a text editor to add the following line to the boot.ini file:

```
c:\linux.ldr="Linux"
```

When you boot NT, the NT loader displays a new line that's labeled "Linux." Simply highlight the new line and press Enter to boot Linux.

TIP If the Windows NT system uses a FAT rather than NTFS file system, you can copy the /boot/linux.ldr file to the proper Windows NT file system without using a floppy disk. Just mount the file system, copy the file, and unmount the file system.

TIP If you recompile your Linux kernel, you must run /sbin/lilo and then repeat the boot sector installation procedure. Otherwise, the NT loader will be unable to find and load the new kernel.

TIP   If you prefer, you can boot Windows NT by using LILO. Just add the Windows NT system to the LILO configuration file, specifying the other and `label` directives. Then, run `/sbin/lilo` to update the boot map and install the revised boot sector.

Other Operating Systems

You can configure Linux to boot, or be booted by, other operating systems, including OS/2, FreeBSD, and NetBSD. The procedure generally resembles that given for Windows NT or Windows 9*x*, depending on whether you prefer to use LILO as the primary bootloader or as a secondary bootloader, respectively. Consult the operating system documentation to determine how to proceed. You'll probably find Usenet newsgroups helpful in resolving any problems and questions you have.

Exam Essentials

Know how to configure a system to dual-boot multiple operating systems   Although the official list of RHCE study points doesn't explicitly require this skill, it's implicit in the study points that concern Red Hat Linux installation. Be sure you're able to configure a multi-boot installation.

Key Term and Concept

Multi-boot installation   A Linux installation that also lets the host PC boot one or more operating systems other than Linux, such as MS Windows or NT.

Sample Questions

1. Which of the following is true of multi-boot installations?

A. MS Windows NT cannot be installed on the same PC as Linux.

B. Other operating systems and Linux must reside on separate hard drives.

C. They're generally easier if you install Linux before installing other operating systems.

D. They're generally easier if you install other operating systems before Linux.

Answer: D. To create a multi-boot installation, you should generally install the non-Linux operating system before installing Linux.

2. Which of the following is true of Windows NT (choose all that apply)?

A. LILO can boot Windows NT.

B. The Windows NT loader can boot Linux.

C. When Linux is installed with Windows NT, Linux cannot be booted via LILO.

D. When Linux is installed with Windows NT, Linux must be booted via a floppy.

Answer: A, B. Both the NT loader and LILO can boot Linux and NT.

Performing Network Installs

When installing Linux to multiple PCs, it's often more convenient to access files residing on a network server rather than on a CD-ROM. This is called a network installation. Network installation reduces the handling of media, which can be inconvenient.

It also allows preparation of custom builds that include updated package files.

Critical Information

You can install Red Hat Linux from distribution media residing on an FTP, HTTP (Web), or NFS server. At one time, Red Hat Linux supported network installation via Samba (SMB). This is no longer the case.

Prior to Red Hat Linux 6.2, the DNS server that resolved host names for the domain that included the server had to be capable of providing a reverse name lookup for the server. The DNS server had to be able to map the IP number of the server to the server's host name. Under Red Hat Linux 6.2, this is no longer necessary.

If the server provides access to the distribution media by means of multiple services, it's useful to store the media only once. The following sequence of commands creates a copy of the distribution media, which is accessible to FTP and HTTP:

```
cp -a /mnt/cdrom/RedHat /home/ftp/pub
ln -s /home/ftp/pub/RedHat /home/httpd/html/RedHat
```

To provide access to the media via NFS, export the /home/ftp/pub/RedHat directory by including the following line in the /etc/exports file:

```
/home/ftp/pub/RedHat (ro)
```

For more information on setting up FTP, HTTP, and NFS services, see Chapter 9, "Primary Network Services."

TIP   You can perform a graphical mode installation via NFS, but not via FTP or HTTP.

To install Red Hat Linux via a network server, create a boot disk from the image file bootnet.img, which resides in the images directory of the distribution CD-ROM. Then, start the installation procedure by booting from this disk. After you select the language and keyboard, the Installation Method screen appears. Select the service that will provide access to the installation media, and click OK.

If you select NFS, the NFS Setup screen appears. Use this screen to specify the host name (or IP number) of the NFS server and the name of the exported directory that contains the RedHat subdirectory of the distribution CD-ROM.

If you select FTP, the FTP Setup screen appears. Use this screen to specify the host name (or IP number) of the FTP server and the name of the directory that contains the RedHat subdirectory of the distribution CD-ROM.

If you selected HTTP, the HTTP Setup screen appears. Use this screen to specify the host name (or IP number) of the HTTP server and the name of the directory that contains the RedHat subdirectory of the distribution CD-ROM.

After you specify the host name (or IP number) of the server and the directory that contains the distribution media, the Configure TCP/IP screen appears. If the client can obtain its network configuration via BOOTP or DHCP, select Use Dynamic IP Configuration and click OK. Otherwise, specify the IP number, netmask, gateway, and DNS server that the client should use, and click OK.

Once you've specified the TCP/IP information, the installation program accesses the distribution media via the server. Thereafter, the installation proceeds as usual.

Exam Essentials

Be thoroughly familiar with, and capable of, Red Hat installation, particularly network installations   This section explained how to install Red Hat Linux via FTP, HTTP, and NFS. Be sure you're able to perform network-based installations of Red Hat Linux.

Key Term and Concept

Network installation   Linux installation from media residing on a
network server.

Sample Questions

1. Which of the following server types can host a network installation
   (choose all that apply)?

   A. FTP

   B. HTTP

   C. NFS

   D. SMB (Samba)

   Answer: A, B, C. You cannot perform a network installation
   using SMB.

2. Which of the following server types can host a graphical network
   installation?

   A. FTP

   B. HTTP

   C. NFS

   D. SMB (Samba)

   Answer: C. Only NFS can be used to host a graphical network
   installation.

Performing Kickstart Installs

A kickstart installation is a special type of installation in which
responses to installation dialog boxes are taken from a script rather
than from user input. When the script is stored on a floppy disk, it has

the name `ks.cfg`; when the script is accessed via NFS, you can specify its name. You can write your own kickstart script, but it's much easier to use the `mkkickstart` program to create a script patterned after a completed installation. You can then revise the script as you like.

Critical Information

Generally, the easiest way to prepare for a kickstart installation is by using the `mkkickstart` program. The program is not installed by default, so the usual first step is to install the `mkkickstart` package using the following command:

```
rpm -Uvh /mnt/cdrom/RedHat/RPMS/mkkickstart*.rpm
```

After installing the `mkkickstart` package, run the `mkkickstart` program as follows:

```
mkkickstart >ks.cfg
```

Notice how the output of the `mkkickstart` program is redirected to the file `ks.cfg`. The `mkkickstart` program will probably display a warning that reminds you to set the static IP address in the configuration file; this is normal.

Here's a sample `ks.cfg` file:

```
lang us
#network --static --ip 10.0.0.2 --netmask 255.255.255.0
%--gateway 10.0.0.1 --nameserver 10.0.0.1
cdrom
device ethernet 3c90x
keyboard us
zerombr yes
clearpart --linux
part swap --size 526
part /space --size 10449
part /boot --size 40
```

```
part /usr --size 2001
part /home --size 4009
part /var --size 503
part / --size 1005
install
mouse genericps/2
timezone US/Pacific
xconfig --server "SVGA" --monitor "viewsonic17gs"
auth --useshadow --enablemd5
lilo --location mbr --linear
%packages
setup
filesystem
basesystem
...and so on...
%post
```

Editing the Configuration File

The configuration file requires some revision before it can be used. Notice that the network line is commented out. You should remove the comment character (#) and revise the IP number, netmask, and gateway. If you want the system to obtain its network configuration via BOOTP or DHCP, specify the following directive:

```
network --bootproto BOOTP
```

or

```
network --bootproto DHCP
```

Table 2.4 describes the other directives shown in the same configuration and a few additional directives you may find useful. Consult the kickstart documentation on the documentation CD-ROM, especially *The Official Red Hat Linux Reference Guide*, to learn more about these and other kickstart directives.

TABLE 2.4: Kickstart Directives

Directive	Meaning
auth —useshadow --enablemd5	Specifies that shadow passwords and MD5 encryption are to be used.
cdrom	Specifies that the installation media is on a local CD-ROM.
clearpart —all	Specifies that all existing partitions should be deleted.
clearpart —linux	Specifies that all existing Linux partitions should be deleted.
device ethernet *device* [--opts "*options*"]	Specifies that the system has the indicated type of Ethernet adapter. The installer consults this directive when unable to successfully identify a network device by probing.
device scsi *device* [--opts "*options*"]	Specifies that the system has the indicated type of SCSI adapter. The installer consults this directive when unable to successfully identify a SCSI interface by probing.
install	Specifies that the installation type is Install rather than Upgrade.
keyboard us	Specifies that the keyboard is type US.
lang us	Specifies the language to be used in any dialog boxes used by the installer to request information.
lilo --append '*anything-needed*'	Specifies options to be appended to the LILO configuration file.
mouse genericps/2	Specifies that the mouse type is PS/2.
network --bootproto bootp	Specifies that the network configuration is to be obtained via BOOTP.

TABLE 2.4: Kickstart Directives *(continued)*

Directive	Meaning
network --bootproto dhcp	Specifies that the network configuration is to be obtained via DHCP.
network --static --ip *ip* --netmask *mask* -gateway *gw* --nameserver *dns*	Specifies a static network configuration.
part /*mount* -size *size*	Specifies that a Linux partition of the specified size (in MB) should be created and mounted as the indicated directory.
part swap --size *size*	Specifies that a swap partition of the indicated size (in MB) should be created.
rootpw --iscrypted *password*	Specifies the root password using encrypted text. This directive has a history of problems and is best avoided.
%packages	Specifies that the following lines name the packages to be installed.
%post	Specifies that the following lines are shell commands to be executed after installation.
timezone US/Pacific	Specifies that the time zone is US/Pacific.
upgrade	Specifies that the installation type is Upgrade rather than Install.
xconfig --server "*server*" --monitor "*monitor*"	Specifies that XFree86 should be configured using the specified X server and monitor.
zerombr yes	Specifies that any existing bootloader should be removed.

Setting Up the Servers

Rather than include the kickstart file on the boot media, you can use a DHCP server to provide it. To do so, specify

```
filename "/home/ftp/pub/ks.cfg";
```

in the /etc/dhcpd.conf file. You can store the kickstart file in a directory other than /home/ftp/pub, if you prefer; simply revise the filename directive accordingly.

If you prefer to have a separate kickstart file for each client system, specify the directive

```
filename "/home/ftp/pub/kickstart";
```

Then, in the directory /home/ftp/pub/kickstart, place the kickstart files, which must have names of the form *xxx.xxx.xxx.xxx-kickstart*, where *xxx.xxx.xxx.xxx* is the IP address of the client system.

When the installation program fetches the kickstart file via DHCP, it assumes that it should perform a network installation from an NFS server. By default, it tries to mount an NFS directory exported by the same host that answered the DHCP query. If you want to use a different host to service the NFS requests, include the following directive in the /etc/dhcpd.conf file:

```
next-server nfserver;
```

where *nfserver* is the host name or IP number of the desired NFS server on which the kickstart file resides. To give the location of installation media, you can specify a kickstart directive of the form

```
nfs --server server directory
```

where *server* specifies the NFS server and *directory* specifies the NFS-exported directory.

Performing the Kickstart Installation

To start the kickstart installation, specify the ks argument at the LILO prompt. Use the command

```
linux ks
```

if the kickstart file is to be obtained from a DHCP or NFS server. Use the command

```
linux ks=floppy
```

if the kickstart file resides on the root directory of the boot floppy disk.

If the kickstart installation needs information that it cannot find in a kickstart directive, it prompts for the information using the dialog box presented by a non-kickstart installation.

Exam Essentials

Understand kickstart installation basics (kickstart file, floppy- vs. network-based, installation media, boot disk preparation, etc.)   Be sure you understand and know how to perform kickstart installations of Red Hat Linux. Be familiar with the kickstart configuration options.

Key Term and Concept

Kickstart installation   A special installation mode that requires little, if any, interaction during installation.

Sample Questions

1. Which of the following is generally the easiest way to create an initial kickstart configuration file?

A. cfgkickstart

B. kickstart

C. mkkickstart

D. setupkickstart

Answer: C. The mkkickstart program is generally the easiest way to create an initial kickstart configuration file.

2. Which of the following kickstart directives is best avoided?

A. auth

B. network

C. rootpw

D. zerombr

Answer: C. The rootpw directive has a history of problems.

Chapter

3

User Administration

Because Linux is a multiuser operating system, a system administrator must know how to create and administer user accounts and how to configure the user environment. Good user administration practices are important to maintaining an effective and secure computing capability.

Creating and Administering User Accounts

One of the primary tasks of a Linux system administrator is the creation and configuration of user accounts. Red Hat Linux provides several kinds of user accounts, so a Red Hat Linux system administrator must know how to choose the proper kind of account for a given user, as well as know how to create and configure the account. Associated with user accounts are *groups*, which define sets of users to which you can extend privileges and permissions.

Critical Information

The /etc/passwd file defines Linux user accounts. Each line in the file describes a single user. Here is a typical /etc/passwd file:

```
root:x:0:0:root:/root:/bin/bash
bin:x:1:1:bin:/bin:
daemon:x:2:2:daemon:/sbin:
adm:x:3:4:adm:/var/adm:
lp:x:4:7:lp:/var/spool/lpd:
sync:x:5:0:sync:/sbin:/bin/sync
```

```
shutdown:x:6:0:shutdown:/sbin:/sbin/shutdown
halt:x:7:0:halt:/sbin:/sbin/halt
mail:x:8:12:mail:/var/spool/mail:
news:x:9:13:news:/var/spool/news:
uucp:x:10:14:uucp:/var/spool/uucp:
operator:x:11:0:operator:/root:
games:x:12:100:games:/usr/games:
gopher:x:13:30:gopher:/usr/lib/gopher-data:
ftp:x:14:50:FTP User:/home/ftp:
nobody:x:99:99:Nobody:/:
xfs:x:100:233:X Font Server:/etc/X11/fs:/bin/false
bill:x:500:500:Bill McCarty:/home/bill:/bin/bash
```

Each line contains several fields, delimited by colons:

Username   The login name associated with the user account.

Password   The login password associated with the user account (if shadow passwords are enabled, only the placeholder x appears).

User ID   A unique numerical ID associated with the user account.

Group ID   The numerical ID associated with the user's home group. Red Hat Linux defines a personal group for each user account.

Full name   The user's full name.

Home directory   The directory that is set at login as the current directory.

Shell   The command interpreter loaded when the user logs in via a command-line interface; the shell is not loaded when the user logs in via X.

Administering User Accounts via the Userconf Tool

The easiest way to administer user accounts is via the Userconf tool, because it automatically performs several otherwise tedious operations. You can launch the Userconf tool by issuing the command

```
userconf
```

If you like, you can run Userconf from X.

The Linuxconf configuration program provides another way to access Userconf. To access Userconf via Linuxconf, issue the command `linuxconf`.

Then, navigate to the user account menu by choosing Config ➤ User Accounts from the Linuxconf menu. The instructions in this chapter assume you're using Userconf; however, you can easily use Linuxconf to perform any of the operations described.

To administer a given kind of user account, highlight the kind you want to administer and press Enter; or, if you're using X, you can simply click the account kind. Ordinary user accounts—often called shell accounts—let the user log in and use the system. To create an ordinary user account, follow these steps:

1. Launch Userconf by issuing the command `userconf`.

2. Choose User Accounts and press Enter; or, if you're using X, click User Accounts. The Users Accounts screen appears. If you're using X, this screen and subsequent screens look somewhat different.

   Depending on the filter settings (in Control ➤ Features), you may see a Filter dialog box. Use the dialog box to limit the user accounts to those you want to see, or press Accept to view all accounts.

3. Click the Add button. The User Account Creation screen appears.

4. Fill in the parameter fields. Refer to Tables 3.1 and 3.2 for information on each field. The privilege fields can have one of three values:

   - Denied, which means the user lacks the privilege

   - Granted, which means the user has the privilege but must confirm authorization by entering the login password

   - Granted/silent, which means the user has the privilege and need not confirm authorization by entering a password

TABLE 3.1: User Account Parameters

PARAMETER	DESCRIPTION
The account is enabled	If checked, the user can log in.
Login name	The login name of the user account. The login name should not contain special characters other than dash (-) or underscore (_). The login name can be as many as 256 characters in length; however, most system administrators assign login names of not more than 8–10 characters in length.
Full name	The user's full name (optional).
Group	The numeric ID of user's home group (optional). By default, a personal group having the same name as the login is created.
Supplementary groups	Additional groups to which the user belongs (optional). By default, no additional groups are assigned.
Home directory	The user's home directory (optional). By default, the *directory/home/login_name* is assigned, where *login_name* is the user's login name.
Command interpreter	The command interpreter (shell), /bin/bash by default (optional).
User ID	The numeric user ID (optional). By default, the next sequential numeric ID is assigned.
Must keep # days	Number of days the user must keep the password, or –1 if the password can be changed immediately.
Must change after # days	Number of days until the user must change the password, or 99999 if the password does not expire.

TABLE 3.1: User Account Parameters *(continued)*

PARAMETER	DESCRIPTION
Warn # days before expiration	Number of days a warning is given before password expiration, or –1 if no warning is to be given.
Account expires after # days	Number of days until the account expires, or –1 if the account never expires.
Expiration date	Expiration date of the account, or blank if the Account Expires After # Days parameter is specified.
Redirect messages to	User account to which e-mail for this account is redirected (optional).
E-mail alias	E-mail addresses (other than the login name) that should be directed to this account (optional).

TABLE 3.2: User Privilege Parameters

PRIVILEGE	DESCRIPTION
May use Linuxconf	The user may access any Linuxconf screen. However, unless the user is explicitly granted permission to activate configuration changes, the user may not do so.
May activate config changes	The user may activate Linuxconf configuration changes.
May shut down	The user may shut down the system. Even without this privilege, a user can use the console to shut down the system by pressing Ctrl+Alt+Delete.
May switch network mode	The user may change system runlevels.

TABLE 3.2: User Privilege Parameters *(continued)*

PRIVILEGE	DESCRIPTION
May view system logs	The user may view system logs.
SuperUser equivalence	The user may issue privileged commands.
Apache administration	The user can configure the Apache Web server.
Mail to Fax manager	The user can configure the Mail to Fax service.
Samba administration	The user can configure Samba.
Message of the day	The user can modify the message of the day.
POP accounts manager	The user can administer POP accounts.
PPP accounts manager	The user can administer PPP accounts.
UUCP manager	The user can administer UUCP accounts.

5. Click the Accept button. The Changing Password dialog box appears.

6. Type the desired password and click the Accept button. The Changing Password dialog box reappears.

7. Confirm the password you previously entered by retyping it. Click the Accept button. The Users Accounts screen reappears.

8. When you're done administering user accounts, click the Quit button.

You can use Userconf to modify ordinary user accounts and to create and modify the following additional types of accounts:

POP user accounts POP user accounts are used by users who access mail via POP from a remote location. POP users don't actually log in to the system, so the POP User Accounts screens don't include the Command Interpreter field. By default, POP users are members of the popusers group.

PPP user accounts PPP user accounts are used by users who log in via PPP from a remote location. The default command interpreter for PPP user accounts is /usr/lib/linuxconf/lib/ppplogin. By default, PPP users are members of the pppusers group.

SLIP user accounts SLIP user accounts are used by users who log in via SLIP from a remote location. The default command interpreter for SLIP user accounts is /sbin/diplogin. By default, SLIP users are members of the slipusers group.

UUCP user accounts Before the advent of the Internet, UUCP was the main way in which Unix computers communicated; a few Linux sites still use UUCP today. UUCP user accounts are used by processes that log in via UUCP from a remote location. The default command interpreter for UUCP user accounts is /usr/sbin/uucico. By default, UUCP users are members of the uucp group. The default home directory of a UUCP user is /var/spool/uucppublic.

Enabling and Disabling User Accounts

If you want to lock out a user, you can disable the user's account. If a user's account is disabled, the user cannot log in or access the POP server. To disable a user account, uncheck the Account Is Enabled box on the Userconf User Information screen. To enable a disabled account, check the Account Is Enabled box on the Userconf User Information screen.

Deleting User Accounts

If a user account is no longer needed, it's better to delete it than merely disable it. By deleting the account, you free the disk space occupied by the user's home directory and its contents.

To delete a user account, perform the following steps:

1. Launch Userconf by issuing the command `userconf`.

2. Choose User Accounts and press Enter; or, if you're using X, click User Accounts. The Users Accounts screen appears.

3. Select the user account you want to delete and press Enter; or, if you're using X, you can simply click the user account. The User Information screen appears.

4. To delete the account, click the Del button. The Deleting Account screen appears.

5. Select the desired option:

- Archive the Account's Data
- Delete the Account's Data
- Leave the Account's Data in Place

The default option, Archive the Account's Data, deletes the user from `/etc/passwd` and creates a gzip-compressed archive in the `/home/oldaccounts` directory, which is automatically created if it does not exist. The file has the name

user-yyyy-mm-dd-xxx`.tar.gz`

where *user* is the user ID, *yyyy-mm-dd* is the current date, and *xxx* is the process ID of the process that performed the deletion.

The option Delete the Account's Data deletes the user's home directory and its contents.

6. Click the Accept button.

WARNING   A user may own files stored in directories other than the user's home directory. If you delete the user account, the files remain. Such files, called orphan files, are owned by the user ID of the deleted user account. If you create a new account that has the user ID of the deleted account, the new user account becomes the owner of the orphan files.

Administering User Accounts via the Command Line

Some administrators prefer to use the command line to administer user accounts. Knowing the relevant commands is helpful, because you can use them to construct scripts that simplify common system administration tasks. The most important commands for administering users are

- useradd, which creates a user account
- userdel, which deletes a user account
- usermod, which modifies a user account
- chfn, which changes the full name field associated with a user account

---

NOTE The full name field contains the so-called gecos information, including name, office location, phone number, and so on.

- chsh, which changes the command interpreter associated with a user account

The *useradd* Command

The useradd command, which is the same program as the adduser command, creates a new user account. The basic form of the command is

```
useradd -d home -e expire -f inactive -g group
↳-G groups -m -s shell -u uid username
```

Only the final argument (username), which specifies the login name, is required. The remaining arguments have these meanings:

-d *home*:	Specifies the user's home directory.
-e *expire*:	Specifies the expiration date of the account. Specified as *mm/dd/yy*.

-f *inactive*:   Specifies the number of days after password expiration that the account is disabled. The default value, -1, prevents the account from being disabled.

-g *group*:   Specifies the user's home group name or number. The default value is 100. Used with the –n flag.

-G *groups*:   A comma-separated list of group names or numbers, specifying supplementary groups of which the user is to be made a member.

-m: Specifies that the user's home directory is to be automatically created.

-n   Specifies that no user private group should be created.

-s *shell*:   Specifies the user's shell. If not specified, the system will launch the default shell when the user logs in.

-u *uid*:   The numerical ID of the user. If not specified, the system chooses the next available user ID.

The *userdel* Command

The userdel command deletes a user account. The form of the command is

    userdel *user*

where *user* is the login name of the user to be deleted. If you want to delete the user's home directory and its contents, issue a command of the form

    userdel -r *user*

For more information on the userdel command, see its man page.

The *usermod* Command

The usermod command lets you modify an existing user account. Its form resembles that of the useradd command:

```
usermod -d home -e expire -f inactive -g group
↳-G groups -1 login -s shell -u uid username
```

All arguments are optional, except the last; however, at least one additional argument must be specified. The argument -1 login lets you change the login name associated with the account. The name of the user's home directory is not affected by this change.

The *chfn* Command

The chfn command lets you change the full name associated with a user account. The form of the command is

```
chfn user
```

where *user* is the login name of the account to be modified. The command will prompt for the following information, known as the gecos information:

- Name
- Office
- Office phone
- Home phone

If you don't wish to specify a value for a prompted field, simply press Enter. If you prefer, you can use the chfn command in non-interactive mode. See its man page for details.

The *chsh* Command

The chsh command lets you change the command interpreter associated with a user account. The form of the command is

```
chsh -s shell user
```

where shell specifies the path of the desired command interpreter and *user* specifies the login name of the user account to be modified. Only approved command interpreters listed in /etc/shells can be specified.

Administering Groups via *userconf*

User groups—often simply called groups—let you associate a set of users, called members. You use the familiar Unix chmod command to specify permissions needed to access files and directories for the owner, members of the owning group, and others.

The /etc/group file defines Linux user groups. Each line in the file describes a single group. Here is a typical /etc/group file:

```
root::0:root
bin::1:root,bin,daemon
daemon::2:root,bin,daemon
sys::3:root,bin,adm
adm::4:root,adm,daemon
tty::5:
disk::6:root
lp::7:daemon,lp
mem::8:
kmem::9:
wheel::10:root
mail::12:mail
news::13:news
uucp::14:uucp
man::15:
games::20:
gopher::30:
dip::40:
ftp::50:
nobody::99:
users::100:
floppy:x:19:
console:x:101:
```

```
utmp:x:102:
pppusers:x:230:
popusers:x:231:
slipusers:x:232:
slocate:x:21:
xfs:x:233:
bill:x:500:
```

Each line contains several fields, delimited by colons:

Group name The name of the group defined by this line of the /etc/group file.

Password An encrypted password associated with the group. Under Linux, group passwords are not commonly used.

Group ID The numerical ID associated with the group.

Members The login names of the group members, if the group contains members.

You can use Linuxconf or Userconf to create groups, change group membership, and delete groups. You can also accomplish these operations by using the command line.

Creating a Group

To create a group by using Userconf, follow this procedure:

1. Launch Userconf by issuing the command `userconf`.

2. Choose Group Definitions and press Enter; or, if you're using X, click Group Definitions.

Depending on the filter settings (in Control ➤ Features), you may see a Filter dialog box. Use the dialog box to limit the user groups to those you want to see, or press Accept to view all groups. The Users Groups screen appears.

3. Click the Add button. The Group Specification screen appears.

4. Fill in the parameter fields. Refer to Table 3.3 for information on each field.

5. Click the Accept button.

TABLE 3.3: Group Parameters

PARAMETER	DESCRIPTION
Group name	The name of the group
Group ID	The numeric group ID
Alternate members	Usernames of group members, separated by one or more spaces (optional)

You can also use Userconf to delete a group and to modify group membership. You can modify group membership by modifying each affected user account or by modifying the group. Generally, it's more convenient to modify the group.

Administering Groups via the Command Line

You can use the command line to administer user groups. Commands let you create a group, delete a group, or modify group membership. To create a group via the command line, issue the groupadd command, which has the following form:

```
groupadd -g groupid group
```

You must specify the name of the group to be created as *group*. If you do not specify a group ID, the next group ID will be used. If you want to create a system group—one with a group ID less than 500—specify -r as an argument before the group name. See the groupadd man page for additional information.

To delete a group via the command line, issue the groupdel command; to modify the name of a group via the command line, issue the groupmod command. To modify membership of a group via the command line, you must manually edit /etc/group or issue the usermod command to adjust the group membership of each affected user. Generally, this means you must issue the command several times; thus it's often more convenient to modify group membership via userconf than from the command line. The usermod command is described earlier in this chapter.

Assigning Passwords

To change the password associated with a user account, do the following:

1. Launch Userconf by issuing the command `userconf`.

2. Choose User Accounts and press Enter; or, if you're using X, click User Accounts. The Users Accounts screen appears.

   Depending on the filter settings (in Control ➤ Features), you may see a Filter dialog box. Use the dialog box to limit the user accounts to those you want to see, or press Accept to view all accounts.

3. Highlight the account you want to modify and press Enter; or, if you're using X, you can simply click the account.

4. Click the Passwd button. The Changing Password dialog box appears.

5. Type the desired password and click the Accept button. The Changing Password dialog box reappears.

6. Confirm the password you previously entered by retyping it. Click the Accept button. The Users Accounts screen reappears.

You can also change the password associated with a user account by using the command line. Issue the `passwd` command, which has the following format:

```
passwd user
```

The program will prompt for the password twice, in order to ensure you typed it correctly.

The `mkpasswd` program is a helpful utility that generates random passwords or assigns a random password to a user account. To generate a random password, issue the following command:

```
mkpasswd
```

The program generates and displays the password. To automatically assign a random password to a user account, issue the command `mkpasswd user`. The command assigns and displays the password.

Exam Essentials

Know how to create different kinds of user accounts   You should be familiar with the various account types, including ordinary user accounts, PPP user accounts, SLIP user accounts, UUCP user accounts, and POP user accounts. You should know how to configure user accounts, how to enable and disable them, and how to assign account passwords. You should also know how to create user groups. You should be able to perform user administration via `userconf` and the command line.

Key Terms and Concepts

Ordinary user account   An account used by a user who logs into the system via the console, TELNET, SSH, or X.

POP user account   An account used by a user who accesses mail via POP from a remote location.

PPP user account   An account used by a user who logs in via PPP from a remote location.

SLIP user account   An account used by a user who logs in via SLIP from a remote location.

User account   A user account provides a means of authenticating a system user and establishes the user's environment and capabilities.

User group   A group defines a set of user accounts.

UUCP user   An account used by a process that logs in via UUCP from a remote location.

Sample Questions

1. Which of the following groups is the default group for PPP users?

A. ppp

B. ppps

C. pppusers

D. users

Answer: C. PPP users, by default, are members of the group pppusers.

2. Which of the following is not a standard component of the gecos field?

A. Home address

B. Home phone

C. Office

D. Office phone

Answer: A. The gecos field does not generally include home address information.

Configuring the User Environment

- **Customizing a User Profile**
- **Sharing Data via a User Private Group**

Because users have a variety of needs and abilities, a user's computing environment should be customized so that the user can access and use computing facilities as efficiently and effectively as possible. Linux lets the system administrator customize a user's environment by means of a user profile. Linux also lets the system administrator configure groups and group memberships to facilitate sharing of data.

Critical Information

When a user logs in, the command interpreter executes several files that configure the user's environment. The files contain commands that set environment variables, adjust the path, create command aliases, and so on. By revising these files, you can configure a user's environment.

System-Wide User Profiles

The files executed when a user whose shell is BASH logs in include

- /etc/bashrc, a file that establishes aliases and functions.

- /etc/profile, a file that sets environment variables and performs other operations, including executing files in the /etc/profile.d directory.

- /etc/profile.d, a directory that contains several small scripts. Those with filenames ending in .sh are executed by /etc/profile.

The files in /etc/profile.d include

- kde.csh, which sets up the KDE environment for C shell users

- kde.sh, which sets up the KDE environment for BASH shell users

- ang.sh, which sets up environment variables used by internationalization facilities

- mc.csh, which sets up the Midnight Commander environment for C shell users

- mc.sh, which sets up the Midnight Commander environment for BASH shell users

You can revise the contents of the /etc/profile.d directory or add and delete files to customize the operations performed when a user logs in.

User Profiles

When you create a user account by using `userconf` or by using the `useradd` command with the -m argument, the contents of /etc/skel are copied to the user's home directory. You can modify the contents of /etc/skel or add and remove files and directories. Doing so makes it possible to customize the user's environment.

The files and directories in /etc/skel are generally hidden files and directories, having names with an initial dot (.). The default files include the following:

`.Xdefaults`   A file that establishes various X options.

`.bash_logout`   A file that clears the screen when the user exits the initial BASH shell.

`.bash_profile`   A file that invokes .bashrc and establishes the path and other environment variables.

`.bashrc`   A file that invokes /etc/bashrc.

`.kde`   A directory that contains a variety of subdirectories and files that are part of the KDE desktop environment and KDE applications, such as the KWM window manager.

`.kderc`   A file that specifies KDE options.

`Desktop`   A directory that contains files that configure the user's KDE desktop.

Sharing Data via a User Private Group

Often, users need to share data that they don't want others to be able to access or modify. A simple way of accomplishing this is to create a group for each set of users who want to share access to data. Then, assign group ownership of the related files or directories to the new group. Finally, assign access permissions that permit members of the group to perform authorized operations, but exclude non-members from doing so.

Red Hat Linux facilitates this operation by assigning each user to a one-member group that includes only the user. This facility, known as the *user private group*, lets you assign a umask value that establishes default access permissions that permit group access. Since the user is the only member of the user's private group, such a umask value does not compromise security. Because of the user private group, when the group ownership of a file or directory is changed to permit shared access, it's often unnecessary to adjust the access permissions.

For example, suppose the users tom, dick, and harry want to have access to the directory bigdeal, but want to prohibit access by others. You could create a group named tdandh (as a reminder of its members) and set the group ownership of the bigdeal directory to tdandh. If necessary, assign permissions of 770 to the directory and you have the desired result.

Exam Essentials

Know how to configure the user environment   You should know how to configure the user environment by modifying the standard scripts that establish the environment.

Be familiar with system and user bash configuration files   You should know the primary scripts that establish the user environment, including /etc/bashrc and /etc/profile and the scripts residing in /etc/profile.d and /etc/skel.

Be capable of using IPChains to implement basic firewalling policies and be familiar with the user private group scheme in Red Hat Linux   This section describes the use of groups to facilitate the sharing of data. You should be familiar with Red Hat's user private group scheme and how to use it to share data.

NOTE   For more information on IPChains, see Chapter 13, "Routing."

Key Terms and Concepts

User private group A group that consists of one member, created by default when the user account is established.

User profile The shell commands executed when a user logs in, logs out, or enters a command shell, and the related files and scripts.

Sample Questions

1. Which of the following directories contains the files copied into the home directory of a newly created user?

   A. /etc/bash

   B. /etc/profile

   C. /etc/skel

   D. /etc/template

   Answer: C. When a new user is created, Red Hat Linux copies the contents of /etc/skel into the user's home directory.

2. What is the term for the group created automatically by Red Hat Linux when a new user account is established?

   A. personal group

   B. private group

   C. user group

   D. user private group

   Answer: D. By default, a new user is assigned to a user private group, which Red Hat Linux automatically creates.

Chapter

4

The Red Hat Package Manager (RPM)

RHCE PREPARATION TOPICS COVERED IN THIS CHAPTER:

▶ **Working with Binary RPM Packages**
(pages 82 – 96)

▶ **Working with Source RPM Packages**
(pages 96 – 99)

One of the most significant contributions of Red Hat Inc. to the Linux community has been Red Hat's support for development of the Red Hat Package Manager (RPM). Prior to RPM, installation of Linux software was largely a matter of hit and miss: Installation of one application often crippled another. Thanks to RPM, Linux system administrators can now install applications with the confidence that the applications will operate correctly and will not conflict with other applications. This chapter explains the operation of the RPM facility and describes how to perform common RPM operations.

Working with Binary RPM Packages

Before RPM, Linux system administrators—like other Unix system administrators—installed programs by downloading TAR files, unpacking them, and compiling source files. Programs often conflicted in their use of common files, and software developers often made assumptions about the placement of files and availability of commands and libraries. Consequently, system administrators regularly spent overtime hours coaxing programs to work.

RPM manages the software installation process by tracking information about installed software programs. Thus, system administrators rarely find that installing one program has broken another.

Critical Information

RPM consists of three components:

- package files

- the RPM database
- the rpm command

Package files replace the TAR files that were used before the advent of RPM. Like TAR files, package files contain the files that must be installed. Unlike TAR files, package files contain information describing the application or service contained in the package. For example, a package file identifies any capabilities, such as libraries or other packages, that must be installed in order for it to install and operate correctly. This information is called *dependency information*. Other information stored in packages includes

- Name and version of the package
- Build date and build host
- Description of the package
- Size and MD5 checksum of each contained file
- Identity of the person or organization that built the package
- Package group to which the package belongs

The name of a package file has a specific structure that resembles the following:

package-version-build.architecture.rpm

where

- *package* is the name of the package contained in the file. This lets you abbreviate the filename to accommodate restrictions imposed by DOS or other file systems that limit the number of characters in a filename.
- *version* is the version number of the package.
- *build* is the build number of the package.
- *architecture* is the computer architecture for which the package is designed.

For example, the package filename gnorpm-0.9-10.i386.rpm indicates that the file contains version 0.9, build 10, of a package named gnorpm intended for the i386 (Intel 386) architecture.

The RPM Database

Once a package is installed, information about the package is stored in the RPM database, which resides in /var/lib/rpm. When you issue an rpm command—for example, a command to install a package or a command to uninstall a package—the RPM facility inspects the package file and the RPM database. Thus, the RPM facility is able to determine whether execution of the command will leave the system in an inconsistent state. If so, the RPM facility suppresses the command and warns the user of the potential danger.

The *rpm* Command

The rpm command is the executable component of the RPM facility. Its host of switches and arguments enable you to perform operations such as

- installing packages
- updating packages
- removing packages
- querying the RPM database
- querying a package file
- building a package file from source code
- validating a package
- validating a package file

When installing, updating, or removing packages, the rpm command performs several checks intended to ensure that the system is left in a consistent state. For example, when installing a package, rpm checks for the following:

- There is sufficient free disk space to accommodate the package.

- Any capabilities required by the package (dependencies) are installed.

- Installation of the package won't overwrite existing files.

Special switches let you override these checks so that you can cope with unusual situations. The remaining sections of this chapter explain the operation of rpm within the context of common operations you'll need to know how to perform.

Necessary Procedures

This section describes several procedures for working with packages. It's particularly important that you master these procedures as part of your preparation for the RHCE exam.

Adding Packages

To install a package, issue a command that has this form:

```
rpm -i package_file_name
```

where *package_file_name* specifies the name of the file containing the package you want to install. If you like, you can list several package names or use shell metacharacters such as * to specify sets of files. For example, here's a typical command:

```
rpm -i gnorpm-0.9-10.i386.rpm gnome-linuxconf-0.23-
 1.i386.rpm
```

The command installs the gnorpm package contained in the package file gnorpm-0.9-10.i386.rpm and the gnome-linuxconf package contained in the package file gnome-linuxconf-0.23-1.i386.rpm. First, of course, the command performs the checks described earlier; if any of the checks fail, the command fails without installing the package that failed the checks.

Many system administrators like to include the -v and -h flags, as in the following example:

```
rpm -ivh gnorpm-0.9-10.i386.rpm gnome-linuxconf-
0.23-1.i386.rpm
```

The -v flag causes the command to print status information as it executes; it's especially helpful when you specify multiple files, because rpm prints a message as it begins installation of each file. The -h flag causes rpm to display 50 hash marks as it installs each package, helping you visualize the progress of each package installation. Here's a typical invocation of rpm that includes these flags:

```
# rpm -ivh gnorpm-0.9-10.i386.rpm
gnome-linuxconf-0.23-1.i386.rpm
gnorpm        ####################################
gnome-linuxconf ####################################
```

One of the advantages of the -vh is that it is very clear what packages have actually been installed. An annoying shortcoming of RPM is that it will exit with an error if a package is already installed. Without the -vh, it is sometimes difficult to tell which packages in a list of packages were installed before RPM aborted.

Another handy RPM feature is support for files stored on FTP servers. Rather than downloading the package file and installing the package, you can install directly from the FTP server by issuing a command that has this form:

```
ftp://server/path
```

where *server* is the host name or IP address of the anonymous FTP server, and *path* specifies the path to the package file. For example, the following command installs a package that resides on Red Hat's anonymous FTP server:

```
rpm -ivh ftp://contrib.redhat.com/i386/RedHat/RPMS/
gnorpm-0.9-10.i386.rpm
```

If you need to access the FTP server by means of a particular account, issue a command that has the form

```
ftp://user:pass@server/path
```

where *user* and *pass* specify the user ID and password, and the remaining tokens have the meaning given previously. If the server listens on a non-standard port, you can use this command form:

```
ftp://user:pass@server:port/path
```

where *port* is the number of the port on which the server listens.

The versions of RPM distributed with Red Hat Linux 6.2 and later support filename globbing, which lets you include wildcard characters. For example, the RPM command to install gnorpm could be written

```
rpm -ivh ftp://contrib.redhat.com/i386/RedHat/RPMS/
↳gnorpm*
```

One more handy RPM feature is that you don't need to specify the package files in any particular order, even if one or more of the specified packages depend on the capabilities of another. The rpm command detects any dependencies and installs the packages in an appropriate order.

If a package requires a capability that's provided neither by a package specified in the same command nor by an installed package, the rpm command prints an error message. For example,

```
# rpm -i gnorpm-0.9-10.i386.rpm
error: failed dependencies:
        usermode >= 1.13 is needed by gnorpm-0.9-10
        librpm.so.0 is needed by gnorpm-0.9-10
```

To resolve a dependency, you must install the appropriate package providing the required capability or upgrade an existing package to a later version. For instance, the error message states that a newer version of the usermode package is required and that the library named librpm.so.0 is required. Later in this chapter, you'll learn how to discover what capabilities a package provides so that you could determine, for example, what package would provide the librpm.so.0 library.

If you try to install a package that conflicts with an existing package or file, you'll see an error message that resembles this one:

```
# rpm -i gnorpm-0.9-10.i386.rpm
file /usr/bin/gnorpm from install of gnorpm-0.9-10
⮑conflicts with file from package gnoway-0.8-5
```

You'll see another sort of error message if you attempt to install a package for which there's insufficient disk space.

Suppose you install a software program distributed by means of a TAR file. Later, a newer version of the software is published, one that uses RPM for distribution. When you install the new package, RPM determines that it will overwrite existing files. Rather than overwrite files RPM recognizes as configuration files, it saves each existing configuration file by appending .rpmsave to its name.

To overcome errors and other exceptions, you may have occasional need for the following special rpm arguments:

- --force, which overwrites newer packages or existing files

- --nodeps, which skips dependency checking

- --replacefiles, which replaces files owned by another package

For example, to install the package gnorpm despite dependency problems, you might issue the command

```
rpm -i --nodeps gnorpm-0.9-10.i386.rpm gnome-
⮑linuxconf-0.23-1.i386.rpm
```

The command will succeed regardless of dependency problems; however, the installed program will not function unless the required files are actually present.

Removing Packages

To remove an installed package, issue a command of the form

```
rpm -e package_name
```

where *package_name* is the name of the installed package. You may find it easier to recall this command form if you think of erasing a package rather than removing it, because the *e* in *erase* corresponds to the -e flag. If you prefer, you can specify the --uninstall flag, which has the same meaning as the -e flag.

TIP   Users unfamiliar with the rpm command often specify a package name where a package filename is needed, and the reverse. Pay careful attention to which is required by each command form.

When the rpm command removes a package, it checks whether the package provides capabilities needed by other packages. If so, it suppresses execution and warns you. If necessary, you can override this check by specifying the --nodeps flag.

When the rpm command removes a package, it also saves any modified configuration files. Thus, when you need a little extra disk space to cope with some emergency, you can easily remove, and later reinstall, some packages.

Performing Updates and Fixes

From time to time, new versions of packages are published. Often, these contain bug fixes or new features that are important. RPM makes it easy to install new versions of packages. To do so, issue a command of the form

```
rpm -Uvh package_file_name
```

where *package_file_name* is the name of the file containing the new version of the package. You can omit the -v and -h flags, if you prefer. The -U flag causes the rpm command to remove the existing package (as though you'd performed an `rpm -e`) and then install the new package (as though you'd performed an `rpm -i`). When the `rpm` command removes the old package, it saves any modified configuration files, renaming them by appending `.rpmsave` to their names. If the package contained in the specified file is not currently installed, the `rpm` command installs it. Therefore, many system administrators use the `-U` flag in place of the `-i` flag; `rpm -U` will install the package if it is absent or update it if it is present.

A related flag, `-F`, lets you update a package only if it's present. For example, the command

```
rpm -Fvh gnorpm-0.9-10.i386.rpm
```

would update the gnorpm package only if the package is installed. The `-F` flag helps you keep your system current. Red Hat maintains a list of updated packages at www.redhat.com/support/errata/. You should monitor the list and apply any fixes that you believe are important to the operation of your system by using the `-F` flag.

Identifying Installed Packages

You can use RPM to learn the version and build numbers of an installed package. To do so, issue a command of the form

```
rpm -q package_name
```

where *package_name* is the name of the installed package. The output consists of a single line that gives the package name, version number, and build number—as in the following example:

```
gnorpm-0.9-10
```

To learn the version ad build number of each installed package, issue the command `rpm -qa`.

Determining File Ownership

You can use RPM to learn which package, if any, owns a particular file. To do so, issue a command of the form

```
rpm -qf filename
```

where *filename* is the name of the file and must include the full path. For example, asking RPM to report the ownership of the file /etc/inittab yields output such as this:

```
# rpm -qf /etc/inittab
initscripts-4.16-1
```

Querying and Verifying Package Contents

The rpm command lets you query and verify package contents in a variety of ways.

Printing a Description of a Package

To print a description of an installed package, issue a command of the form

```
rpm -qi package_name
```

where *package_name* is the name of the installed package.

To print this information for a package file, issue a command of the form

```
rpm -qip package_file_name
```

where *package_file_name* is the name of the package file.

Listing Contained Files

To list the files contained in an installed package, issue a command of the form

```
rpm -ql package_name
```

where *package_name* is the name of the installed package.

To list the files contained in a package file, issue a similar command having the form

```
rpm -qlp package_file_name
```

Printing Scripts

To print the pre-installation and post-installation scripts associated with a package file, issue a command of the form

```
rpm -qp --scripts package_file_name
```

where *package_file_name* is the name of the file that contains the package.

Verifying Package Contents

RPM maintains a record on each file contained in an installed package. The record contains the file size, ownership, permissions, the MD5 checksum of each file, and other information. If the file is a symbolic link, the record contains the path to which the link refers; if the file is a device file, the record contains the associated major and minor device numbers.

By means of these records, you can determine which files, if any, have been modified since installation of a package by issuing a command of the form

```
rpm -V package_name
```

where *package_name* is the name of the installed package. The output consists of one line for each file. Each line has three fields:

- Status, which indicates the status of the file. Table 4.1 describes the flags used to indicate status.

- Configuration, which contains a *c* if the file is a configuration file and a space otherwise.

- Filename, which gives the path and name of the file.

TABLE 4.1: Package Verification Flags

Code	Meaning
.	No change.
5	MD5 checksum has changed.
D	Device major or minor number has changed.
G	Owning group has changed.
L	Link path has changed.
M	File modes have changed.
S	File size has changed.
T	Modification time has changed.
U	Owning user has changed.

Here's an example that shows the status of the contents of the setup package:

```
# rpm -V setup
S.5....T c /etc/exports
S.5....T c /etc/hosts.allow
S.5....T c /etc/hosts.deny
etc.
```

You can compare against package files rather than the database, if you prefer. This option is useful if you suspect the database may be corrupt. To do so, issue a command of the form

```
rpm -Vp package_file_name
```

where *package_file_name* is the name of the package file.

You can also verify the status of every installed package. To do so, issue the command rpm --verify -a.

Verifying Package Authenticity

GNU Privacy Guard (GPG) is an open source program similar to the more familiar Pretty Good Privacy (PGP) program, which lets you authenticate electronic documents. Authors of RPM packages can sign their work with a GPG key. If you've installed the GPG package, you can verify the authenticity of a signed package file. To do so, issue a command of the form

```
rpm -K package_file_name
```

where *package_file_name* is the name of the package file. You'll need to download and install Red Hat's GPG key; you can find the key on the Contacts page of their Web site, www.redhat.com.

Finding the Package that Provides a Given Capability

Red Hat Linux 6.2 and later include the rpmdb-redhat package that contains an alternate RPM database describing the contents of the release. If you install this package, you can use the rpm command's special --redhatprovides flag to determine which package owns a particular file. This capability is helpful in resolving dependencies. For example, suppose you try to install a package but receive an error message stating that a particular library is required—say, libsample .so.1. The following command identifies the package containing the missing library:

```
rpm -q --redhatprovides libsample.so.1
```

Exam Essentials

Possess a thorough knowledge of the rpm command and its switches, particularly those related to the installation and querying of packages RPM is one of the most important facilities of Red Hat Linux. You should be thoroughly familiar with packages, package files, and using RPM to install and query packages. In particular, be sure you understand package dependencies and how to resolve dependency problems by installing appropriate packages or using the `--force` option.

Key Terms and Concepts

Build number   The serial build number that distinguishes various builds of a given version of a software application.

Capability   A resource provided by a package.

Dependency   A resource required by a package.

Package   The files and scripts that comprise an installable application.

Package file   A file that contains a package.

Version number   The serial version number associated with a software application.

Sample Questions

1. What filename would be associated with a package containing build 1 of version 2 of the xyz application for Intel-compatible PCs?

A. `xyz-1-2.i386.rpm`

B. `xyz-2-1.i386.rpm`

C. `xyz-1-2-i386.rpm`

D. `xyz-2-1-i386.rpm`

Answer: B. The version number precedes the build number, and the architecture is delimited by dots.

2. Which of the following command forms uninstalls a package?

A. `rpm -e` *package*

B. `rpm -f` *package*

C. rpm −i *package*

D. rpm −u *package*

Answer: A. The -e flag (erase) specifies that a package should be uninstalled.

Working with Source RPM Packages

Ordinary RPM packages contain binary executable files. RPM also supports source RPM package files, which contain source code and which must therefore be compiled before installation. Because you can generally configure a variety of options at compile time that are not available thereafter, source RPM packages afford greater flexibility than binary RPM packages. You'll find source RPMs on the auxiliary CD-ROM that's part of the Red Hat Linux distribution; you can also download them from ftp://contrib.redhat.com and other sites.

Critical Information

Source RPMs have names of this form:

package-version-build.src.rpm

As you can see, the name of a source RPM differs from that of a binary RPM in that it ends in .src.rpm rather than merely .rpm.

When you install a source RPM, its files are installed under the /usr/src/redhat directory tree, which contains these subdirectories:

- BUILD: The source RPM is uncompressed, untarred, and patched here.

- RPMS: When you compile a source RPM, the new binary RPM is saved here. The directory contains subdirectories for each supported architecture.

- SOURCES: The source code—usually contained in a TAR file—and patches reside here.

- SPECS: This directory contains SPEC files that list package sources, patches, compile-time options, post-install steps, and package information related to a source RPM.

- SRPMS: When you create a new source RPM, it is saved here.

To build a binary RPM from a source RPM, move to the SPECS directory and issue a command of the form

```
rpm -bb spec_file
```

where *spec_file* is the name of the SPEC file associated with the source RPM. Table 4.2 describes other useful rpm command flags related to source RPMs.

TABLE 4.2: Source File Flags of the rpm Command

Flag	Meaning
-bp	%prep stage: unpack and patch source
-bl	%files stage: check that files exist
-bc	%build stage: make install
-bb	builds binary package
-ba	builds binary and source packages
--test	check syntax of SPEC file

If a SPEC file is contained within a TAR file, you need not unpack the TAR file. Instead, replace the -b flag with -t and specify the TAR file that contains the SPEC file. The rpm command supports both uncompressed and gzip-compressed TAR files.

You need not install a source RPM in order to compile it. Simply specify a command of the form

```
rpm --recompile source_package_file
```

where *source_package_file* is the name of the source RPM. To compile an uninstalled SRPM, build a corresponding binary RPM, and clean up the source files, issue a command of the form

```
rpm --rebuild source_package_file
```

where *source_package_file* is the name of the source RPM.

Exam Essentials

Be familiar with the basic elements of source (*.src.rpm) RPM packages   You should understand the concepts involved in working with source RPM packages. You should also be able to build a binary package from a source RPM package.

Key Term and Concept

Source RPM Packages   Unlike ordinary RPM packages, which contain binary code, source RPM packages contain source code and provide greater flexibility than ordinary RPM packages.

Sample Questions

1. What filename would be associated with an RPM source package containing build 1 of version 2 of the application xyz for Intel-compatible PCs?

   A. xyz-1-2.i386.rpm

   B. xyz-1-2.i386.src.rpm

C. xyz-1-2.src.i386.rpm

D. xyz-1-2.src.rpm

Answer: D. The architecture is not part of the name of a source RPM package file, because a single source distribution generally provides support for all architectures.

2. Which of the following command forms builds a binary RPM based on directives contained in a SPEC file?

A. rpm —bb *spec_file*

B. rpm —bs *spec_file*

C. rpm —bt *spec_file*

D. rpm —bz *spec_file*

Answer: A. The –bb flag specifies that a binary RPM package file should be built according to the directives in the given SPEC file.

Chapter

5

The File System

A typical Red Hat Linux system holds many directories and files. To efficiently administer such a system, you must know where important files, and which kinds of files, are stored. This chapter describes the Red Hat Linux file system layout, which generally follows the recommendations of the File System Hierarchy Standard.

▶ Navigating the Red Hat Linux File System Layout

If you're familiar with the layout of the Red Hat Linux file system, you can quickly locate the files and directories you need. This will save you time on the RHCE exam and make you a more efficient system administrator.

Critical Information

Like other Unix systems, Red Hat Linux has a hierarchical file system. The top-most directory—known as the *root directory*—of the file system contains several other directories, sometimes called subdirectories. These directories, in turn, generally contain subdirectories and files.

The directory structure is not arbitrary. For packages to work properly, the location of important files and directories must be standardized. The File System Hierarchy Standard codifies common practices and suggests improved practices for the structure of directories. The File System Hierarchy Standard is available via the Web, at http://pathname.com/fhs.

Though designed with Linux systems in mind, the standard is applicable to Unix systems in general. Distributors of Linux generally follow the recommendations of the File System Hierarchy Standard. However, the standard is somewhat loose and subject to interpretation. Consequently, two distributions that are held to follow the standard may nevertheless differ significantly in the structure of their file systems. Red Hat Linux follows the standard closely. The *Official Red Hat Linux Reference Guide* explains the standard and how Red Hat Linux implements the standard's recommendations.

The Root Directory

The root directory (/) of a Linux system is the directory that contains all other directories and files. Other directories may be separately mounted and, therefore, may or may not be present at system start-up. Therefore, the file system that contains the root directory must contain all files necessary to operate the system in single-user mode. The root directory also contains all files needed to shut down and recover or repair the system.

The following directories are essential and must be part of the root file system:

- /bin, which contains binary files used by the system administrator and other users

- /dev, which contains device files

- /etc, which contains host-specific configuration data

- /lib, which contains system libraries

- /sbin, which contains binary files used by the system administrator

A boot or rescue floppy disk may contain only the essential directories on its root file system, which may be the only file system contained on the media. However, Linux systems typically include several other directories, which may be used as mounting points for non-root file systems or which may contain directories and files that reside on the root file system. Some commonly used directories include

- /boot, which contains files needed by the boot loader when booting the system. These files could be placed in the root partition.

However, Red Hat Inc. recommends that they be placed in a separate partition to overcome common PC BIOS limitations on the location of boot data.

- /home, which contains users' home directories.

- /lost+found, which contains files recovered during file system rebuilds.

- /mnt, which contains mount points for temporarily mounted file systems.

- /proc, which contains system information.

- /root, which contains the home directory of the root user.

- /tmp, which contains temporary files.

- /usr, which contains shareable files not essential to basic system operation.

- /var, which contains non-shareable files not essential to basic system operation.

/bin: Essential Binary Files

The /bin directory contains binary files that are essential to system operation in single-user mode. These files are generally commands that may be used by the system administrator and by users. Similar files not required for single-user mode are placed in /usr/bin.

/boot: Boot Loader Files

Many PCs contain BIOS code that cannot load a boot record unless the boot record is stored below a given cylinder (usually 1024) of a disk drive. Red Hat recommends that you avoid boot problems by placing boot loader files in a separate partition and placing the partition on a region of the disk that is accessible to the BIOS.

The /boot partition generally contains the first stage of the Linux loader (LILO) in its MBR, located on the first cylinder of the partition. It also contains files such as the following:

- LILO's second stage, which resides in the file boot.b

- the Linux kernel, generally named `vmlinuz*`
- module information that identifies system modules by name
- the system map file that records the location of kernel modules and symbols
- copies of disk areas overwritten by the loader during its installation

/dev: Device Files

The Linux /dev directory includes a variety of *device files*, which provide interfaces to hardware devices. Not every device file corresponds to an installed device; an installation script (/dev/MAKEDEV) creates a standard set of device files, whether the associated device is installed or not.

Table 5.1 summarizes some of the most important common device files. In addition, there are device files that correspond to the following:

- various mice (for example, /dev/psaux)
- memory and I/O ports (for example, /dev/mem)
- various audio and multimedia devices (for example, /dev/audio)
- specialized serial cards (for example, /dev/ttyC)
- proprietary CD-ROM drives (for example, /dev/cdu31a)

TABLE 5.1: Important Device Files

DEVICE FILE	DEVICE
console	System console
cua*	Deprecated—originally referred to a serial port
fd*	Floppy drive
hd*	IDE hard disk or CD-ROM
lp*	Parallel port
md*	RAID array

TABLE 5.1: Important Device Files *(continued)*

DEVICE FILE	DEVICE
null	Null output device
ramdisk	RAM disk
sd*	SCSI hard disk
sr*	SCSI CD-ROM
st*	SCSI tape
tpqic*, ntpqic*, rft*, nrft*	QIC tape
tty*	Terminal or pseudoterminal
ttyS*	Serial port
vc*	Contents of a tty device, such as a virtual console
zero	All binary 0s input device

/etc: Host-Specific Configuration Files

The /etc directory contains files and directories that are specific to the local host. Traditionally, some binary files had resided in /etc; these are now found in /sbin and /usr/sbin. Some of the most important files and subdirectories are summarized in Tables 5.2 and 5.3, respectively.

TABLE 5.2: Important Files in /etc

FILE	CONTENTS
adjtime	Time synchronization data
fdprm	Floppy diskette parameters
fstab	File system table
gettydefs	Log in terminal characteristics

TABLE 5.2: Important Files in /etc *(continued)*

FILE	CONTENTS
group	User groups
inittab	System startup configuration
ld.so.conf	System library cache
lilo.conf	Linux loader configuration
motd	Message of the day
mtab	Mounted file system table
mtools.conf	Configuration of mtools utilities
nsswitch.conf	List of sources for information on users, hosts, networks, and services
passwd	User accounts
profile	Shell initialization script
securetty	List of secure log in terminals
shadow	User account encrypted passwords, if shadow passwords enabled
shells	List of approved shells
syslog.conf	System log configuration
exports	NFS exports configuration
ftp*	FTP configuration files
host.conf	Host name resolution configuration (see also resolv.conf)
hosts	List of known hosts
hosts.allow	List of hosts allowed access to services
hosts.deny	List of hosts denied access to services

TABLE 5.2: Important Files in /etc *(continued)*

FILE	CONTENTS
hosts.equiv	List of trusted hosts
inetd.conf	Configuration of Internet superserver, inetd
networks	List of known networks
printcap	Printer configuration
protocols	List of known protocols
resolv.conf	Host name resolution configuration (see also host.conf)
rpc	List of RPC services
services	List of TCP/IP services

TABLE 5.3: Important Subdirectories of /etc

SUBDIRECTORY	CONTENTS
cron*	Configuration of cron service
httpd	Configuration of http (Web) service
pam.d	Configuration of PAM, Red Hat's security library
pcmcia	Configuration of PCMCIA slots and devices
ppp	Configuration of the PPP service
rc.d	System initialization files
security	Security configuration
skel	User environment template files
sysconfig	System configuration
X11	X Window System configuration, including XF86Config file

/home: User Home Directories

The /home directory contains home directories of users other than root (whose home directory is /root). By default, a user's home directory is a subdirectory of /home and has the same name as the user's login. However, you may prefer to structure the /home directory differently, particularly if a system has many user accounts. For example, a university might place students' home directories under /home/student and faculty members' home directories under /home/faculty, mounting disk volumes at these mount points.

/lib: Shared Libraries and Kernel Modules

The /lib directory contains libraries and modules needed to boot the system and run programs residing in the /sbin and /bin directories; other libraries reside in /usr/lib, /usr/X11R6/lib, and elsewhere. Modules reside in subdirectories of /lib/modules; each such subdirectory is named according to the version and build number of the kernel with which the modules are associated. For example, modules for build 15 of the Linux 2.2.9 kernel might be found in /lib/modules/2.2.9-15.

/lost+found: Recovered Files

When you recover a file system, files and file data may be partially recovered. For example, the recovery utility may recover a file's data but not the file's name. Such files are placed by the utility in the /lost+found subdirectory of the root directory of the file system.

/mnt: Mount Point for Temporarily Mounted File Systems

The /mnt directory exists as the standard parent directory of a set of directories for temporarily mounting file systems. Standard subdirectories include cdrom, a mount point for CD-ROM file systems, and floppy, a mount point for file systems residing on floppy disk.

/proc: System Information Virtual File System

The Linux /proc directory is a pseudo file system provided by the kernel, containing files and directories that let system administrators and programmers access system information. Some information in the

/proc directory can be modified to configure system operation. Some of the most important files and subdirectories in the /proc directory are summarized in Table 5.4.

TABLE 5.4: Important Files and Subdirectories of /proc

FILE OR SUBDIRECTORY	CONTENTS
[*number*]	A directory that contains files and subdirectories that describe the process having the same ID as the directory name
cpuinfo	Various architecture-dependent information
devices	Major device numbers and device groups
dma	Registered ISA DMA channels in use
filesystems	File system types supported by the kernel
interrupts	Information on interrupts and IRQs
ioports	Registered input/output ports
kcore	System physical memory contents
kmsg	Kernel message log
ksyms	Kernel exported symbols and definitions
loadavg	Average number of jobs in the run queue
meminfo	Memory allocation information
modules	List of loaded modules
net	Network status information
pci	Configuration of PCI devices
scsi	Status of SCSI input/output system
self	Information on the process accessing the /proc file system

TABLE 5.4: Important Files and Subdirectories of /proc *(continued)*

FILE OR SUBDIRECTORY	CONTENTS
stat	Kernel and system statistics
sys	Kernel variables, some of which can be modified to configure kernel operation
uptime	The system uptime and idle time
version	The version number of the running kernel

/sbin: Essential System Binaries

The /sbin directory contains essential system binary files used by the system administrator; that is, files needed for system startup, shutdown, and operation in single-user mode.

/tmp: Temporary Files

The /tmp directory contains *temporary files* and subdirectories that are automatically deleted by the tmpwatch utility when they've not been used for a specified period of time (by default, 10 days).

/usr: Shareable Files

The /usr file system may not be available, so it contains no files or directories that are essential for system operation. Normal operation of the system does not require modification of files in /usr, so its contents are shareable; often, for example, the /usr partition is an NFS-exported partition that resides on a remote system. Table 5.5 summarizes some important subdirectories of /usr.

TABLE 5.5: Important Subdirectories of /usr

SUBDIRECTORY	CONTENTS
/usr/X11R6	X Window System binary files
/usr/bin	Commands used by ordinary users

TABLE 5.5: Important Subdirectories of /usr *(continued)*

SUBDIRECTORY	CONTENTS
/usr/dict	Dictionary
/usr/doc	Documentation
/usr/games	Game-related binary files
/usr/include	Header files
/usr/info	Texinfo documentation files
/usr/lib	Programming libraries
/usr/local	Local files not part of the operating system
/usr/man	Man pages
/usr/sbin	System binaries not required to start, shut down, or run the system in single-user mode
/usr/share	Architecture-independent files
/usr/src	Source code

/var: Non-Shareable Files

Like the /usr file system, the /var file system may not be available and so it contains no essential files or directories. Unlike /usr, however, /var contains files that are modified during system operation—for example, log files. Table 5.6 summarizes important subdirectories of /var.

TABLE 5.6: Important Subdirectories of /var

SUBDIRECTORY	CONTENTS
/var/cache	Application cache files
/var/lock	Lock files

TABLE 5.6: Important Subdirectories of /var *(continued)*

SUBDIRECTORY	CONTENTS
/var/log	Log and accounting files
/var/run	System information files
/var/spool	Spool files, including those for cron, lpd, and mail
/var/tmp	Temporary files
/var/yp	NIS files

Exam Essentials

Be familiar with Red Hat Linux file system layout   You should know the principal directories of the Red Hat Linux file system layout and their contents. You should also know what the File System Hierarchy Standard is and why it's important.

Key Terms and Concepts

Device file   A file that provides an interface to a hardware device.

Temporary file   A file that is used for a relatively short period and then deleted.

Sample Questions

1. Which of the following directories contains the ifconfig command?

   A. /bin

   B. /sbin

C. /usr/bin

D. /usr/sbin

Answer: B. The ifconfig command is used by the system administrator to configure network interfaces, a function operation critical to system operation. Therefore, the command resides in /sbin.

2. Where might modules associated with version 2.4.2 of the Linux kernel reside?

A. /lib/2.4.2

B. /lib/modules/2.4.2-2

C. /modules/2.4.2

D. /modules/2.4.2-2

Answer: B. The modules reside in a subdirectory of /lib/modules named for the kernel version and build with which they're associated.

Chapter

6

System Initialization and Configuration

RHCE PREPARATION TOPICS COVERED IN THIS CHAPTER:

he RHCE exam is a hands-on exam that includes troubleshooting and configuration sessions. Because many system problems involve system initialization and configuration, these are among the most important topics to RHCE candidates. For the same reason, they're also important to system administrators generally.

Configuring System Initialization

When Red Hat Linux is booted, it automatically performs a variety of checks and then starts specified services. A Red Hat Linux administrator must be able to configure what checks are performed and what services are started. A thorough knowledge of system initialization is also important to system troubleshooting and recovery. This section explains the system initialization scripts and several tools that you can use to configure them.

Critical Information

Red Hat Linux generally follows the system initialization procedure inaugurated under AT&T SysV Unix. When a Red Hat Linux system boots, the system executes two main scripts:

- /etc/rc.d/rc.sysinit
- /etc/rc.d/rc

Essentially, the /etc/rc.d/rc.sysinit script initializes file systems and devices. It is a large script that invokes many commands. It also invokes the /etc/rc.d/rc.serial script, if one exists. The /etc/rc.d/rc.serial script initializes serial ports; it is used when special initialization must be performed—for example, when a multi-port serial card is installed.

Essentially, the /etc/rc.d/rc script initializes services. It is invoked at system startup and whenever the system *runlevel* is changed. It invokes an appropriate set of *runlevel scripts* that start and stop facilities and services. On system startup, it invokes the /etc/rc.d/rc.local script after all other runlevel scripts have executed. The contents of the /etc/rc.d/rc.local script are locally defined; you can use it to perform special initialization operations.

System initialization scripts may log error messages. If the system doesn't properly start up, you should examine /var/log/messages for relevant error messages.

The /etc/rc.d/rc.sysinit Script

The /etc/rc.d/rc.sysinit script initializes file systems and devices. It also performs several other operations. Here is a step-by-step guide to the operations performed by the script:

1. Checks for an /etc/sysconfig/network script, which sets environment variables describing the network configuration. If the script exists, it executes it; otherwise it sets environment variables that turn off networking and sets the host name to localhost.

2. Sources the file /etc/rc.d/init.d/functions, which contains a group of shell functions. These functions are used by scripts in the /etc/rc.d/init.d directory.

3. Displays welcome banner that includes a prompt for interactive startup.

4. Sets the logging level.

5. Mounts the /proc file system, configures kernel parameters by using sysctl, and sets the system clock.

6. Loads the default keymap if /etc/sysconfig/console/default.kmap exists; otherwise it loads the keymap specified in /etc/sysconfig/keyboard.

7. Runs the /sbin/setsysfont script, which sets the default system font.

8. Activates the swap partitions specified in /etc/fstab.

9. Sets the host name and the NIS domain name, if applicable.

10. If there is a problem with the root file system, remounts the root file system in read-only mode and checks its status. If a serious error is found, the script starts a shell that enables you to attempt to repair the damaged file system.

11. Sets up configured ISA plug-and-play devices.

12. Remounts the root file system in read-write mode.

13. Checks disk quotas on the root file system.

14. Sets up /etc/mtab, which lists mounted file systems, and /etc/HOSTNAME, which identifies the host.

15. Sets up support for loadable kernel modules.

16. Loads the sound module if a sound card is specified in /etc/conf.modules; loads the MIDI module if a MIDI interface is specified in /etc/conf.modules.

17. Loads the RAID devices specified in /etc/raidtab.

18. Checks the non-root file systems. If a serious error is found, the script starts a shell that enables you to attempt to repair the damaged file system. Otherwise, the script checks disk quotas on the non-root file systems and mounts those specified in /etc/fstab as automatically mountable. It then turns on disk quota checking if the disk quota package is installed.

19. Removes unneeded temporary files of various sorts, such as lock files.

20. Initializes serial ports by running the script /etc/rc.d/rc.serial, if it exists. The /etc/rc.d/rc.serial script generally contains setserial commands that configure serial devices. It is not generally needed to configure standard PC serial ports and is included mainly for compatibility with older Linux releases.

21. Loads the SCSI tape module if a SCSI tape drive is present.

22. Creates the header file /boot/kernel.h, under some circumstances.

23. Creates symbolic links for /boot/System.map-*kernel_version*.

24. Copies the kernel ring buffer messages to /var/log/dmesg so that they can be read subsequently.

The */etc/rc.d/rc* Script

During system startup, the init process invokes /etc/rc.d/rc. sysinit and then invokes /etc/rc.d/rc. The /etc/rc.d/rc script sets a new runlevel and then runs a series of scripts associated with the specified runlevel. The scripts are contained in the directories that have names matching the regular expression /etc/rc.d/rc?.d. The name of each directory corresponds to that of the associated runlevel. Table 6.1 summarizes the runlevels used by Red Hat Linux.

TABLE 6.1: Summary of Runlevels

Runlevel	Description
0	System halt
1	Single-user mode
2	Multiuser mode, no NFS
3	Full multiuser mode
4	Unused
5	Full multiuser mode, with X login
6	System reboot

Runlevel Scripts

Each /etc/rc.d/rc?.d directory contains a series of symbolic links that refer to scripts in the /etc/rc.d/init.d directory called runlevel scripts. The most common runlevel scripts, which are used to start and stop system services, are summarized in Table 6.2. If you've installed optional packages, you may find other scripts in addition to those described in Table 6.2. The point of using symbolic links to refer to the scripts is that several symbolic links can refer to a single script file. If the script requires revision, only one file must be changed, which is a more convenient and less error-prone method than changing several files.

TABLE 6.2: Description of Common Runlevel Scripts

Script	Description
anacron	Runs commands at specified intervals; unlike crond, it does not assume that the system is continuously operational.
apmd	Advanced power management service, which monitors battery power levels.
atd	AT server, which processes commands specified via the at command.
autofs	Automatically mounts file systems.
crond	Cron server, which runs commands at user-specified intervals.
gpm	Mouse support for text mode programs.
halt	Reboots or halts the system.
httpd	Apache Web server.
inet	A variety of basic TCP/IP services, run under control of inetd.
keytable	Loads the keyboard map.
killall	Kills running services.
kudzu	Checks at boot time for hardware changes.

TABLE 6.2: Description of Common Runlevel Scripts *(continued)*

Script	Description
linuxconf	A hook that allows linuxconf to perform specified actions on system startup and shutdown.
local	The /etc/rc.d/rc.local script, which has locally specified contents.
lpd	LP service, which provides access to remote printers.
named	DNS server, which provides host name and IP address lookups.
netfs	Mounts network file systems.
network	Activates and deactivates network interfaces.
nfs	Network File System (NFS) server, which provides file sharing.
pcmcia	Activates and deactivates PCMCIA support.
portmap	Manages RPC connections used, for example, by NFS and NIS.
postgresql	Database management system.
random	Saves and restores status of random number generator, to yield better-quality random numbers.
reboot	Symbolic link to halt script.
routed	RIP client and server, which automatically update routes.
rstatd	RSTAT server, which provides performance metrics.
rusersd	RUSERS server, which helps locate users.
rwhod	RWHO server, which lists logged-in users.
sendmail	Mail server.

TABLE 6.2: Description of Common Runlevel Scripts *(continued)*

Script	Description
single	Puts the system in single-user mode.
smb	Samba (SMB) server, which provides authentication and file and printer sharing.
sound	Saves and restores sound card mixer settings.
sshd	SSH server, which provides secure logins and remote command execution.
syslog	Starts and stops system logging.
xfs	The X Window system font server.

Most of the scripts accept arguments that control their operation. The most common arguments are

- start, which causes the script to start the associated service
- stop, which causes the script to stop the associated service
- restart, which causes the script to restart the associated service
- reload, which causes the script to reread its configuration file
- status, which causes the script to report the status of the associated service

The Linuxconf program uses these scripts to start and stop services. You can also manually invoke them to control services. For example, you could shut down the Web server (httpd service) by issuing the command

```
/etc/rc.d/init/d/httpd stop
```

Or you could restart the server by issuing the command

```
/etc/rc.d/init/httpd restart
```

TIP   It's important to use the scripts in /etc/rc.d/init.d rather than controlling services some other way. For example, it's possible to start the Web server by issuing the command /usr/sbin/httpd. However, if you do so, Linux won't be able to clean up lock files and process identification files when you shut down the service. Worse, unless you use the runlevel scripts, you may unintentionally start multiple instances of a server.

The Symbolic Links in */etc/rc.d/rc?.d*

The symbolic links in /etc/rc.d/rc?.d have names such as K05keytable and S40atd. Links having names beginning with *K* are passed the stop argument when they are executed by /etc/rc.d/rc; links having names beginning with *S* are passed the start argument. Generally, the directory associated with a given runlevel will include either a *K*-script or an *S*-script for each installed service.

The two-digit number in the script names, called the *priority*, indicates the sequence in which scripts in a given directory are run; for example, the script K10xfs is run before the script K15gpm.

When a runlevel script terminates, it reports a completion status. The possible values of the completion status are

- OK, which means that the script successfully started the associated service
- Passed, which means that the script encountered errors, but was able to recover and successfully start the associated service
- Failed, which means that the script was unable to start the associated service

The completion values appear on the console during system startup.

Operation of the */etc/rc.d/rc* Script

The /etc/rc.d/rc script sets the specified runlevel and invokes the runlevel scripts appropriate to the specified new runlevel. Here is a detailed step-by-step guide to the operations it performs:

1. Sources the file /etc/rc.d/init.d/functions, which contains a group of shell functions. These functions are used by scripts in the /etc/rc.d/init.d directory.

2. Determines the current and previous runlevels.

3. Checks and notes whether user confirmation mode is set.

4. Sets the runlevel to the specified value.

5. Tells Linuxconf the current runlevel.

6. Finds the /rc/rc.d/rcn.d directory, where *n* is the new runlevel.

7. Runs the kill script for each running service.

8. Runs the start script for each service not already running.

During system startup, the init process invokes /etc/rc.d/rc after completion of /etc/rc.d/rc.sysinit, based on the configuration of the /etc/inittab file.

The */etc/rc.d/rc.local* Script

The /etc/rc.d/rc.local script is a special script run by symbolic links in the directories associated with runlevels 2, 3, and 5. Its start priority is 99, which means it runs after all other runlevel scripts. By default, it

- creates the /etc/issue file
- creates the /etc/issue.net file

The /etc/issue file is listed when a user logs in by using a local console. By default, the file reports the release of Red Hat Linux and the kernel version:

```
Red Hat Linux release 6.0 (Hedwig)
Kernel 2.2.13-0.7 on an i686
```

The /etc/issue.net file is listed when a user logs in by using a remote console—for example, by initiating a Telnet session. By default, the file also reports the release of Red Hat Linux and the kernel version. However, it's considered good practice to change the contents of /etc/issue.net so that would-be hackers gain less information about your system. You may also want to display a banner stating any restrictions on system use.

You can easily modify the /etc/rc.d/rc.local script to put a different message in /etc/issue.net or to perform other host-specific initialization. Since the script is executed last, all other system services associated with the current runlevel should be operational when the script executes.

The *init* Process and the */etc/inittab* File

The init process is responsible for spawning login processes and managing the system runlevel. Its configuration file, /etc/inittab, determines the services that should be active at each defined runlevel.

Managing Runlevels

You can determine the current runlevel by issuing the command

```
runlevel
```

Its output consists of the previous runlevel followed by the current runlevel. For example, the output

```
5 3
```

indicates that the previous runlevel was 5 and the current runlevel is 3.

To change the runlevel, issue the command

```
init n
```

where *n* is the desired runlevel. The command form

```
telinit n
```

has the same effect. The distinguishing feature of `telinit` is its ability to specify that the change of runlevel should occur after a specified interval. For example, the command

```
telinit -t 60 3
```

specifies that the runlevel should be set to 3 after a delay of 60 seconds.

You can switch to runlevel 6, which causes the system to reboot, any of the following ways:

- issue the command `telinit 6` or `init 6`
- issue the command `shutdown -r now`
- issue the command `reboot`
- press Ctrl+Alt+Del

The `shutdown` command provides several useful options. In place of now, you can include an argument of the form *+min*, where *min* specifies the number of minutes until the reboot takes place. You can also include an argument of the form `-t` *sec*; this option causes the command to warn users of the impending shutdown seconds (*sec*) before it takes place.

You can switch to runlevel 0, which causes the system to halt, any of the following ways:

- issue the command `telinit 0` or `init 0`
- issue the command `shutdown -h now`
- issue the command `halt`

The options *+min* and `-t` *sec* can be used with the `-h` argument of the `shutdown` command.

The /etc/inittab File

The /etc/inittab file determines the processes that should be active at each runlevel. Lines in the file have the form

id:runlevels:action:process

The fields are

- id, a unique 1–4 character identification. For login processes, id should be the tty suffix of the corresponding tty.

- runlevels, a list of runlevels for which the action should be taken. If omitted, the action is taken for each runlevel.

- action, which specifies the action to be taken. Table 6.3 summarizes the available actions.

- process, which specifies the program to be executed.

Lines beginning with a hash mark (#) are ignored.

TABLE 6.3: Actions Specifiable in /etc/inittab

Action	Description
boot	The specified process is executed during system boot. The runlevels field is ignored.
bootwait	The process is executed during system boot; init waits for its termination. The runlevels field is ignored.
ctrlaltdel	The process is executed when init receives the SIGINT signal, meaning that someone on the system console has pressed the Ctrl+Alt+Del key combination.
initdefault	Specifies the initial runlevel, which is entered after system boot. The process field is ignored.
kbrequest	The process is executed when init receives a signal from the keyboard handler that a special key combination was pressed on the console keyboard.

TABLE 6.3: Actions Specifiable in /etc/inittab *(continued)*

Action	Description
off	No action taken.
once	The process is executed once when the specified runlevel is entered.
ondemand	The process is executed whenever the specified runlevel (a, b, or c) is called. However, no runlevel change will occur.
powerfail	The process is executed when the power goes down. The init process will not wait for the process to finish.
powerfailnow	This process is executed when init is told that the battery of the external UPS is almost exhausted.
powerokwait	This process is executed when init is informed that the power has been restored.
powerwait	The process is executed when the power goes down. The init process will wait for the process to finish.
respawn	The process is restarted whenever it terminates.
sysinit	The process is executed during system boot, before any boot or bootwait entries. The runlevels field is ignored.
wait	The process is executed once when the specified runlevel is entered; init will wait for its termination.

If you change the contents of /etc/inittab, you must instruct the init process to reread the file. To do so, issue the command init q.

Configuring Special Hardware

In addition to the network script and the network-scripts subdirectory, the /etc/sysconfig directory contains scripts that contain configurations for a variety of system facilities. Table 6.4 summarizes these.

TABLE 6.4: Files and Directories in /etc/sysconfig

File/Directory	Description
apmd	Contains Advanced Power Management configuration.
clock	Contains clock configuration, indicating whether the clock is set to UCT.
console	Contains console configuration, including key maps (directory).
init	Contains system startup configuration, including how service startup status should be reported.
keyboard	Contains keyboard configuration, including the identity of the default key map.
mouse	Contains mouse configuration, including the type of mouse and whether 3-button emulation is required.
network	Contains network configuration, including the host name and gateway.
network-scripts	Contains network configuration scripts (directory).
pcmcia	Contains PCMCIA configuration, including whether PCMCIA should be loaded on boot.
sendmail	Contains sendmail configuration, including whether sendmail runs as a daemon.

TABLE 6.4: Files and Directories in /etc/sysconfig *(continued)*

File/ Directory	Description
soundcard	Contains sound configuration, including the sound card type.
static-routes	Contains static routes, including the associated device, network address, and gateway.

The Linuxconf program lets you configure most of these facilities. If you prefer, most of the files can be safely revised by using a text editor. However, the sound configuration is an exception. You should use the Sndconfig utility to configure sound; you should not manually edit the /etc/sysconfig/soundcard file.

Advanced Power Management (APM) Configuration

APM helps conserve electrical power. It is especially useful for battery-operated computers, such as laptops; however, many modern desktop computers also support APM, which you can use to shut down peripherals that aren't being used. When used with a laptop, APM detects low battery conditions and dims the display, slows the CPU clock, and turns off peripherals to save power. The file /etc/sysconfig/apmd contains the APM configuration, which is referenced by the script /etc/rc.d/init.d/apmd.

PCMCIA Configuration

The PCMCIA service manages PCMCIA cards. The file /etc/sysconfig/pcmcia contains PCMCIA service configuration information, which is referenced by the script /etc/rc.d/init.d/pcmcia. Configuration information for PCMCIA devices resides in /etc/pcmcia. If you recompile the Linux kernel of a system that uses PCMCIA, you must also recompile and install the PCMCIA package.

Plug-and-Play Configuration

Plug-and-play devices are designed to be automatically configured by cooperation between the BIOS and operating system. Linux, however, does not fully support plug-and-play for ISA interface cards.

When using Linux with a BIOS that supports plug-and-play, set the BIOS to indicate that the operating system does not support plug-and-play. You can then configure ISA plug-and-play cards by following this procedure:

1. Issue the command

```
pnpdump >/etc/isapnp.conf
```

This command dumps the configuration of each installed plug-and-play card to the specified file, /etc/isapnp.conf.

2. Using a text editor, revise the /etc/isapnp.conf file. The file contains commented lines for each possible configuration of each plug-and-play device. You must un-comment the desired configuration for each device. You must also un-comment the line at the end of the device configuration, which specifies that the device is active.

3. Issue the command

```
isapnp /etc/isapnp.conf
```

This command configures installed plug-and-play cards according to the configuration given in /etc/isapnp.conf. The Linux boot sequence issues this command to configure plug-and-play devices during system startup.

Sound Configuration

The sndconfig command detects and configures most plug-and-play sound cards. The command places sound configuration information in /etc/conf.modules and /etc/isapnp.conf as well as /etc/sysconfig/soundcard.

If you're using the GNOME desktop manager under X, the GNOME sound manager, esd, will manage your sound card and allow multiple applications to simultaneously access it. However, if you execute an application that is not aware of esd, it may conflict with other applications. To avoid this, invoke the application by using the esddsp wrapper. Start the application by issuing the command

```
esddsp application
```

where *application* is the name or path of the application. The KDE application Kaudioserver performs a function similar to that of esd.

Necessary Procedures

This section gives several important procedures for configuring runlevel control of services.

Configuring the Runlevel

To change the system runlevel, issue the command

```
init n
```

where *n* is the desired new runlevel. Refer back to Table 6.1 for a summary of the runlevels used by Red Hat Linux.

You can use Linuxconf to select the initial runlevel that the system assumes when booted. To do so, select Config ➤ Miscellaneous Services ➤ Initial System Services. The Init Default Runlevel screen appears. Click the radio button corresponding to the desired default runlevel, and click Accept. The next time you boot the system, it should enter the specified runlevel.

Associating Services with Runlevels

In principle, you could associate a service with its runlevels by creating and manipulating symbolic links in the /etc/rc.d/rc?.d directories. However, because such a process would be tedious and error-prone, several utilities are available to facilitate the task. These include

- Chkconfig, a command-line utility
- Ksysv, a KDE-based utility
- Ntsysv, a text-mode graphical utility
- Tksysv, an X-based utility

The most important of these tools are Chkconfig and Ntsysv; the other tools require support, such as X, which may not be available when configuring services. Chkconfig provides more functions than Ntsysv; Chkconfig lets you

- List installed services
- Add a service
- Delete a service
- Associate a service with a runlevel

Listing Services

To list the installed services and their associated runlevels, issue the command

```
chkconfig --list
```

Each service is listed, followed by its status for each of the possible runlevels.

You may find it more convenient to issue this command, which sorts the output by the name of the service:

```
chkconfig --list | sort
```

Adding a Service

To add a service, you must first ensure that the associated init.d script contains special comments. The first comment is a line that tells Chkconfig the runlevels for which the service should be started and the start and stop priority numbers. The comment line contains the tokens # `chkconfig:` and then lists the runlevels. For example, the following comment specifies that a service runs at runlevels 2 and 5 and has start priority 20 and stop priority 80:

```
# chkconfig: 25 20 80
```

The second comment consists of one or more lines that describe the service. Each line other than the last must end with a backslash (\), which is the comment continuation character. For example, here's a typical comment, which describes the random service:

```
# description: Saves and restores system entropy
↳ pool for
# higher quality random number generation.
```

To add the service, issue the command

```
chkconfig --add name
```

where *name* is the name of the service. Chkconfig creates the required symbolic links according to the comments in the `init.d` script.

Deleting a Service

To delete a service, issue the command

```
chkconfig --del name
```

where *name* is the name of the service. Chkconfig deletes the associated symbolic links.

Associating a Service with Runlevels

To associate a service with one or more runlevels, issue the command

```
chkconfig name reset
```

where *name* is the name of the service. Chkconfig creates the required symbolic links, according to the comments in the `init.d` script. If you prefer, you can explicitly set a service to run, or not run, at specified levels regardless of the contents of the associated `init.d` script. To specify levels at which the service should run, issue the command

```
chkconfig --level levels name on
```

where *name* is the name of the service and *levels* is a series of digits that specify the runlevels. For example, the command

```
chkconfig --level 35 lunch on
```

specifies that the hypothetical service `lunch` will run at levels 3 and 5.

To specify levels at which the service should not run, issue the command

```
chkconfig --level levels name off
```

where *name* is the name of the service and *levels* is a series of digits that specify the runlevels. For example, the command

```
chkconfig --level 24 lunch off
```

specifies that the hypothetical service `lunch` will not run at levels 2 and 4.

Exam Essentials

Be able to configure and troubleshoot system initialization This section explains the system initialization scripts and several tools that you can use to configure them. Although the official list of RHCE study points does not explicitly include the ability to configure and troubleshoot system initialization, the performance-based components of the RHCE exam are likely to require these skills. Be sure you know how to configure and troubleshoot system initialization.

Be able to configure and troubleshoot runlevel control of services
Although the official list of RHCE study points does not explicitly include the ability to configure and troubleshoot system runlevel control of services, the performance-based components of the RHCE exam are likely to require these skills. Be sure you know how to configure and troubleshoot runlevel control of services, including being able to use the chkconfig utility.

Key Terms and Concepts

Priority   The priority of a runlevel script determines the sequence in which it is run. The priority of a service is encoded in the names of symbolic links to the service's runlevel script.

Runlevel   Red Hat Linux defines several runlevels. You can associate services with runlevels. By setting the system runlevel, you can conveniently start and stop sets of services.

Runlevel script   A runlevel script starts or stops a service associated with one or more runlevels.

Sample Questions

1. Which of the following files specifies what processes are active at various runlevels?

    A. /etc/init

    B. /etc/inittab

    C. /etc/initprocess

    D. /etc/process

    Answer: B. The /etc/inittab file specifies the processes active at various runlevels.

2. Which of the following programs can be used to configure the system even if X is not available?

A. Chkconfig

B. Gurble

C. Ksysv

D. Tksysv

Answer: A. The Chkconfig program can be used to configure runlevel scripts even if X is not available.

▶Configuring Networking

In addition to the AT&T SysV Unix-style startup scripts, Red Hat Linux uses several other sets of scripts during system initialization, most of which concern networking. This section describes these scripts and explains how to use them to configure network startup.

Critical Information

When the `/etc/rc.d/init.d/network` network startup script runs, it brings up the configured network interface devices. It does so by invoking a set of scripts stored in the `/etc/sysconfig/network-scripts` directory. Table 6.5 summarizes these scripts, which can perform a variety of operations besides bringing up network interfaces.

TABLE 6.5: Scripts in /etc/sysconfig/network-scripts

Script	Description
chat-*	Chat scripts for PPP and SLIP connections.
ifcfg-*	Stores the configuration of the associated interface; for example, ifcfg-eth0 stores the configuration of the first Ethernet card and ifcfg-lo stores the configuration of the TCP/IP dummy loopback device.

TABLE 6.5: Scripts in /etc/sysconfig/network-scripts *(continued)*

Script	Description
ifdhcp-done	Configures /etc/resolv.conf if DHCP is used.
ifdown-*	Brings down the associated protocol; for example, ifdown-ppp brings down PPP.
ifdown-post	Brings down a specified device.
ifup-*	Brings up the associated protocol; for example, ifup-ppp brings up PPP.
ifup-aliases	Adds IP aliases for a specified device.
ifup-post	Brings up a specified device, adding static routes and aliases and setting the host name.
ifup-routes	Adds static routes for a specified device.

The *ifcfg-** Scripts

Each ifcfg-* script stores the configuration for a network interface. The scripts /sbin/ifup and /sbin/ifdown use these configuration scripts to bring up or bring down, respectively, an interface. For example, a system that has an Ethernet network interface will store the interface configuration in /etc/sysconfig/network-scripts/ ifcfg-eth0; if the system has a second Ethernet network interface, the interface configuration will be stored in /etc/sysconfig/ network-scripts/ifcfg-eth1, and so on. To bring up the first Ethernet card, you can issue the command

    /sbin/ifup ifcfg-eth0

or simply

    /sbin/ifup eth0

The command supplies the ifcfg- prefix if you omit it.

TIP The ifup and ifdown scripts use the ifconfig command (described in a subsection below), which is a privileged command. Therefore, ordinary users cannot execute the ifup and ifdown scripts, unless you specify that the associated interface is user controllable. However, non-privileged users may require a simpler user interface than that provided by the ifup and ifdown scripts. Such users may prefer to use the usernet and usernetctl commands, which are available to them if the interface is user controllable. See the usernet and usernetctl man pages for details.

The ifcfg-* scripts contain commands that set the values of environment variables that specify the network configuration. For example, here's a typical ifcfg-eth0 script:

```
DEVICE="eth0"
IPADDR="192.168.1.3"
NETMASK="255.255.255.0"
ONBOOT="yes"
BOOTPROTO="none"
```

If you used Linuxconf to establish the network configuration, the file likely contains statements that set a variety of IPX-related environment variables, even if your system is not configured for IPX. The sample configuration corresponds to a static Ethernet configuration. It includes

- the device name, DEVICE=eth0

- the IP address, IPADDR=192.168.1.3

- the network subnet mask, NETMASK=255.255.255.0

- a parameter indicating that the device should be started when the system boots, ONBOOT=yes

- a parameter indicating that the configuration is static, BOOTPROTO=none

A static Ethernet configuration may also include

- a network address, NETWORK=192.168.1.0

- a network broadcast address, BROADCAST=192.168.1.255

If you configure an interface to obtain its configuration via DHCP, the contents of the file are somewhat different:

- the device name, DEVICE=eth0

- the boot protocol, BOOTPROTO=dhcp

- a parameter indicating that the device should be started when the system boots, ONBOOT=yes

You can revise the network configuration via Linuxconf or Netcfg, or you can modify the files by using a text editor.

The */etc/sysconfig/network* Script

Global network configuration information affecting each interface is stored in /etc/sysconfig/network. Here's a typical /etc/sysconfig/network file:

```
NETWORKING=yes
FORWARD_IPV4="yes"
HOSTNAME="athlon.azusapacific.com"
GATEWAY="192.168.1.1"
GATEWAYDEV="eth1"
```

The file indicates that networking is active and that the system will route packets. The host name of the system is athlon.azusapacific.com; its default gateway is 192.168.1.1, which is accessible via the Ethernet interface known as eth1. If the system used NIS, the file would also indicate the NIS domain with which it's associated.

The *ifconfig* Command

The ifconfig command reports the status of a network interface and lets you add or remove an interface. It's run by the /etc/sysconfig/network-scripts ifup and ifdown scripts.

Reporting Network Interface Status

To report the status of network interfaces, issue the command

    ifconfig

The output of the command resembles the following:

```
eth0  Link encap:Ethernet  HWaddr 00:40:05:68:02:30
      inet addr:192.168.100.2  Bcast:192.168.100.255
      ⮑Mask:255.255.255.0
      UP BROADCAST RUNNING MULTICAST  MTU:1500
      ⮑Metric:1
      RX packets:1601111 errors:0 dropped:0
      ⮑overruns:0 frame:0
      TX packets:1549740 errors:49 dropped:0
      ⮑overruns:0 carrier:98
      collisions:952 txqueuelen:100
      Interrupt:10 Base address:0x6100


lo    Link encap:Local Loopback
      inet addr:127.0.0.1  Mask:255.0.0.0
      UP LOOPBACK RUNNING  MTU:3924  Metric:1
      RX packets:75545 errors:0 dropped:0 overruns:0
      ⮑frame:0
      TX packets:75545 errors:0 dropped:0 overruns:0
      ⮑carrier:0
      collisions:0 txqueuelen:0
```

Table 6.6 describes the fields included in the report.

TABLE 6.6: Fields in ifconfig Output

Field	Description
Link encap	The type of interface
Hwaddr	The hardware address (MAC) of the interface
Inet addr	The IP address of the interface
Bcast	The broadcast address for the network
Mask	The netmask for the subnet
Status	The interface status (for example, UP BROADCAST RUNNING MULTICAST)
MTU	The maximum transfer unit size (bytes)
Metric	The interface metric, used by some routing protocols
RX packets	The number of packets received, the number of errors, dropped packets, overruns, and bad frames
TX packets	The number of packets transmitted, the number of errors, dropped packets, overruns, and dropped carriers
Collisions	The number of Ethernet collisions
Txqueuelen	The transmit queue length
Interrupt	The IRQ of the interface
Base address	The I/O port address of the interface

If you want to report the status of a particular network interface, issue a command of the form

```
ifconfig if
```

where *if* is the name of the interface. For example, the command

```
ifconfig eth0
```

reports the status of the eth0 interface.

Adding and Dropping Network Interfaces

To add an interface, specify a command of the form

```
ifconfig device ipaddr
```

where *device* is the name of the device and *ipaddr* is the IP address of the interface. For example, the command

```
ifconfig eth0 192.168.1.1
```

establishes an Ethernet interface with IP address 192.168.1.1. You can specify several additional options. For instance, the command

```
ifconfig eth0 192.168.1.1 netmask 255.255.255.0
↳broadcast 192.168.1.255
```

establishes an Ethernet interface with IP address 192.168.1.1, network subnet mask of 255.255.255.0, and network broadcast address of 192.168.1.255.

To drop an interface, specify a command of the form

```
ifconfig device down
```

where *device* is the name of the device. For example, the command

```
ifconfig eth0 down
```

drops the eth0 interface.

WARNING   When you reconfigure an interface by using ifconfig, your changes are lost when the system is rebooted, because the system initialization scripts issue the ifconfig command with parameter values specified in the network configuration files. You should understand the ifconfig command so that you understand the operation of these scripts. You'll issue the ifconfig command primarily for troubleshooting network problems and making other temporary network reconfigurations. To permanently change the network configuration, you should use a configuration utility or edit the network configuration files.

The *netstat* Command

The netstat command reports a variety of network-related information. For example, the command

```
netstat -r -n
```

reports the kernel's routing table. Here is a typical output:

```
Kernel IP routing table
Destination    Gateway       Genmask           Flags  MSS Window
↳irtt Iface
192.168.1.3    *             255.255.255.255 UH       0  0
↳0 eth1
192.168.100.3 *             255.255.255.255 UH       0  0
↳0 eth0
192.168.100.0 *             255.255.255.0   U        0  0
↳0 eth0
192.168.1.0    *             255.255.255.0   U        0  0
↳0 eth1
127.0.0.0      *             255.0.0.0       U        0  0
↳0 lo
default        192.168.1.1 0.0.0.0           UG       0  0
↳0 eth1
```

The output shows several destinations accessible via network interfaces. In the example, the first two lines describe interfaces installed in the system. The following two lines describe networks available via these interfaces; the Genmask column gives the network mask associated with each network. The next-to-last line describes the loopback network, associated with the dummy loopback device. The last line shows the default route, used for network addresses that do not match a defined destination address. Table 6.7 describes the flags that appear in the fourth column of the output.

TABLE 6.7: Flags Reported by netstat

Flag	Description
G	Route establishes a gateway.
U	The associated interface is up.
H	The route specifies a route to a single host, not a network.
D	The entry was created in response to an ICMP message.
M	The entry was modified in response to an ICMP message.

Another useful form of the netstat command reports connections to hosts outside a masqueraded network. To view this report, issue the command

```
netstat -M
```

The output resembles the following:

```
IP masquerading entries
prot   expire source                 destination   ports
tcp 14:53.71 bigtop.azusapacific.com home.apu.edu  1047 ->
↳ssh (63685)
```

The output shows the protocol (TCP), the expiration time of the masqueraded connection (14:53.71), the local host (`bigtop.azusapacific.com`), destination (`home.apu.edu`), port (1047), and service (`ssh`).

The *arp* Command

The `arp` command lets you view or modify the kernel's *Address Resolution Protocol (ARP)* table, which maps IP addresses to *hardware (MAC) addresses* of interfaces. The `arp` command is especially helpful in detecting and dealing with duplicate IP addresses. However, hosts appear in the ARP table only after they've been sent Ethernet packets.

To view the ARP table, issue the command

```
arp -a
```

Output of the command resembles the following:

```
bigtop.azusapacific.com (192.168.1.90) at
↳00:E0:98:77:08:40
  [ether] on eth1
```

The report indicates the host name, IP address, Ethernet address, and interface associated with systems on a locally accessible network.

To delete the ARP entry for a host, issue a command of the form

```
arp -d host
```

where *host* is the host name of the system you want to delete from the table. To specify an ARP entry for a host, issue a command of the form

```
arp -s host mac_addr
```

where *host* is the host name of the system you want to delete from the table, and *mac_addr* is the hardware (MAC) address you want to associate with the host. For example, to specify an ARP entry for the host happy, with MAC address 00:E0:98:77:08:41, issue the command

```
arp -s happy 00:E0:98:77:08:41
```

Exam Essentials

Understand the role of the scripts and configuration files under `/etc/sysconfig/network-scripts`   You should be familiar with `/etc/sysconfig/network` and the scripts that reside in `/etc/sysconfig/network-scripts`. You should also be familiar with the functions that these scripts perform and with the syntax and operation of the principal network configuration commands, including `ifconfig`, `netstat`, and `arp`.

Key Terms and Concepts

Address Resolution Protocol (ARP)   A protocol used to resolve IP addresses to MAC addresses.

MAC address   The hardware address assigned to a device by the manufacturer.

Sample Questions

1. Which of the following is the protocol that resolves IP addresses to network interface devices?

   A. ARP

   B. ICMP

   C. IP

   D. TCP

   Answer: A. The ARP protocol resolves IP addresses to the MAC addresses associated with hardware devices.

2. Which of the following is the command used to configure a network interface?

A. arp

B. ifconfig

C. netstat

D. tcpdump

Answer: B. The ifconfig command configures a network interface.

▶ Configuring the File System and Disk Quotas

When a Linux system boots, it mounts one or more file systems. File systems sometimes fail to mount properly, owing to hardware errors or changes to a disk's partition table. It's important that you understand how the mounting process works so that you can repair a broken system and configure the file systems you want to be mounted at boot time.

Disk space quotas are a policy mechanism designed to facilitate sharing of disk space. An administrator can assign a user or group a fixed amount of disk space that the user cannot exceed. By limiting the amount of disk space that a user (or group) can consume, an administrator can prevent a greedy user from taking more than his or her share.

Critical Information

The /etc/fstab file describes the file systems associated with a Linux system. Here are the contents of a typical /etc/fstab file:

```
/dev/hda1       /dos        msdos    defaults      0 2
/dev/hda5       /boot       ext2     defaults      1 2
/dev/hda6       /usr        ext2     defaults      1 2
```

```
/dev/hda7      /home        ext2     defaults       1 2
/dev/hda8      /var         ext2     defaults       1 2
/dev/hda9      /            ext2     defaults       1 1
/dev/hda10     swap         swap     defaults       0 0
/dev/hda11     /space       ext2     defaults       1 2
/dev/fd0       /mnt/floppy  ext2     noauto         0 0
/dev/cdrom     /cdrom1      iso9660  noauto,ro      0 0
/dev/hdd       /cdrom2      iso9660  noauto,ro      0 0
none           /proc        proc     defaults       0 0
none           /dev/pts     devpts   mode=0622      0 0
```

Each line in the file describes a file system. The fields are

- the device file.

- the mount point.

- the file system type. Table 6.8 summarizes the file system types supported by Linux.

- the mount options. Table 6.9 summarizes the available options.

- the dump flag. The value 1 indicates a file system that should be automatically included in a system dump; the value 0 indicates a file system that should not be included.

- the file system check sequence. The value 1 indicates the root file system; the value 2 indicates a non-root file system that should be automatically checked; and the value 0 indicates a file system that should not be automatically checked.

TABLE 6.8: Linux File System Types

File System Type	Description
adfs	Acorn RiscOS file system
affs	AmigaOS file system
coda	Coda, an advanced network file system similar to NFS
devpts	A virtual file system for pseudoterminals

TABLE 6.8: Linux File System Types *(continued)*

File System Type	Description
ext2	The standard Linux file system
hfs	Apple Macintosh file system
hpfs	IBM OS/2 file system
iso9660	The standard CD-ROM file system
minix	Tannenbaum's MINIX file system
msdos	Uncompressed MS-DOS file systems
ncpfs	Novell NetWare file system
nfs	Unix network file system
ntfs	Microsoft Windows NT file system
proc	The /proc virtual file system
qnx4fs	QNX file system
romfs	Read-only file system for RAM disks
smbfs	Microsoft SMB (LAN Manager) file system
sysv	SCO, Xenix, and Coherent file system
ufs	BSD, SunOS, FreeBSD, NetBSD, OpenBSD, and NeXTstep file system
umsdos	Linux file system running on top of MS-DOS file system
vfat	Microsoft Windows 9x file system

TABLE 6.9: Mount Options

Option	Description
async	Perform all input and output asynchronously.
atime	Update inode access times on the file system.
auto	Automatically mount the file system in response to mount -a.
defaults	Enable the options rw, suid, dev, exec, auto, nouser, and async.
dev	Interpret character or block special devices on the file system.
exec	Permit execution of binary files on the file system.
noatime	Do not update inode access times on the file system.
noauto	Do not automatically mount the file system in response to mount -a.
nodev	Do not interpret character or block special devices on the file system.
noexec	Do not permit execution of binary files on the file system.
nosuid	Set-user-id and set-group-id permissions of files in the file system are not effective.
nouser	An ordinary user may not mount the file system (default).
remount	Remount a mounted file system, to enable a different set of options. Often used to remount a read-only file system in read-write mode.
ro	Mount the file system in read-only mode.
rw	Mount the file system in read-write mode.
suid	Set-user-id and set-group-id permissions of files in the file system are effective.

TABLE 6.9: Mount Options *(continued)*

Option	Description
sync	Perform all input and output synchronously.
user	Permit an ordinary user to mount the file system. Implies the options noexec, nosuid, and nodev.

Disk Quotas

Disk space quotas place limits on the amount of disk space a user or group can use. In the /etc/fstab file, you specify the partitions for which disk quotas are enabled. Only Linux Ext2 partitions support disk quotas; you cannot enable quotas for other file system types.

The quota facility uses a pair of files stored in the mount directory of a quota-enabled file system:

- quota.user, which stores quotas assigned to users
- quota.group, which stores quotas assigned to groups

For example, if a partition is mounted as /home, the files would be named /home/quota.user and /home/quota.group. The quotacheck command updates the contents of these files to reflect actual disk space usage. If the files do not exist, the command creates them. Unlike most Unix files, these files contain binary information and cannot be directly edited. To establish a quota for a user or group, you use the edquota command. You can view the contents of the files by issuing the repquota command.

Quota tracking is initiated when the system boots. Commands in the /etc/rc.d/rc.sysinit script update usage data and turn on quota checking. Quotas can be established for individual users or for groups. Two types of limits can be defined:

- Soft limits: Users or groups that exceed the *soft limit* are notified by e-mail when the warnquota program is run.

- Hard limits: Users or groups that exceed the *hard limit* are prevented from using additional disk space.

You can define a *grace period* that works with soft limits. If the user continues to exceed the soft limit upon expiration of the grace period, the user is prevented from using additional space. You can specify limits on the number of disk blocks used, on the number of files (inodes) used, or both.

Consider the following example. Assume that user bob has the following limits:

- soft disk space limit: 10000 blocks

- hard disk space limit: 12000 blocks

- soft inode limit: 100

- hard inode limit: 120

Finally, suppose that a seven-day grace period is in effect and that bob currently has 5000 blocks of disk space and 50 inodes in use. If bob increases his disk usage to 11000 blocks, he'll receive an e-mail message the next time the quotacheck command is run. If bob fails to reduce the number of blocks within seven days or if he increases his usage to 12000 blocks, he'll be prevented from using additional disk space until he reduces his usage below his soft quota.

Necessary Procedures

This section gives procedures for implementing and administering disk quotas.

Implementing Quotas

To implement quotas, you follow these steps:

- Configure the kernel

- Install the quota package

- Revise /etc/fstab
- Establish the quota files
- Set quotas
- Turn on quota checking

Configuring the Kernel

In order to support quotas, a system's kernel must be properly configured. Specifically, the kernel must have been compiled with the CONFIG_QUOTA option enabled. Standard Red Hat Linux kernels include this option; however, if you compile your own kernel, you must enable it or you'll be unable to use quotas.

Installing the *quota* Package

The quota package is part of the Red Hat Linux base component and is generally installed during installation. To check whether the package is installed, issue the command rpm -qi quota.

The command will print a short description of the package or a message stating that the package is not installed.

To install the quota package, move to the directory that contains it and issue the command rpm -Uvh quota*.rpm.

The /etc/rc.d/rc.sysinit file performs the following steps when the system is booted:

- Runs quotacheck on the root file system
- Runs quotacheck on all other local file systems
- Turns on quota checking

Revising */etc/fstab*

To specify that a partition supports disk quotas, you must revise the partition's description in /etc/fstab. Here's a sample file:

```
/dev/hda8     /          ext2     defaults      1 1
/dev/hda5     /boot      ext2     defaults      1 2
/dev/hda6     /home      ext2     defaults      1 2
```

```
/dev/hdc       /mnt/cdrom     iso9660 noauto,owner,ro    0 0
/dev/hda7      /usr           ext2    defaults           1 2
/dev/fd0       /mnt/floppy    ext2    noauto,owner       0 0
none           /proc          proc    defaults           0 0
none           /dev/pts       devpts  gid=5,mode=620     0 0
```

To specify that the /home partition supports user disk quotas, revise its line as follows:

```
/dev/hda6    /home    ext2 usrquota 1 2
```

To specify that the /home partition supports group disk quotas, you would revise its line as follows:

```
/dev/hda6    /home    ext2 grpquota 1 2
```

To specify that the /home partition supports both user and group disk quotas, you would revise its line as follows:

```
/dev/hda6    /home    ext2  defaults,usrquota,grpquota 1 2
```

Once you've revised the partition options, you must remount the partition. For example, to remount the /home partition, issue the command mount -o remount /home.

TIP   If you prefer, you can specify the usrquota or grpquota option by using Linuxconf. Go to Config ➢ File Systems ➢ Access Local Drive, select the desired partition, and specify the desired option or options on the Volume Specification screen.

Establishing the Quota Files

Once you've specified the partition or partitions that support disk quotas, you must establish the quota files quota.user and quota .group in each such partition. To do so, issue the quotacheck command:

```
quotacheck -avug
```

The command may require several minutes to complete its task of accumulating and storing a record of the disk space used by each user account and group.

To avoid a denial of service attack, you should verify that the created quota.user and quota.group files have read and write permissions only for their owner, which should be root.

NOTE The files maintained by quotacheck must be kept in sync with the file systems. If the system is improperly shut down, the system will automatically run quotacheck when rebooted.

Setting Default Quotas

You're now ready to set quotas for users or groups. Bear in mind that you can set quotas only for partitions that support them and only of the supported type or types. For example, if you configure the partition to support *user quotas*, you can set only user quotas, not group quotas.

Before setting quotas for particular users or groups, you may prefer to set default quotas. Default quotas apply to any user or group whose quota has not been set. To set default quotas, perform the following steps:

1. Launch Linuxconf by issuing the command linuxconf.

2. Select Config ➤ File Systems ➤ Set Quota Defaults. The Default Quota for Users and Groups screen appears. If you're using X, the screen will look somewhat different.

3. Specify the desired default limits and grace periods. A limit of zero (0) means there is no limit. Click the Accept button to save your changes.

WARNING Using linuxconf to set default quotas overwrites limits entered manually. It's best to set default quotas only once, before setting specific user quotas.

Setting a User Quota

To set a quota for a user, issue the command

```
edquota -u user
```

where *user* is the login name of the user. The edquota command launches the default editor (specified by the $EDITOR environment variable), which displays a series of lines resembling the following:

```
Quotas for user bill:
/dev/hda6: blocks in use: 1236, limits (soft = 0,
↳hard = 0)
              inodes in use: 235, limits (soft = 0,
↳hard = 0)
```

To specify a limit, change the appropriate number, save the file, and exit the editor. A limit of zero (0) means there is no limit. For example, you might revise the limits imposed on the user bill as follows:

```
Quotas for user bill:
/dev/hda6: blocks in use: 1236, limits (soft = 8000,
↳hard = 10000)
              inodes in use: 235, limits (soft = 0,
↳hard = 0)
```

To verify that the quota has been set, issue the command

```
quota -u user
```

where *user* is the login name of the user. You should see the same information you entered by using the editor.

Setting a Group Quota

To specify a *group quota*, issue the command

```
edquota -g group
```

where *group* is the name of the group. The `edquota` command launches the default editor (specified by the `$EDITOR` environment variable), which displays a series of lines resembling the following:

```
Quotas for group users:
/dev/hda6: blocks in use: 12436, limits (soft = 0,
↳hard = 0)
            inodes in use: 2135, limits (soft = 0,
↳hard = 0)
```

To revise a limit, change the appropriate number, save the file, and exit the editor. A limit of zero (0) means there is no limit.

To verify that the quota has been set, issue the command

```
quota -g group
```

where *group* is the name of the group. You should see the same information you entered by using the editor.

Setting the Grace Period

To set the grace period, issue the command

```
edquota -t
```

The edquota command launches the default editor (specified by the `$EDITOR` environment variable), which displays a series of lines resembling the following:

```
Time units may be: days, hours, minutes, or seconds
Grace period before enforcing soft limits for users:
/dev/hda6: block grace period: 7 days, file grace
↳period: 7 days
```

To revise a limit, change the appropriate number or time unit, save the file, and exit.

Setting Quotas for Multiple Users

You can use one user account as a template for setting quotas for other accounts. To do so, follow these steps:

1. Issue the command

```
edquota -p user
```

where *user* is the login name of the user account you want to use as a template. This establishes the specified user account as a template.

2. Issue the command

```
edquota user
```

where *user* is the login name of the user account you want to use as a template. The edquota command launches the default editor. Set the desired limits, save the file, and exit the editor. This establishes the desired quota for the template user account.

3. Issue the command

```
edquota -p user user1 user2 ...
```

where *user* is the login name of the user account you want to use as a template, and the remaining arguments are login names of user accounts you want to have the same quota as the template account.

Turning On Quota Checking

Finally you're ready to actually turn on quota checking. Quota checking will be turned on when the system is booted. However, you can turn on quota checking without rebooting by issuing the command quotaon -av.

This command turns on both user and group quotas. To turn on only user quotas, issue the command quotaon -avu.

Similarly, to turn on only group quotas, issue the command `quotaon -avg`.

To turn off quotas, issue the command `quotaoff -av`.

This command turns off both user and group quotas. To turn off only user quotas, issue the command `quotaoff -avu`.

Similarly, to turn off only group quotas, issue the command `quotaoff -avg`.

Administering Quotas

Once quotas are set up, you can use commands that report on the status of quotas.

Viewing Quota Reports

To view the quota assigned to a user, issue the command

```
quota -u user
```

where *user* is the login name of the user. The resulting report resembles the following:

```
Disk quotas for user test (uid 510):
    Filesystem blocks   quota   limit   grace   files
    ↳quota   limit   grace
    /dev/hda6    804  150000  200000            152
    ↳0        0
```

A user can view his or her own quota by issuing the similar command `quota`.

However, only root can view the quotas of other users. To view the quotas for multiple users, issue the command `repquota -a`.

Setting Quotas and NFS

If you export a directory via NFS, you can establish disk quotas that limit the disk space or inodes used by NFS users. Simply apply the desired limits to the local user account to which NFS maps the remote users. For example, if remote users are mapped to the local user nfsuser, set quotas on the nfsuser account.

Exam Essentials

Understand quotas, quota concepts, and be able to implement user and group quotas You should be able to implement and administer disk quotas for users and groups.

Key Terms and Concepts

Grace period Once the grace period has expired, a user in violation of a soft limit is prohibited from using additional disk space.

Group quota A disk quota assigned to a user group.

Hard limit When the hard limit is exceeded, the user is prohibited from using additional disk space.

Soft limit When the soft limit is exceeded, the user is warned to reduce disk usage and the grace period is initiated.

User quota A disk quota assigned to a user.

Sample Questions

1. Which of the following choices correctly identifies the actual user quota file associated with a partition mounted as /space?

   A. /quota.user

   B. /user.quota

C. /space/quota.user

D. /space/user.quota

Answer: C. The user quota file is named quota.user and resides in the mount directory of the quota-enabled file system.

2. Which of the following commands sends e-mail to users in violation of disk quotas?

A. quotacalc

B. quotacheck

C. quotaupdate

D. quotawarn

Answer: B. The quotacheck command updates the quota file contents and sends e-mail to users in violation of quotas.

Scheduling Jobs

The job-scheduling system lets the system administrator, and ordinary users, schedule jobs for automatic execution at specified intervals and times. By default, a Red Hat Linux system runs several jobs that facilitate system administration. As a Red Hat Linux system administrator, you need to know how to manage the job-scheduling system. You also need to understand the jobs that are automatically configured to run on your behalf. This section describes the job-scheduling system and the default jobs it runs.

Critical Information

The job-scheduling system includes two programs: Cron and Anacron. *Cron* is useful primarily for servers and systems that run continuously. *Anacron* is more useful for desktops and systems that run intermittently.

The Cron System

The Cron system lets users schedule jobs for automatic execution at specified times and intervals. The jobs run using the owning user's login; by default, the results of jobs are sent to the owning user via e-mail. A utility program lets a user run a text editor to specify what jobs to run and when to run them.

The Cron system consists of the following components:

- /usr/sbin/crond, the Cron daemon, which runs continuously

- /etc/crontab, the system Cron table, which specifies default jobs defined by Red Hat

- /usr/bin/crontab, the program that lets users create and manage Cron table entries

- /var/spool/cron, the directory that holds Cron files created by users

- /etc/cron.d, the directory that holds Cron files created by package installation scripts

- /etc/cron.allow and /etc/cron.deny, files that let you restrict access to the Cron system

User Crontabs

When a user accesses the Cron system, the system creates the file /var/spool/cron/*user*, where *user* is the login name of the user. This file—called the Cron file, Cron table, or Crontab—contains entries that specify which jobs to run and when to run them.

By default, ordinary users are allowed to access the Cron system. However, the system administrator can restrict this privilege. If the file /etc/cron.allow exists, only users listed in the file can access the Cron system. Similarly, if the file /etc/cron.deny exists, no user listed in the file can access the Cron system.

The System Crontab?

In addition to the user Crontab files stored in /var/spool/cron, the Cron system has a system Cron file, stored in /etc/crontab. Here are the contents of a typical /etc/crontab file:

```
SHELL=/bin/bash
PATH=/sbin:/bin:/usr/sbin:/usr/bin
MAILTO=root
HOME=/

# run-parts
01 * * * * root run-parts /etc/cron.hourly
02 4 * * * root run-parts /etc/cron.daily
22 4 * * 0 root run-parts /etc/cron.weekly
42 4 1 * * root run-parts /etc/cron.monthly
```

The format of the /etc/crontab file differs slightly from that of the user Crontab files. It includes a user id field, which specifies the user ID under which the associated command is run. The user id field is the sixth field of each line, placed just before the command field.

The default Red Hat Linux /etc/crontab file contains four command lines, each of which specifies the run-parts script as the command to be run. The run-parts script takes a single argument, which is a directory. The script executes the files contained in the specified directory. The /etc/crontab file uses run-parts to execute hourly, daily, weekly, and monthly jobs. Thus, it's not necessary to edit the /etc/crontab file; you merely place the script you want to execute—or a symbolic link to the script—in one of the /etc/cron.* directories. As root, however, you can edit the file by using a text editor; you don't need to use the crontab command.

TIP If you change the /etc/crontab file, the Cron system will detect the changed modification date of the file. You do not need to restart or signal the Cron daemon.

Red Hat Linux also has a set of system Crontab files stored in /etc/cron.d; these files are created by package installation scripts. They have the same format as /etc/crontab. The modutils package, for example, installs the file /etc/crond.d/kmod:

```
# rmmod -a is a two-hand sweep module cleaner
*/10 * * * *    root    /sbin/rmmod -as
```

This file runs the rmmod command every 10 minutes, unloading unused modules.

Hourly Cron Jobs

The /etc/crontab file designates the /etc/cron.hourly directory as the location for scripts that will be executed hourly. By default, that directory is empty. However, you can add your own hourly scripts to the directory.

Daily Cron Jobs

By default, Red Hat Linux runs several daily Cron jobs: logrotate, makewhatis, locate, and tmpwatch.

The Logrotate Job   The daily logrotate job is a simple script that invokes the logrotate command:

```
#!/bin/sh
/usr/sbin/logrotate /etc/logrotate.conf
```

The logrotate command allows automatic rotation, compression, removal, and mailing of log files.

The Makewhatis Job   The whatis command provides access to a database of key words found in man pages. For example, if you issue the command

```
whatis rm
```

the command responds with

```
rm (1)                - remove files or directories
```

The same database supports the apropos command, which lists man pages related to a specified topic. For example, if you issue the command

```
apropos cron
```

the command responds with

```
cron(8)     - daemon to execute scheduled commands
crontab(1) - maintain crontab files for
↳individual users
crontab(5) - tables for driving cron
```

You can also invoke the apropos command by using the command form

```
man -k topic
```

where *topic* specifies the subject in which you're interested.

In order to maintain the database used by whatis and apropos, the makewhatis command must be run periodically.

The Locate Program The locate command makes it possible to find the directory in which a file resides, given the name of the file or pattern that matches the name. For example, to find directories containing files having names including the characters *linux.words*, issue the command

```
locate linux.words
```

Output of the command resembles the following:

```
/usr/dict/linux.words
/usr/doc/words-2/README.linux.words
/usr/doc/words-2/README2.linux.words
```

Unlike the find command, which provides a similar capability, the locate command uses a database. The database speeds execution of the locate command relative to that of the find command. However, the database must be regularly updated in order to be useful, and will not reflect files added since the most recent update.

The Tmpwatch Job   Another daily task shouldered by the Cron system is the deletion of stale temporary files. The script `/etc/cron.daily/tmpwatch`, executed daily, invokes the following command:

```
/usr/sbin/tmpwatch 240 /tmp /var/tmp /var/catman/cat?
```

The `tmpwatch` command deletes files that have not been accessed in 10 days (240 hours), residing in the `/tmp`, `/var/tmp`, and `/var/catman/cat?` directories.

Weekly Cron Jobs

The Red Hat Linux Cron system executes one weekly job by default, `/etc/cron.weekly/makewhatis.cron`.

Monthly Cron Jobs

The `/etc/crontab` file designates the `/etc/cron.monthly` directory as the location for scripts that will be executed monthly. By default, that directory is empty. However, you can add your own monthly scripts to the directory.

A Desktop Job Scheduler: Anacron

The Cron utility assumes that a system is continuously powered on. If you install Cron on a desktop system that's powered on intermittently, you may find that Cron jobs are seldom executed. For instance, a Cron job scheduled to run at 2 A.M. will run only if the system is powered on at that time. When you power on a system that has Anacron installed, Anacron will execute any jobs skipped during the time the system was powered off.

The Anacron utility is not as flexible as Cron. It cannot schedule jobs at intervals smaller than one day nor guarantee the time at which a job is run. Moreover, it does not run continuously as a daemon; it must be executed in a startup script, initiated manually, or defined as a Cron job.

To start Anacron, issue the command

```
anacron -s
```

The −s flag, which specifies serial execution, causes Anacron to start jobs one at a time. This avoids clogging the system with a backlog of jobs. When you install the `anacron` package, a System V `init` script named anacron is placed in the `/etc/rc.d/init.d` directory. You can use Linuxconf or another configuration utility to configure Anacron to start when the system boots.

The Anacron utility's configuration file, `/etc/anacrontab`, is generally edited by hand. Its format is simpler than that of the Crontab file, as shown by the following typical Anacrontab file:

```
SHELL=/bin/sh
PATH=/usr/local/sbin:/usr/local/bin:/sbin:/bin:
↳/usr/sbin:/usr/bin

# These entries are useful for a Red Hat Linux system.
1       5       cron.daily      run-parts /etc/cron.daily
7       10      cron.weekly     run-parts /etc/cron.weekly
30      15      cron.monthly    run-parts /etc/cron.monthly
```

The file can contain lines that assign values to environment variables; the first two lines of the example set the value of the SHELL and PATH environment variables. The lines that specify Anacron jobs have four fields:

- `period`, which specifies the execution interval in days
- `delay`, which specifies a delay in minutes before the job is started
- `job identifier`, a string that uniquely identifies the Anacron job
- `command`, which specifies the command to be executed and any command arguments

Necessary Procedures

A user who is allowed to access the Cron system can perform these operations:

- Revise the entries in the user's Crontab.

- List the existing jobs in the user's Crontab.
- Delete the user's Crontab.

Editing the User Crontab

A user can edit the user's Crontab entries by issuing the command

```
crontab -e
```

Similarly, the root user can edit a user's Crontab entries by issuing a command of the form

```
crontab -u user -e
```

where *user* is the login name of the user whose Crontab is to be edited.

In response to the crontab -e command, the Cron system launches the default system editor. If you prefer to use a different editor, you can set the environment variable EDITOR before issuing the crontab command. For example,

```
export EDITOR=/usr/bin/pico
crontab -e
```

lets the user edit the Crontab by using the Pico editor.

A user can remove the user's Crontab entirely, by issuing the command

```
crontab -r
```

The root user can remove a user's Crontab by issuing a command of the form

```
crontab -u user -r
```

where *user* is the login name of the user whose Crontab is to be removed.

Format of the Crontab File

The *Crontab file* may contain these sorts of lines:

- comment lines
- environment settings
- Cron commands

Within a line, leading spaces and tabs are ignored. Blank lines and lines beginning with a hash mark (#) are considered comment lines and are ignored by the Cron system.

Specifying Environment Settings

Environment setting lines have the following form:

```
name = value
```

Such lines specify environment variable names and associated values. A Cron job can access these environment variables. Several environment variables are available without explicit definition:

- SHELL is bound to /bin/sh
- LOGNAME is bound to the user's login name
- HOME is bound to the user's home directory, as specified in /etc/ passwd

You can specify a new value for the SHELL or HOME environment variable. However, you cannot specify a new value for the LOGNAME environment variable.

By default, the output of a Cron job is sent via mail to the owning user. However, you can override this action by specifying a value for the MAILTO environment variable. By defining the variable this way:

```
MAILTO=" "
```

no output will be sent. If you bind the MAILTO environment variable to an e-mail address, the output will be sent to the specified address. For example, if you specify

MAILTO="admin@bigtop.azusapacific.com"

the output of Cron jobs will be mailed to admin@bigtop .azusapacific.com.

Specifying Cron Commands

The command lines in the Crontab have the following form:

minute hour day_of_month month day_of_week command

The lines contain six fields, each separated by one or more spaces from adjacent fields. Table 6.10 describes the first five fields, which specify the interval or time of execution of the specified command. The Cron system checks its Crontab files every minute and executes entries with time specifications that match the current date and time. A field that contains an asterisk (*) matches any value.

TABLE 6.10: Date Fields in the Crontab File

Field	Description
minute	A value from 0 to 59, or *
hour	A value from 0 to 23, or *
day_of_month	A value from 1 to 31, or *
month	A value from 1 to 12, where 1 denotes January, or *
day_of_week	A value from 0 to 7, where either 0 or 7 denotes Sunday, or *

(Additional options will be covered in this chapter.)

A Crontab entry is considered to match the current time when the minute and hour fields match the current time and the month field matches the current month. An entry is considered to match the current date when either the day-of-month field matches the current day of month or the day-of-week field matches the current day of week: It is not necessary that both the day of month and day of week match. If both the time and date match the current time and date, the specified command is executed. Table 6.11 describes some sample Crontab entries.

TABLE 6.11: Sample Time Specifications in the Crontab File

Time Specification	Meaning
5 12 * * *	Run at 5 minutes after noon, every day.
5 * * * *	Run at 5 minutes after each hour.
15 17 1 * *	Run at 5:15 P.M. on the first of each month.
45 16 * * 5	Run at 4:45 P.M. on each Friday.
00 15 * 12 5	Run at 3:00 P.M. on each Friday in December.

You can also specify ranges and lists of numbers. For example, 8-10 in the hour field would match 8, 9, and 10 A.M. Similarly, 8-10,13 in the hour field would match 8, 9, and 10 A.M. and 1 P.M.

You can specify step values, which are used with ranges. For example, 0-10/2 in the hour field refers to 0, 2, 4, 6, 8, and 10 A.M. The specification */2 means that the specified command should be executed every two hours.

If you prefer, you can use names in the month and day-of-week fields. To do so, use the first three letters of the month or day, in either upper or lower case. For example,

```
0 19 * dec fri
```

specifies execution at 7 P.M. on each Friday in December. You cannot use ranges or lists of month or day names; if you want to specify a range or list, you must use numbers.

The final field of each Crontab line specifies the command. If you include a percent sign (%) in the command, only the portion of the field before the percent sign is executed. Any remaining characters in the command are sent as standard input to the command; subsequent percent signs in the command are replaced by newline characters. To embed a percent sign in a command, precede it with a backslash (\), which escapes the special meaning of the percent sign.

Listing the User Crontab

A user can list the contents of the user's Crontab by issuing the command

```
crontab -l
```

The output is listed in the format of the Crontab.

The root user can list the contents of a user's Crontab by issuing a command of the form

```
crontab -u user -l
```

where *user* is the login name of the user whose Crontab is to be listed.

Exam Essentials

Understand the Cron system and be capable of setting up the scheduled jobs using Cron   You should understand the Cron system and be capable of working with established Cron jobs and setting up new ones. Although the official list of RHCE study points does not mention Anacron, you should be familiar with it as well.

Key Terms and Concepts

Anacron   A job-scheduling system suitable for systems that run intermittently.

Cron   The standard Linux job-scheduling system. Cron is best suited for systems that run continuously.

Crontab File   A Crontab file specifies the times or intervals at which Cron jobs run.

Sample Questions

1. Which of the following is a standard Cron job that is run weekly?

A. Anacron

B. Locate

C. Makewhatis

D. Tmpwatch

Answer: C. The Makewhatis job runs weekly to update the database of man page information for use by the `apropos` and `whatis` commands.

2. Which of the following commands can be issued by a user to list the contents of the user's Crontab?

A. `crontab -d`

B. `crontab -l`

C. `crontab -p`

D. `crontab -v`

Answer: B. The −1 argument instructs the `crontab` command to list the user's Crontab.

Administering System Logs

Red Hat Linux logs important events to disk files. As a system administrator, you need to be able to analyze these files, which can help you to anticipate and prevent or troubleshoot system problems. You also need to be able to configure system logging and manage the log files, which can become large over time, especially if the system is busy. You should retain system log files for a reasonable period of time; often, the easiest way to determine if an unfamiliar type of log entry is unusual is to discover how long it's been occurring.

Critical Information

A Red Hat Linux system has two system logging processes:

Syslogd   The main system logging process

Klogd   The process that logs kernel messages

The main system logging process is Syslogd, which is started at system boot time by the initialization script `/etc/rc.d/init.d/syslog`. When an important event occurs and an application needs to log a message, it sends the message to Syslogd, which logs the message. Generally, logging the message entails writing it to the file `/var/log/messages`. However, Syslogd can take a variety of other logging actions. For example, Syslogd can log the event to a file other than `/var/log/messages`, display the message on the system console, send a message to a logged-on user, and so on. The Syslogd configuration file is `/etc/syslog.conf`.

Another important system logging process is Klogd, which handles kernel messages. Klogd generally passes received messages to Syslogd, which logs them in the usual manner. However, by specifying appropriate command-line arguments, you can configure Klogd to log kernel messages to a designated file, if you prefer. Klogd is started by the same `/etc/rc.d/init.d/syslog` script that starts Syslogd.

System Log Files and Entries

By default, most message types are logged to the file /var/log/
messages, the system log file. You can view the most recent entries in
the system log file by issuing a command of the form

```
tail -n /var/log/messages
```

where *n* is the number of lines you want to view. The system log typically contains a wide variety of message types. Here is a typical entry:

```
May 10 15:10:00 www named: named startup succeeded
```

Each entry has the general form

```
time_stamp host application[process_ID]: message
```

where

- *time_stamp* is the date and time at which the message was
  received.

- *host* is the name of the host that originated the message.

- *application* is the name of the application that sent the message.

- *process_ID* is the process number of the application that sent the
  message.

- *message* is the message contents.

Some common message types include

- authorization failures

- failed su commands

- hardware errors, such as timeouts

- logins via FTP, SSH, and Telnet

- mail activity

- startups and shutdowns of processes and services

If you're looking for a particular type of log message in a large log file, you may find the grep command handy. Issue a command of the form

```
grep string /var/log/messages | more
```

where *string* is a string of text common to log messages of the type you're interested in. The grep command will display only those log entries that contain the specified text.

Configuring System Logging

The file /etc/syslog.conf contains the system logging configuration. Each entry in the file specifies a class of log messages and a corresponding logging action. Entries have the general form

$$facility.priority \ [; \ facility.priority \ ...] \ action$$

where

- *facility* specifies the class of application that originates the messages. You can specify multiple facilities by separating each facility from the others with a comma (,).

- *priority* specifies the priority associated with the messages.

- *action* specifies the action to be taken with respect to messages from the given facility and having the given priority.

Table 6.12 summarizes the keywords used to refer to facilities that originate log messages. Table 6.13 summarizes the keywords and symbols used to refer to message priorities. Table 6.14 summarizes the keywords and symbols used to designate logging actions.

TABLE 6.12: Facilities and Their Designations

Facility Designation	Description
auth	Messages from user authorization facilities.
authpriv	Messages from privileged user authorization facilities; ordinary users should not see these messages.

TABLE 6.12: Facilities and Their Designations *(continued)*

Facility Designation	Description
cron	Messages from the Cron facility.
daemon	Messages from daemons and TCP services.
kern	Messages from the kernel.
lpr	Messages from the printer facility.
mail	Messages from the mail facility.
news	Messages from Internet news.
syslog	Messages from system logging.
user	Messages from user-defined facilities.
uucp	Messages from the Unix-to-Unix Copy Program (UUCP).
local0-local7	Messages from locally defined facilities.
*	Messages from any facility.

TABLE 6.13: Message Priority Designations

Message Priority	Priority	Description
debug	1	Log debug messages and messages of higher priority.
info	2	Log info messages and messages of higher priority.
notice	3	Log notice messages and messages of higher priority.
warning	4	Log warning messages and messages of higher priority.

TABLE 6.13: Message Priority Designations *(continued)*

Message Priority	Priority	Description
err	5	Log err messages and messages of higher priority.
crit	6	Log crit messages and messages of higher priority.
alert	7	Log alert messages and messages of higher priority.
emerg	8	Log emerg messages and messages of higher priority.
*	N/A	Log all messages, irrespective of priority.
=priority	N/A	Log messages of only the specified priority.
!priority	N/A	Ignore messages of the specified priority and higher.
!=priority	N/A	Log all messages except those of the specified priority.

TABLE 6.14: Logging Action Designations

Action Designation	Description
absolute path	Log messages to the specified file.
/dev/console or /dev/ttyn	Log messages to the specified terminal.
@host	Log messages to the remote host.
Userid	Send messages to the specified user, if the user is logged in. You can specify multiple user IDs by separating each user ID from the others with a comma.
*	Send messages to all logged-in users, via the wall command.

Boot Log

When the Linux kernel boots, it displays boot messages on the system console. These messages are stored in the kernel ring buffer, which is overwritten when full. You can view the kernel ring buffer by issuing the command dmesg.

To prevent the loss of potentially important boot messages, the initialization scripts save the contents of the kernel ring buffer in the file /var/log/dmesg, the boot message file, which can be viewed by issuing the command more /var/log/dmesg.

The system boot log is particularly helpful in troubleshooting problems related to device drivers. If a hardware device is not functioning properly, check the system boot log to see whether the driver loaded and initialized without error.

Log Rotation

If a system is busy, its log files can quickly grow to become large and cumbersome to work with. To control the size of system logs, the Cron facility runs a daily job that rotates log files, /etc/cron.daily/ logrotate. The logrotate script simply executes the logrotate command, which can manipulate log files in several ways. For instance, it can do the following tasks:

- Rotate log files

- Compress log files to minimize disk space used

- Mail log files to a specified user

Rotating a log file involves establishing a series of log files. When the current log file reaches a specified age, it is renamed rather than deleted. So, the current log file is always a manageable size. By using log rotation, several generations of log files can be retained for convenient access. The logrotate configuration file is /etc/logrotate.conf. By default, logs are rotated weekly, and four weeks of logs are retained in addition to the current log.

Red Hat Linux also uses the `logrotate` utility to maintain logs other than the system log. The relevant configuration files reside in `/etc/logrotate.d`; the name of this directory is specified in the `/etc/logrotate.conf` file.

The Swatch Utility

When a system is busy, log files can rapidly become large and, therefore, too time-consuming to examine manually. The Swatch utility, distributed as part of the Red Hat PowerTools collection, monitors log files and can take specified action when a given type of event message is logged. For example, Swatch can send an e-mail message, call a pager, and so on.

A similar utility, Logwatch, is also distributed as part of the Red Hat PowerTools collection. The Logwatch utility can process Samba logs as well as system logs.

Exam Essentials

Be familiar with system logging   Although the official list of RHCE study points does not mention system logging, you should be familiar with system logging. An understanding of system logging can help you troubleshoot a variety of system problems, which is an important skill tested by the performance-based components of the RHCE exam. Moreover, you must be able to configure network services, some of which create system log entries.

Key Term and Concept

Log rotation   Log rotation controls the size of log files by beginning a new log at regular intervals.

Sample Questions

1. Which of the following is the name of the configuration file for system logging?

A. `/etc/syslog.conf`

B. `/etc/syslog/syslog.conf`

C. `/var/log/syslog.conf`

D. `/var/syslog/syslog.conf`

Answer: A. The system logging configuration file resides in `/etc`.

2. Which of the following files contains the contents of the kernel's ring buffer at the conclusion of system startup?

A. `/var/boot`

B. `/var/boot.log`

C. `/var/log/dmesg`

D. `/var/dmesg.log`

Answer: C. The kernel ring buffer is written to `/var/log/dmesg` at the conclusion of system startup. The file `/var/boot.log` contains kernel messages logged during recent system startups.

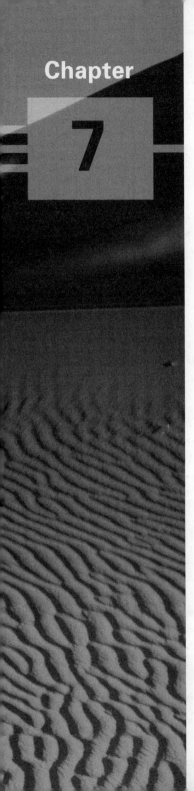

Chapter

7

The Kernel, Modules, and Libraries

RHCE PREPARATION TOPICS COVERED IN THIS CHAPTER:

he principal component of Red Hat Linux is the
Linux kernel. This chapter explains basic kernel concepts, such as
monolithic and modular kernels, and describes the process for building a Linux kernel. It also explains the basic commands for working
with loadable kernel modules. This chapter also explains shared
libraries and the dynamic loader, which are essential to almost every
Linux program.

Working with the Linux Kernel and Modules

The Linux operating system takes its name from its kernel, the
Linux kernel. The kernel is the most basic component of an operating
system. Much of a typical kernel is resident in memory at all times,
whereas other operating system components are loaded when needed
and then discarded. The kernel manages system resources such as the
processor, memory, and devices and provides services used by other
components of the operating system.

Critical Information

Unlike the kernels of most commercial operating systems, the Linux
kernel is distributed in source form. This lets system administrators
compile custom kernels that closely match the unique requirements of
host systems. Being able to build a custom kernel offers promise of
improved system efficiency and performance, but the system administrator must understand the Linux kernel if these advantages are to
be realized.

Kernel Versions

Releases of the Linux kernel are designated by three numbers—for example, Linux 2.4.3. These numbers are called

- the major version (2)
- the minor version (4)
- the patch level (3)

New *major versions* are released every several years and provide significant improvements in kernel capability and performance. However, because the kernel architecture may change with the release of a new major version, non-kernel software designed to work with a previous major release may need to be reconfigured or even modified.

Minor versions are released more frequently than major versions. Software doesn't generally need to be reconfigured or modified to work with a new minor version of the kernel.

At any time, two releases of Linux are undergoing development. The release with an even minor number is called the *stable release*—for example, Linux 2.4.3. Development of the stable kernel focuses more on fixing defects than on adding new features. The release with an odd minor number is called the *developmental release*—for example, Linux 2.5.10. Development of this release focuses on new—and sometimes experimental—features. Therefore, as the release names suggest, the developmental release tends to be less stable than the stable release. System administrators generally do not install a developmental release, except on computers that provide non-critical functions.

The third number making up the kernel version number is the *patch level*. Patch releases occur even more frequently than minor releases, particularly patch releases of the developmental release. Sometimes several patches are released in a single week.

Linux kernels are released via the Linux Kernel Archive Web site, www.kernel.org. Red Hat Inc. downloads released kernels and repackages them as RPMs for easy distribution and installation. Red Hat Inc. also specially configures the kernel and applies patches that modify and extend functionality.

In addition to the major-minor-patch versioning of Linux kernels, Red Hat Inc. encourages use of what they call the *extraversion code*, which distinguishes differently configured versions of the same kernel release. As explained in the next chapter, you can specify an extraversion code when you build a Red Hat Linux kernel. The extraversion code takes the form of a sequential number and a short descriptive name. For example, build #20 of a Linux 2.4.6 kernel supporting SMP might be named 2.4.6-20smp. Using the extraversion code facilitates having several Linux kernels on a single system. When you build a new kernel, you can keep a copy of the old kernel on the system. That way, if the new kernel fails to operate properly, you can simply reboot the system by using the old kernel, rather than perform some more elaborate recovery operation.

Custom Kernels

Many Red Hat Linux users and system administrators never compile a Linux kernel. Instead, they download and install kernel updates in package form. However, you may want to build a custom kernel for reasons such as these:

- You want to configure an especially secure system and therefore want to disable unneeded capabilities that might present a security risk. For example, you plan to use a Linux system as a router and therefore don't need or want some of the capabilities included in the standard Red Hat Linux kernel.

- You want to enable capabilities not available in the standard Red Hat Linux kernel, such as advanced routing options.

- You want to alter operating parameters not configurable during operation. For example, you want to use more than 1GB of RAM and therefore need to reconfigure the balance between user-space and kernel-space memory.

- You're curious to learn more about the Linux kernel. Building a custom kernel is a good way to do so.

Originally, the Linux kernel was a *monolithic* kernel, a kernel that resides in a single file. You can still build a monolithic kernel if you choose, but most Linux kernels are now *modular* kernels that reside in a set of files called *modules*. A modular Linux kernel can load modules when they're needed and unload them when they're no longer needed. Typically, any modules not needed during boot are compiled as modules rather than being incorporated into the kernel. Such modules include peripheral device drivers, supplementary file systems, and so on.

TIP   If you choose to build and use a monolithic kernel, you should remove all device probes from /etc/rc.d/rc.sysinit and remove the module sweeper script, /etc/cron.d/kmod.

Kernel-Related Files

Several sets of files are closely related to the Linux kernel, including the boot files, the kernel source files, and utilities needed to build the Linux kernel.

Boot Files

The Linux boot files reside in the /boot file system so that they can be accessed by PC BIOS code that's incapable of accessing every sector on a large hard disk. The principal Linux boot files are

- vmlinu*, the Linux kernel, which can have an arbitrary name. Generally, the name includes *vmlinux* or *vmlinuz*. If LILO is used to boot the system, the kernel filename will be referenced in the /etc/lilo.conf file.

- boot.b, LILO's second stage.

- initrd, a file containing a RAM disk that contains drivers (modules) available to the kernel at boot time. This file is often needed to boot from a SCSI hard drive; otherwise it is not generally needed for normal system operation.

- boot.*nnnn*, a backup copy of the original master boot record, before the installation of LILO. The file is not needed for normal system operation. The *nnnn* part of the name is the hexadecimal device number of the hard drive—for example, boot.0300 or boot.0305.

- System.map, a file needed by utilities that read the /proc file system and to debug the kernel.

Kernel Source

Red Hat publishes RPMs that contain the Linux kernel. A standard installation of Red Hat Linux includes the kernel package, which contains a precompiled modular kernel and associated modules. On the Intel 386 platform, the standard installation also includes the kernel-pcmcia-cs package, which contains the daemon and drivers needed to support PCMCIA cards.

To build a custom kernel, you must install two packages containing the kernel source:

- kernel-source
- kernel-headers

To install the packages, move to the directory that contains them and issue the command

```
rpm -Uvh kernel-source-*.i386.rpm kernel-headers-
*.i386.rpm
```

When installed, the files of these packages reside in /usr/src/linux-*version*, where *version* is the version of the Linux kernel contained in the package. If you want to view kernel documentation without installing the kernel source and headers, which are relatively large, you can install the kernel-doc package. That package contains the kernel files that otherwise reside in /usr/src/linux/Documentation, but it places them in /usr/doc.

If you prefer to work from a source RPM, you can install the package kernel-source-*version*.src.rpm, where *version* is the version number of the Linux kernel contained in the package. This package contains the source files as released on www.kernel.org plus patches applied by Red Hat Inc. The package installs the source files in the /usr/src/redhat directory.

The RPM packages that contain the Linux kernel source install their files in the /usr/src directory. The binary RPMs place their files in the linux-*version* subdirectory—for example, linux-2.4.2—and the (optional) source RPM places its files in the redhat subdirectory. As a convenience, the installation script of the kernel package creates the symbolic link /usr/src/linux, which refers to the /usr/src/ linux-*version* directory. The directory contains about two dozen files and directories; Table 7.1 describes several of the most important ones.

TABLE 7.1: Important Files and Directories in /usr/src/linux

File or Directory	Description
arch/i386/config.in	Current kernel configuration options, as written by kernel configuration program or script
arch/i386/boot/bzImage	Compiled kernel image
Documentation	Directory containing a variety of useful documentation
README	README file for Linux kernel

If you want to build a kernel from sources that have not been packaged by Red Hat Inc. as an RPM, you can download a TAR file from the Linux Kernel Archives Web site, www.kernel.org. Download the file into the /usr/src directory and then install it by issuing the following commands:

```
cd /usr/src
mkdir linux-version
rm linux
ln -s linux-version linux
tar zxvf linux-version.tar.gz
```

where *version* is the version of the Linux kernel contained in the TAR file. Once the file is installed, you can build the kernel by following the procedure given later in this chapter.

NOTE Some kernel archives store kernels compressed using the BZIP utility, which yields smaller archive files. For instructions on using the BZIP utility, see its man page.

Utilities Needed to Build the Linux Kernel

To build the Linux kernel, you must have available the C compiler, certain software development utilities, and certain libraries. The required packages are

- egcs-*version*.i386.rpm, the GNU C compiler

- cpp-*version*.i386.rpm, the GNU C preprocessor

- dev86-*version*.i386.rpm, an 80x86 assembler and linker

- make-*version*.i386.rpm, the GNU make utility

- glibc-devel-*version*.i386.rpm, header files and libraries for the standard C library

- ncurses-*version*.i386.rpm, the ncurses library, which provides a terminal-independent application programming interface for character-mode video displays

- ncurses-devel-*version*.i386.rpm, headers files and libraries for development using ncurses (needed only when building the kernel by using the menuconfig utility)

In each case, *version* stands for the version number of the package.

To install these packages, move to the directory containing them and issue the command

```
rpm -Uvh egcs-*.i386.rpm \
  cpp-*.i386.rpm \
  dev86-*.i386.rpm \
```

```
make-*.i386.rpm \
glibc-devel-*.i386.rpm \
ncurses-*.i386.rpm \
ncurses-devel-*.i386.rpm
```

Kernel Modules

Kernel modules are files that contain dynamically loadable kernel components, such as device drivers. Linux 2.0 required external assistance to load and unload modules; however, Linux 2.2 introduced the kmod thread that automatically loads modules when needed.

The standard location for kernel modules is the directory /lib/ modules/*version*, where *version* is the version number of the associated Linux kernel. The Red Hat extraversion code ensures that the modules of differently configured kernels of the same release do not conflict. The kernel modules directory contains several subdirectories. These typically include the following:

- block, which contains modules related to block devices

- cdrom, which contains modules related to CD-ROM devices

- fs, which contains modules related to file systems

- ipv4, which contains modules related to TCP/IP networking

- misc, which contains a variety of module types

- net, which contains modules related to networking

- pcmcia, which contains modules related to PCMCIA support

- scsi, which contains modules related to SCSI devices

- video, which contains modules related to video and video devices

A kernel module subdirectory may itself contain one or more subdirectories.

Necessary Procedures

This section gives several important procedures for working with the Linux kernel and modules, including the procedure for compiling the Linux kernel.

Determining the Kernel Version

To view the version and extraversion code of the running kernel, issue the command uname -r. The output of the command consists of simply the kernel version and extraversion code. For example: 2.4.5-15.

The modules associated with the sample kernel reside in /lib/modules/2.4.5-15.

Listing Loaded Modules: *lsmod*

To see what modules are currently loaded, issue the lsmod command, which lists resident modules. The output of the command reports

- the name of each module
- the size of each module
- a count of the number of uses of the module
- the names of other modules referring to the module

Unloading Idle Modules: *rmmod*

When a module has been idle for not more than 10 minutes, the /etc/cron.d/kmod cron jobs will unload it, unless you've disabled the job. However, you can unload an idle module at any time by issuing the command

```
rmmod module
```

where *module* is the name of the idle module you want to unload. You can specify several modules, separating each module name from adjacent module names by one or more spaces. The order in which multiple modules are specified is irrelevant; the rmmod module removes the modules simultaneously. If a module is in use or referred to by a loaded module, it cannot be removed.

To remove all idle modules, issue the command rmmod -a.

Loading Modules: *modprobe* and *insmod*

To load a module, issue a command of the form

> modprobe *module.o*

or, more simply:

> modprobe *module*

where *module.o* is the name of the object file that contains the compiled module. If the module accepts or requires parameters, include them on the command line—for example:

> modprobe fancycard.o irq=11 align=no

If the specified module requires other modules, modprobe will automatically find and load them by searching the database built by the depmod command, described in a subsequent subsection.

The modprobe command has two main modes of operation. In one, it can probe using a single module name or a series of candidate module names. When you specify a series and modprobe successfully loads a candidate module, it ceases probing. To initiate probing, issue a command of the form

> modprobe -t *dir pattern*

where *dir* specifies a subdirectory of /lib/modules/*version* and *pattern* is a regular expression that specifies the names of the candidate module files. For example, to load a module from the /lib/modules/2.4.5-15/net directory, where the currently running kernel is version 2.4.5-15, issue the command

> modprobe -t net '*'

In its other main operating mode, the modprobe command attempts to load every candidate module contained in a particular directory. For instance, to attempt to load every module in the /lib/modules/ 2.4.5-15/misc directory, issue the command

```
modprobe -a -t misc '*'
```

Of course, it's unlikely that you'd ever want to attempt to load every module. Instead, you'd specify a pattern that identifies only the relevant module files.

Like the modprobe command, the insmod command loads a kernel module. However, the insmod command does not attempt to load dependent modules. Therefore, the modprobe command is more commonly used, except in scripts that handle module dependencies in their own fashion rather than rely on modprobe, such as scripts that execute during system startup when the module dependency database may not have been updated.

Updating the Module Dependency Database: *depmod*

The ability of the modprobe command to correctly identify modules that depend on other modules and load them as a group is quite convenient. However, proper operation depends on having an up-to-date list of modules that identifies the other modules that each module requires. The depmod command constructs a database that contains this information. The /etc/rc.d/rc.sysinit script invokes the depmod command to establish such a database whenever the system is booted. The form of the command to be issued is

```
depmod -a
```

which completely rebuilds the module database.

Configuring Modules: The */etc/conf.modules* File

The /etc/conf.modules file lets you specify a variety of parameters that control the operation of depmod and modprobe. For example, you can specify

- aliases that let you refer to modules by more convenient names
- default parameters to be passed to a module when it is loaded
- shell commands to be executed when a module is loaded or unloaded

Here is a typical /etc/conf.modules file:

```
alias sound emu10k1
alias parport_lowlevel parport_pc
alias eth0 3c90x
alias eth1 3c90x
options opl3 io=0x388
pre-install emu10k1 insmod soundcore
post-remove emu10k1 rmmod soundcore
```

This file defines four aliases. It allows the emu10k1 module to be referred to as sound. It defines an option passed to the opl3 module when the module is loaded; this option specifies that the input/output port is 0x388. Finally, it specifies commands executed when the emu10k1 module is loaded (pre-install) and unloaded (post-install).

The /etc/conf.modules file can contain these types of lines:

- Parameter definition lines of the form

    parameter = value

A parameter definition line defines a parameter and binds it to the specified value. The following types of parameter definitions are allowed:

  - depfile=*directory*, which specifies the location of the module dependency database generated by depmod.

- path=*directory*, which specifies a directory to be searched for modules.

- path[*type*]=*directory*, which specifies a directory containing modules of the specified type. The value of *type* can be used with the -t argument of the modprobe command.

- Option lines of the form

  options *module* *symbol*=*value*

  where *module* specifies the name of a module, *symbol* specifies an argument known to the module, and *value* specifies the value of the argument. Option lines specify arguments to be sent to modules. Multiple pairs of symbols and values can be specified; separate each pair from adjacent pairs by one or more spaces.

- Alias lines of the form

  alias *alias_name* *actual_name*

  An alias line establishes an alias, or alternative name, for a module.

- Pre-install lines of the form

  pre-install *module* *command*

  A pre-install line specifies a command to be executed before the specified module is installed.

- Install lines of the form

  install *module* *command*

  An install line specifies a command to be executed to install the specified module.

- Post-install lines of the form

  post-install *module* *command*

  A post-install line specifies a command to be executed after the specified module is installed.

- Pre-remove lines of the form

> pre-remove *module command*

A pre-remove line specifies a command to be executed before the specified module is removed.

- Remove lines of the form

  remove *module command*

A remove line specifies a command to be executed to remove the specified module.

- Post-remove lines of the form

  post-remove *module command*

A post-remove line specifies a command to be executed after the specified module is removed.

- A keep line of the form

  keep

A keep line indicates that any paths specified by parameter lines are to be used in addition to, rather than as replacements for, the default module path.

The /etc/conf.modules file can also contain comments. Empty lines and all text following a hash mark (#) are ignored.

Building a Linux Kernel

This section explains the procedure for configuring, building, and installing the Linux kernel. To help you keep your place, procedurally important subsections are titled with a step number that indicates their place in the overall process:

1. Changing to the kernel source directory

2. Recovering the default configuration (optional)

3. Defining the extraversion code

4. Specifying the kernel configuration options

5. Building the kernel and modules

6. Installing the kernel and modules

7. Creating the boot driver ramdisk

8. Revising the LILO configuration

9. Creating a new boot disk

Step #1: Changing to the Kernel Source Directory

Configuring the kernel, like building and installing the kernel, is done from the root directory of the kernel source tree, /usr/src/linux. To begin configuring the kernel, you should change to that directory:

```
cd /usr/src/linux
```

Step #2: Recovering the Default Configuration

If you have already built a kernel on the local host, you may want to simply tweak the kernel configuration. However, if you've not previously built a kernel, you should recover the default Red Hat Linux kernel configuration. To do so, issue the commands

```
cp configs/kernel arch/i386/defconfig
make mrproper
make oldconfig
```

where *kernel* is the name of the file in the configs directory that corresponds to the standard kernel on which you want to base your new kernel. The make mrproper command removes old configuration files and the results of previous builds. The make oldconfig command sources the config.in file, referring to the defconfig file to determine default values for parameters.

Step #3: Defining the Extraversion Code

As explained earlier in this chapter, Red Hat Inc. recommends that you define an extraversion code that distinguishes differently configured kernels of the same version. To do so, edit the file /usr/src/linux/Makefile. The first few lines of the file should resemble the following:

```
VERSION = 2
```

```
PATCHLEVEL = 2
SUBLEVEL = 12
EXTRAVERSION = -20
```

Add some descriptive text following the -20 in the fourth line, which specifies the Red Hat build number. For example, if the new kernel supports Wireless Access Protocol (WAP), you might revise the line to read

```
EXTRAVERSION = -20WAP
```

The extraversion code is reported by `uname` and determines the subdirectory of `/lib/modules` into which kernel modules are installed, preventing conflicts between modules of similar kernels.

Step #4: Specifying the Kernel Configuration Options

The kernel configuration options reside in the file `/usr/src/linux/ .config`. In principle, you could modify this file by using a text editor. However, Linux provides three utilities that make kernel configuration much simpler:

- `config`
- `menuconfig`
- `xconfig`

To use one of these utilities, issue a command of the form

```
make utility
```

where `utility` is the name of one of the three utilities.

The `config` utility is the oldest of the three utilities. It is a text-based, question-and-response utility that is available as a part of many Linux distributions. However, most users find it clumsy to use. A significant drawback is that `config` provides no way to modify a response once entered. So, if you discover you've responded incorrectly, you must exit the procedure (by typing Ctrl+C) and start over.

The `menuconfig` utility is a favorite among system administrators. Like `config`, it has a text-based interface and so can be used remotely—for example, over a `telnet` or `ssh` connection. However, `menuconfig`—as its name suggests—provides a menu-based interface that lets you cycle through configuration options until you arrive at a configuration you approve of. Thus, it's much less clumsy to use than the `config` utility. It also includes a useful help facility that explains the selected configuration option.

If the host system supports X, you can use the `xconfig` utility. The `xconfig` utility has an attractive and easy-to-use interface that fully supports a mouse or other X-supported pointing device. Like `menuconfig`, it provides a help facility.

The remaining subsections of this section briefly explain the configuration options provided by the Linux kernel. Relatively more attention is given to configuration options you're more likely to work with, especially those that you may need to use in the RHCE exam exercises.

Many configuration options provide three alternatives:

- Yes, which inserts support for the option into the kernel
- No, which omits support for the option
- Module, which compiles a loadable module that provides support for the option

The responses are typically abbreviated as *y* for yes, *n* for no, and *m* for module. In general, you should respond *y* to options needed at boot time, *m* to options needed during operation or likely to be needed in the future, and *n* to other options. An option is considered enabled if you respond *y* or *m*.

Here are some guidelines for choosing kernel options:

Code Maturity Level   You should generally enable Prompt for Development and/or Incomplete Code/Drivers. Some Linux facilities, such as NFS, may not operate correctly without support provided by development code.

Processor Type and Features   Select the highest processor family that includes the CPU of your system; turn math emulation off, unless your CPU is a 386 or 486SX; and turn Symmetric Multiprocessing Support (SMP) off, unless your system's motherboard has multiple CPUs installed.

If you unnecessarily enable math emulation or SMP, your kernel may require somewhat more memory or your system may operate somewhat more slowly.

Loadable Module Support   You should generally enable Loadable Module Support.

Step #5: Building the Kernel and Modules

To build the kernel and modules, issue the following sequence of commands:

```
make bzImage
make modules
```

The commands perform the following operations:

- `make bzImage` compiles the kernel.

- `make modules` compiles loadable modules.

The commands generally take some time to execute. You may prefer, then, to execute them as a single command so that you need not monitor the system to see when it's time to enter the next command. Here's how to do so:

```
make bzImage modules
```

After building a kernel for the first time, you can use an alternative set of commands. First, create your kernel configuration in the usual way by using `make config`, `make menuconfig`, `make xconfig`, or `make oldconfig`. Then, issue the commands

```
make dep
make clean
make bzImage
make modules
```

or issue the single command

```
make dep clean bzImage modules
```

The make dep command propagates your configuration choices through the source tree, and the make clean command removes the results of previous builds. The order in which these two commands are given does not matter. The remaining two commands have their usual effect.

Step #6: Installing the Kernel and Modules

When the build is complete, install the kernel and modules by issuing commands of the following form:

```
cp /usr/src/linux/arch/i386/boot/bzImage
↳/boot/vmlinuz-version
make modules_install
cp /usr/src/linux/System.map /boot/System.map-version
cp /usr/src/linux/.config /boot/config-version
```

where *version* is the version and extraversion code associated with the new kernel. The last command is not absolutely necessary. However, it's handy to have a copy of a kernel's configuration stored with the kernel.

Step #7: Creating the Boot Driver Ramdisk File

If the system uses SCSI or RAID devices during boot, you should create a ramdisk file containing appropriate drivers. The kernel loads the ramdisk file and accesses drivers as needed during boot-up.

To create the ramdisk file, issue a command of the form

```
mkinitrd /boot/initrd-version.img version
```

where *version* is the version and extraversion code associated with the new kernel. The mkinitrd command examines the modules library lib, automatically selects the proper modules, creates the ramdisk file, and packs the modules into the ramdisk file.

Step #8: Revising the LILO Configuration

To boot the new kernel, you generally must revise the LILO configuration. Using a text editor, add lines of the following form to /etc/lilo.conf:

```
image=/boot/vmlinuz-version
  label= vmlinuz-version
  root=/dev/xxx
  initrd=/boot/initrd-version.img
  read-only
```

where *version* is the version and extraversion code associated with the new kernel and *xxx* is the root partition of the Linux system. If you prefer some other label text, specify a different value for label.

After saving the modified file, run the LILO boot map installer:

```
/sbin/lilo -v
```

Step #9: Creating a New Boot Disk

Whenever you install a new kernel, you should create a new boot disk that contains it. To do so, issue a command of the form

```
mkbootdisk -device /dev/fd0 -verbose version
```

where *version* is the version and extraversion code associated with the new kernel. If you want to write the kernel to a floppy drive other than /dev/fd0, specify the device file of the desired floppy drive, for example, /dev/fd1.

After creating the boot disk, boot the system by using LILO and check that it operates properly. If you can't boot the system using the new kernel, boot the system using the old kernel by specifying the label of the old kernel in response to the LILO prompt.

Exam Essentials

Understand essential kernel concepts, such as monolithic versus modular kernels, initial ramdisks, etc.   You should be familiar with basic kernel concepts such as monolithic versus modular kernels, boot driver ramdisks, kernel version numbers, and the kernel extraversion code.

Be able to install kernel sources and development tools needed in order to rebuild the Linux kernel   You should be familiar with the files, directories, and packages related to the Linux kernel. You should also be able to build and install the Linux kernel.

Key Terms and Concepts

Developmental kernel   A developmental kernel is a kernel version that is undergoing major development.

Extraversion code   An extraversion code is a string added to the version number of a Linux kernel that uniquely qualifies the version number in order to avoid conflicts between the modules of kernel instances sharing the same version number.

Major version   The major version of the Linux kernel changes less rapidly than the minor version. The current major version of the Linux kernel is 2.

Minor version   The minor version of the Linux kernel changes more rapidly than the major version. An even minor version is assigned to a stable kernel; an odd minor version is assigned to a developmental kernel.

Modular kernel   A modular kernel consists of multiple components, called modules, some of which can be loaded dynamically.

Module   A module is a part of the Linux kernel, such as a device driver, that can be loaded dynamically.

Monolithic   A monolithic kernel consists of a single unit that is loaded all at once.

Patch level   The patch level of a program or of the Linux kernel is the sequential number of the latest applied patch.

Stable kernel   A kernel that is undergoing limited development aimed primarily at repairing bugs.

Sample Questions

1. If you respond *m* to the prompt for a device driver, which of the following is true?

   A. The driver is compiled as a loadable module.

   B. The driver is compiled as part of the kernel.

   C. The driver is not compiled.

   D. You cannot respond *m* to the prompt for a device driver.

   Answer: A. The response *m* compiles support for a driver or other facility as a loadable kernel module.

2. The file that defines the value of the extraversion code is which of the following?

   A. /usr/src/linux/make

   B. /usr/src/linux/Make

   C. /usr/src/linux/makefile

   D. /usr/src/linux/Makefile

   Answer: D. The value of the extraversion code is defined in /usr/src/linux/Makefile.

Configuring the Loader

Next to the kernel and modules, the most important part of a Linux system is the dynamic loader and its shared libraries. Almost every program uses one or more library routines that the loader supplies when the program is loaded. If the loader is misconfigured, programs—even basic commands, such as ls, that are crucial to system operation—will fail to run.

Critical Information

The programming language C is the most popular language for writing Linux programs. However, C programs as written by a programmer are not immediately ready for execution, because computers do not process C programs. Instead, a computer requires programs to be expressed in a form known as *machine language*. The machine language accepted by one computer model is closely related to the computer's internal architecture and, thus, not generally compatible with machine languages accepted by other computers. Therefore, a computer program must undergo a transformation—generally, a series of transformations—before it can be executed. Programs written in a scripting language such as Perl, Python, or the BASH shell can be executed immediately. That's the primary distinction between a scripting language and ordinary programming languages.

The form of program written by a programmer is called *source code*. A special program called a *compiler* transforms source code into a form known as *object code*. Object code closely resembles machine language but, like source code, it is not executable. A programmer doesn't generally write code to handle common operations such as counting the number of characters in a text string; otherwise, the programmer would be writing the same code again and again. Instead, common operations are written once and organized as a *library*. When a programmer needs to perform one of these operations, the programmer simply writes a reference to the library routine. This speeds the programming process and reduces programming errors.

A special program called a *linker* combines object code with the necessary library routines to create a *statically linked* executable program. A statically linked executable is ready to run.

Statically linked programs suffer several disadvantages. For example, every executable program that uses the library routine to count the number of characters in a text string must contain the machine language instructions to perform this operation. If a system contains thousands of programs that use dozens or hundreds of library routines, considerable disk space is wasted in multiply storing the routines. Moreover, suppose an error is found in a library routine: Every program that uses the routine contains the erroneous code. Fixing the defect requires linking every program that uses the erroneous routine to a corrected library.

A generally better approach is to *dynamically link* programs. A dynamically linked program does not contain the library routines it references. Instead, it contains special *stubs* that specify the library routines the program needs. When a dynamically linked program is loaded, a special *dynamic loader* resolves the program's library references. The system keeps one copy of a dynamically loaded routine in its virtual memory; all programs that use the routine share access to the same copy.

Dynamically linked programs save disk space, because programs do not contain redundant copies of library routines. Moreover, fixing a defective library routine is as simple as replacing the containing library: Every subsequent reference to the routine will resolve to the corrected copy. Dynamically linked programs do execute slightly more slowly, but the difference is seldom significant.

X programs that use the Motif library are often distributed in statically linked form, but the aversion to dynamic linking has nothing to do with performance. The software license of the Motif library restricts its distribution. Statically linked executables do not run afoul of the license.

Linux Shared Libraries

Linux executable program files generally use a structure known as *ELF* (executable and linking format). However, older executable files sometimes use a format known as a.*out*. One complication of this inconsistency is that several system libraries exist separately in both ELF and a.out formats. Eventually, support for a.out will likely disappear.

The Linux linker is known as /usr/bin/ld. At one time, Linux had separate dynamic loaders for a.out files (/lib/ld.so) and ELF files (/lib/ld-linux.so-1). However, Linux now uses a single dynamic loader, /lib/ld-*version*.so, to support both file formats. For compatibility, Red Hat Linux includes both the old and new versions of the Linux dynamic loader.

Linux shared libraries are stored in several directories, such as

- /lib, the main shared libraries
- /usr/lib, supplementary shared libraries
- /usr/i486-linux-libc5/lib, shared libraries for use with the old version of the C standard library, libc5
- /usr/X11R6/lib, shared libraries related to XFree86
- /usr/i486-linuxaout/lib, a.out shared libraries

Static library files have names of the form *libname*.a, where *libname* is the name of the library. Dynamic library files are specially named in a manner designed to achieve upward compatibility with new releases of shared libraries. The name of a shared library generally has the form *libname-major.minor.patch*.so, where

- *libname* is the name of the library.
- *major* is the major release number of the library.
- *minor* is the minor release number of the library.
- *patch* is the patch level of the library.
- so indicates that the file is a shared library.

For example, the standard C library might reside in a file named
libc-2.1.1.so. If a library has been freshly released, the patch level
or minor release level may be omitted and the filename will have the
form *libname-major.minor.*so or *libname-major.*so.

In addition to the library file, there are two symbolic links that point
to the library file:

- *libname.*so

- *libname.*so.*major*

Programs are linked against one or the other of the symbolic links
rather than against the library file. Thus, the loader is able to locate
the required library even if the patch level or minor release numbers
change.

Necessary Procedures

This section gives several procedures associated with shared libraries.

Adding a Shared Library

When you install an RPM package that includes a shared library, the
installation script should automatically update the shared library
configuration. However, if you install a non-RPM package, you may
need to revise the shared library configuration manually.

The shared library configuration resides in the file /etc/ld.so.conf,
which contains a list of directories that contain shared libraries, one
directory on each line. Here are the contents of a typical ld.so.conf file:

```
/usr/lib
/usr/i486-linux-libc5/lib
/usr/X11R6/lib
/usr/i486-linuxaout/lib
```

Notice that the main library shared directory, /lib, is not listed; if it could not be found, essentially no commands, including those needed to update the shared library configuration, would work. Therefore, the location of this library is built into the loader and need not be specified in the configuration file.

To add a directory to the shared library configuration, use a text editor to add a line specifying the directory name to /etc/ld.so.conf. Then, issue the command

```
ldconfig -v
```

This command is necessary, because the loader keeps a cache of directory and library names in the file /etc/ld.so.cache. The cache improves performance but must be rebuilt by the ldconfig command so the loader will begin searching the newly specified directory.

Viewing Library References

To determine the dynamic libraries needed by a program, issue a command of the form

```
ldd programfile
```

where *programfile* is the name of the program. For example, to determine the dynamic libraries required by the rm command, issue the command

```
# ldd /bin/rm
    libc.so.6 => /lib/libc.so.6 (0x40019000)
    /lib/ld-linux.so.2 => /lib/ld-linux.so.2
    ↪(0x40000000)
```

The sample output shows that the rm command requires version 6 of libc and that the loader resolved this reference to /lib/libc.so.6. The output also shows that the current version of the Linux dynamic loader is version 2.

Specifying Library Paths

If the loader is unable to locate a library required by a program, it prints an error message and halts the loading process. If the library resides on the system, you can inform the loader of its location by setting the environment variable LD_LIBRARY_PATH. For example, to specify that the loader should search the directories /usr/local/lib and /usr/local/otherlib for required libraries, issue the command

```
export LD_LIBRARY_PATH=/usr/local/lib:/usr/local/
↪otherlib
```

The specified directory or directories are searched in addition to the default directories, which therefore need not be explicitly specified.

Exam Essentials

Be familiar with shared libraries and the loader   Although the official list of RHCE study points does not mention shared libraries or the loader, you should be familiar with these topics. You should be able to view library references, add a shared library, and specify library paths.

Key Terms and Concepts

a.out   The a.out format is an object file format popular in early Linux versions.

Compiler   A compiler is a program that translates source code to machine code, for example, the C compiler.

Dynamic linking   Dynamic linking is linking performed when a program is loaded. Linking combines an object module with library members it uses to form a complete program.

Dynamic loader   A dynamic loader is a loader capable of dynamic linking.

ELF   ELF is the object file format currently used by Linux systems.

Library   A library is a file that contains object modules—called library members—that can be combined with other object modules to form programs.

Linker   A linker is a program that can be used to combine object modules and library members to form programs.

Machine language   Machine language is the set of operating codes understood by a given processor model or, more generally, any set of operating codes understood by some processor model.

Object code   Object code is a form intermediate between source code and machine language.

Source code   Source code is the program form that programmers work with.

Static linking   Static linking is linking of an object module with all required library members so that no references to libraries or dynamic linking are necessary when the resulting program is loaded.

Stub   A stub is a piece of code that acts as a placeholder.

Sample Questions

1. To update the shared library configuration, you must issue which command?

   A. ld

   B. ld.so

   C. ldconfig

   D. ldd

   Answer: C. The ldconfig command rebuilds the loader's shared library cache.

2. What is the predominant form of Linux executables?

   A. a.out

   B. COFF

   C. ELF

   D. IBCS

   Answer: C. The predominant form of Linux executables is ELF; some older executables use the a.out format.

Chapter

8

Single-User and Rescue Modes

RHCE PREPARATION TOPICS COVERED IN THIS CHAPTER:

A significant portion of the RHCE exam requires you to troubleshoot and fix broken system configurations. To do so, you must boot the system in single-user or rescue mode, find the problem, and fix it. This chapter explains single-user and rescue mode operation and gives general procedures for troubleshooting systems.

Using Single-User Mode

From time to time, you may attempt to boot a Linux system only to find that the system won't boot. You may see error messages pointing to problems such as

- missing or corrupt LILO installation
- kernel panic
- missing or corrupt kernel
- damaged file system
- inability to enter runlevel 2, 3, or 5
- unknown root password

To fix the system, you must boot it. Unless the system is suffering from a hardware problem, you'll probably be able to boot it using either single-user mode or rescue mode.

Once you succeed in booting the system, you can study its configuration files and logs to determine the cause of the problem, fix the problem, and reboot the system. The next section explains single-user mode and single-user mode recovery procedures. The following section explains rescue mode and rescue mode recovery procedures.

Critical Information

Single-user mode provides a simple way to recover from problems that do not affect LILO, the kernel, or the root file system. Problems with non-root file systems, runlevels, and failing services can often be repaired in single-user mode.

Entering Single-User Mode

To enter single-user mode, respond *linux* **single** or *linux* **emergency** at the boot prompt, where *linux* is the label associated with your kernel in the LILO configuration file. If you prefer a shorter response, you can type *linux* **s**, which is equivalent to *linux* **single**.

The boot parameter—s, single, or emergency—is passed to the init process, which places the system in single-user mode when system startup is complete. If you specify the emergency parameter, init also omits loading of initial processes; this option is helpful if your /etc/inittab file is incorrect.

The system does not prompt for a password, but places you in a shell with root privileges.

TIP Because anyone with access to the system console can boot a system in single-user mode and obtain privileged access, you should maintain good physical security of computer systems. Alternatively, you can configure the system BIOS to boot only from the hard drive, restrict access to the system BIOS, lock the system case, and configure LILO to restrict access to single-user mode.

Accessing the Single-User Mode Environment

When you enter single-user mode as explained in the preceding subsection, only the root file system is mounted, and the PATH environment variable may not be set to its usual value. Therefore, you may need to type the full path name of commands you want to execute.

You won't initially have access to commands stored in /usr/bin and /usr/sbin, for example; only commands residing in /bin and /sbin are available.

Examining Configuration Files

Generally, when a system fails to properly boot, it has been wrongly configured. You have—or another system administrator has—made an error in revising a configuration file or in using linuxconf or another configuration utility. Here are some configuration files that you should examine in your search for the problem:

- /etc/conf.modules
- /etc/fstab
- /etc/inittab
- /etc/lilo.conf
- /etc/rc.d/*
- /etc/yp.conf, if the system uses NIS

Pay particular attention to /etc/fstab and /etc/lilo.conf, which—when wrongly configured—are common causes of system startup problems.

Necessary Procedure

This section gives a general troubleshooting procedure for single-user mode.

General Single-User Mode Procedure

Here's a general troubleshooting procedure for single-user mode:

1. Boot in single-user mode by responding *linux* **s** to the boot prompt image label.

2. When the system is booted, you'll have access to a BASH shell session that has only the root partition mounted.

3. Identify the available partitions: `fdisk -l`.

4. Check the non-root file systems: `e2fsck -y /dev/xxx`, where *xxx* is the partition on which the root file system resides.

5. If LILO is damaged or missing, mount the `/boot` partition: `mount /dev/xxx /boot`, where *xxx* is the partition on which the root file system resides.

6. Find and fix any wrongly configured facilities. Be sure to check `/etc/lilo.conf` and `/etc/fstab`.

7. If `/etc/lilo.conf` or the kernel has changed, run the `lilo` map installer: `/sbin/lilo`.

8. Reboot the computer: `shutdown -r now`.

Exam Essentials

Know how to boot into or enter and use the single-user mode
Although the official list of RHCE study points does not mention single-user mode, you should be able to boot into or enter and use single-user mode. Being able to do so is essential to trouble-shooting and repairing many kinds of system problems.

Key Term and Concept

Single-user mode   Single-user mode is a special mode intended to help a system administrator repair a damaged system.

Sample Questions

1. Which of the following responses to the Linux boot prompt causes Red Hat Linux to enter single-user mode?

    A. `linux 1`

    B. `linux rescue`

C. linux single

D. linux single-user

Answer: C. You can enter single-user mode by responding **linux s,** **linux single**, or **linux emergency** to the LILO boot prompt.

2. Which of the following directories is not generally available when running in single-user mode?

A. /

B. /bin

C. /sbin

D. /usr/sbin

Answer: D. The /usr file system is not generally available when operating in single-user mode.

Using Rescue Mode

*R*escue mode is useful when you cannot boot a system, even in single-user mode. Rescue mode supplies a root file system taken from a ramdisk image, so you have access to common shell commands even if no partitions on the system's hard disk can be mounted. With skill and insight, you can use these commands to find and fix the problem.

Critical Information

To use the Red Hat Linux 6.1 or later rescue facility, boot the system by using the installation floppy disk or the installation CD-ROM. In response to the boot prompt, reply **linux rescue**.

The rescue facility will ask you to choose your language and keyboard style. It will then attempt to locate the RPMS and base directories of the Red Hat Linux distribution media. If the system's CD-ROM drive contains a distribution CD-ROM, the system will enter rescue mode. Otherwise, the rescue facility will prompt you for the location of these directories, which may be a CD-ROM drive or local hard drive. Generally, you should insert an installation CD-ROM in the CD-ROM drive and direct the rescue mode facility to that device. However, if the system contains a readable file system holding the RPMS and base directories, you can direct the rescue facility to the partition on which the file system resides.

TIP   You can use a bootnet.img floppy as a rescue disk, obtaining the rescue environment from a suitably configured NFS server.

Accessing the Rescue Mode Environment

The commands available in rescue mode are a small subset of those generally available under Red Hat Linux. This subsection highlights several especially useful commands, explaining how they're useful in troubleshooting and recovery.

The *fdisk* Command

The fdisk command will tell you what partitions exist on local hard drives. You need to know this information in order to know what partitions to check and then mount. To report the existing partitions on local hard drives, issue the command

```
fdisk -l
```

The partition type will help you determine the partitions of interest. Here's a typical output of fdisk:

```
Disk /dev/hda: 255 heads, 63 sectors, 2489 cylinders
Units = cylinders of 16065 * 512 bytes

    Device Boot   Start     End    Blocks   Id  System
/dev/hda1    *        1     127   1020096    6  FAT16
/dev/hda2            128    2489  18972765    5  Extended
/dev/hda5            128     132     40131   83  Linux
/dev/hda6            133     387   2048256   83  Linux
/dev/hda7           1091    1157    538146   82  Linux swap
```

In the example, partitions hda5 and hda6 are Linux partitions that you'd want to check and possibly mount.

The *e2fsck* Command

The e2fsck command checks a Linux file system for damage and, optionally, repairs simple damage. To check a file system, issue a command of the form

```
e2fsck -y /dev/xxx
```

where *xxx* is the partition that contains the file system. The -y flag instructs e2fsck to automatically attempt to repair damage, rather than prompt you for each error found; without the flag, the command can become tiresome when a file system contains numerous errors.

Linux stores information about file systems in special areas called *superblocks*. If a file system is corrupt, you can sometimes recover it by instructing Linux to use an alternate superblock. To do so, you must know the location of the alternate superblock; usually, they are written at intervals of 32768 blocks, so the first alternate superblock is likely to be located in block 32769. To instruct e2fsck to attempt to recover a file system by using superblock 32769, issue a command of the form

```
e2fsck -b 32769 -y /dev/xxx
```

where *xxx* is the partition that contains the file system.

NOTE   Prior to Red Hat Linux 6.2, superblocks were written at intervals of 8192 blocks.

You can use the dumpe2fs command to learn the location of alternate superblocks of an undamaged file system. If you're concerned about the possibility of file system damage, you should run the command on each of your file systems and retain the output so that it's available during recovery procedures.

The *lilo* Command

The lilo command installs the LILO boot loader and updates the boot map. Normally you perform these operations by issuing the command

```
/sbin/lilo
```

However, when operating in rescue mode, the root file system of the local hard disk is not mounted as the root directory. Running lilo in the usual way would not properly update the /boot directory of the local hard drive. Instead, you should issue a command of the form

```
/sbin/lilo -r path
```

where *path* is the current mount point of the root file system of the local hard drive. For example, if the root file system of the local hard drive is mounted as /mnt/hd, issue the command

```
/sbin/lilo -r /mnt/hd
```

Alternatively, you can issue the chroot command to establish a changed-root environment, and then issue the lilo command in the ordinary manner:

```
chroot /mnt/hd
/sbin/lilo
```

The *mknod* Command

Some commands, such as fdisk, will not function unless the necessary device files exist. Unfortunately, the rescue mode environment does not include the complete set of device files normally available. However, you can create device files by using the mknod command. For example, the command

```
mknod /dev/hda
```

creates the device file /dev/hda. The mknod command available in the rescue mode environment can generally determine the proper major and minor device numbers for a device, so you generally need not specify them. The rescue mode mount command shares this convenient capability.

The *sync* Command

When operating in rescue mode, you generally cannot shut down the system in the usual, orderly way by using the shutdown command. However, if you abruptly power off or reset the system, you may corrupt one or more file systems. So, a modified shutdown procedure must be used.

When you're ready to restart the system, issue a sequence of commands of the following form:

```
sync
sync
sync
cd /
umount fs1 fs2 ...
```

where *fs1*, *fs2*, . . . represent mounted file systems of the local hard drive. When the umount command completes, you can power off or reset the system.

Necessary Procedure

This section gives a general troubleshooting procedure for rescue mode.

General Rescue Mode Recovery Procedure

Here's a general troubleshooting procedure for rescue mode:

1. Boot from a system boot disk or the installation CD-ROM. Respond **linux rescue** to the prompt for the boot image label. When the system is booted, you'll have access to a BASH shell session that has no mounted local file systems—that is, no file systems from the hard drive.

2. Create a mount point for the local file systems: mkdir /mnt/hd.

3. Identify the available partitions: fdisk -l.

4. Check the root file system: e2fsck -y /dev/*xxx*, where *xxx* is the partition on which the root file system resides. You may need to first create the device file by issuing the command mknod /dev/*xxx*.

5. Mount the root file system: mount /dev/*xxx* /mnt/hd, where *xxx* is the partition on which the root file system resides.

6. Establish a changed-root environment, making your work more convenient: chroot /mnt/hd.

7. If LILO is damaged or missing, mount the /boot partition: mount /dev/ *xxx* /boot, where *xxx* is the partition on which the root file system resides.

8. Fix any wrongly configured facilities by using the pico editor. Be sure to check /etc/lilo.conf and /etc/fstab.

9. If /etc/lilo.conf or the kernel has changed, run the lilo map installer: /sbin/lilo.

10. Commit the changes: sync; sync; sync.

11. Unmount any mounted file systems: cd /; umount /boot.

12. Reset the computer.

Exam Essentials

Know how to boot into and use the rescue environment for system recovery   You should know how to boot into and use rescue mode. Knowing how to do so is critical to being able to troubleshoot and repair many kinds of problems, particularly problems related to partitions and file systems.

Key Terms and Concepts

Rescue mode   Rescue mode is a special mode that provides facilities that help you repair a damaged system.

Superblock   A superblock is a special block of data that describes the content and structure of a file system.

Sample Questions

1. Which of the following commands can create device files when in rescue mode?

   A. fdisk

   B. lilo

   C. mount

   D. sync

   Answer: C. The rescue mode versions of the mknod and mount commands can create device files.

2. Which of the following is a likely location for an alternate superblock under Red Hat Linux 6.2?

   A. block 8193

   B. block 16385

   C. block 32769

   D. block 65537

   Answer: C. Under Red Hat Linux 6.2, superblocks are generally stored every 32768 blocks; therefore, block 32769 is likely to be the first alternate superblock.

Chapter

9

Primary Network Services

RHCE PREPARATION TOPICS COVERED IN THIS CHAPTER:

his chapter is one of the most important chapters of this book—perhaps the *most* important chapter—from the standpoint of your preparation for the RHCE exam. One of the three RHCE exam components requires you to install and configure a specified set of network services. Your ability to excel in that component of the exam depends upon your grasp of the material in this chapter, which explains primary network services and how to install, configure, and troubleshoot them.

Working with Apache

The Apache Web server is the most popular Web server on the Internet. Like most other Linux network services, Apache is a TCP/IP network service. This section explains TCP/IP network services, and then explains how to install and configure Apache.

Critical Information

All primary Linux network services are TCP/IP services—that is, services based on the TCP/IP family of protocols. A TCP/IP service has an associated number known as a port; ports are numbered from 0 to 65535. The ports of common TCP/IP services are termed *well-known ports*; the file /etc/services contains a list of these ports.

Under Linux, only privileged users can access ports 0 to 1023, which are therefore known as *privileged ports*. This restriction improves system security by preventing a non-privileged user from substituting a phony service in place of a real one. When a client accesses a service bound to a privileged port, the client has some confidence that the service has not been compromised.

To understand how port numbers are used, consider how you address mail to someone living in an apartment: You write the street address and an apartment number. An IP number resembles the street address in this analogy; many services may be available on the host bound to the IP number. A port number identifies a particular service in much the same way that an apartment number identifies a particular unit within an apartment complex.

When a client accesses a service, the client uses a port on the client host. To pass information to the client, the server uses the client host's IP address and the client's port number. Thus, four elements are involved in communication between a client and server:

- the server host IP address

- the server port

- the client host IP address

- the client port

Collectively, these elements are referred to as a *socket*.

Accessing a service involves a standard process, called the *bind-listen-connect-accept process*:

1. The server process *binds* itself to a port on the server host and begins *listening* for client requests.

2. A client process requests an available port on the client host and uses it to *connect* to the server process via the server process's port.

3. The server process *accepts* the connection by requesting an available port on the server host and informing the client to communicate using that port.

A TCP/IP service can operate either of two ways: stand-alone or inetd. A stand-alone service runs continuously as a daemon process. An inetd service runs under the control of the inetd process and is started only when a client request arrives. The service runs only as long as necessary to satisfy the request and then terminates. If a service is heavily used or requires a relatively long time to start, it's best run as a stand-alone service. However, services that are seldom used and quick to start can be run more efficiently as inetd services, because they consume resources such as memory only when running.

To specify that a service runs as an inetd service, you specify the service in inetd's configuration file, /etc/inetd.conf. The inetd service binds itself to the service's designated port and listens for client requests. When one is received, the inetd service starts the proper server and hands off the request.

The Apache Web Server

Apache is an HTTP 1.1–compliant, open-source Web server that is widely used. The March 2000 Netcraft survey (www.netcraft.com) showed that over 7.8 million Web sites, about 61 percent of Web sites surveyed, were running Apache; in contrast, only about 21 percent of Web sites were running Microsoft's Internet Information Server.

Apache is fast and reliable. Moreover, many third-party modules that extend its functionality are available. You can obtain information about these modules from the Apache Modules Registry Web site, modules.apache.org.

To avoid U.S. export restrictions, Apache does not include support for Secure Socket Layer (SSL), an important Web technology that enables secure transactions. However, you can obtain Apache-SSL, a version of Apache that includes support for SSL, from the Apache-SSL project Web site, www.apache-ssl.org, or from ftp.zedz.net. Alternatively, you can use the Apache SSL module, mod_ssl, or purchase a commercial version of Apache that provides SSL support, such as that sold by Red Hat Inc.

Installation

To install the standard version of Apache, move to the directory containing the RPM packages and issue the following command:

```
rpm -Uvh apache-*.rpm
```

If you need to be able to compile Apache modules, you should also install the apache-devel package:

```
rpm -Uvh apache-devel*.rpm
```

TIP If you prefer accessing Apache documentation from your local hard drive rather than via the Web, you can install the apache-manual package, which places important Apache documents in /home/httpd/html/manual/.

Basic Configuration

The configuration files for Apache reside in /etc/httpd/conf. They are

- access.conf

- httpd.conf

- srm.conf

At one time, each file contained directives of a particular sort. More recent versions of Apache have relaxed restrictions on file content, so the presence of three files can be viewed as a mere historical artifact.

The current version of Red Hat Linux places all the configuration information in the file httpd.conf; the other two files contain only comment lines, which have a hash mark (#) as the first non-blank character. The httpd.conf file has three main sections, which are marked off by comments:

- Section 1, the global environment

- Section 2, the main server configuration

- Section 3, virtual host configurations

The directives included in Section 1 affect the operation of the server as a whole, including the main configuration and all virtual host configurations. Directives in Section 2 affect only the main server configuration. Directives in Section 3, if present, affect only the virtual host configuration to which they pertain. The next several subsections examine the `httpd.conf` file and its directives more closely.

Section 1: The Global Environment

The directives in Section 1 let you specify configuration options that affect all server configurations, such as

- the type of configuration: stand-alone or `inetd` (generally stand-alone)

- the names and locations of available Apache modules

- the number of server processes to start, and the minimum and maximum number to maintain

Unless you want to operate the server in `inetd` mode, install custom modules, or modify the number of server processes, you may not need to modify the directives in Section 1.

Section 2: The Main Configuration

Section 2 of the `httpd.conf` file contains directives that affect the operation of only the main configuration of the server; the directives do not affect the operation of virtual hosts, if any are configured. Primary configuration items include:

- the host name of the server

- the port number on which the server listens (generally port 80)

- the user and group IDs under which the daemon runs (generally nobody)

- the type of logging desired: logging by IP address or host name (generally logging by IP address, which is more efficient)

- the location of the root directory (generally `/home/httpd/html`)

- the name of users' HTML subdirectory (generally `~/public_html` or `~/www`)

- the path where CGI scripts reside

- the location of icons used when formatting directory indexes

- configuration options for special content handlers

Generally, you should revise the ServerName directive, which specifies the name of the host with which the server is associated, and the ServerAdmin directive, which specifies the e-mail address of the server administrator. You may need to change other directives, depending on your requirements.

Section 3: The Virtual Host Configuration

Virtual hosting, also known as multi-homing, is an important Apache feature that lets a single Web server respond to several IP addresses or host names. For example, a single instance of Apache could be configured to respond to queries directed to www.able.com and www.baker.com. Virtual hosting lets two or more organizations share a single Web server. If you want to configure Apache to support virtual hosts, you must revise the directives in Section 3 of the httpd.conf file. You should specify the following:

- the IP address, or addresses, of the virtual hosts
- the e-mail address of the administrator of each virtual host
- the host name of each virtual host
- the names of the log files associated with each virtual host
- the location of the document root and CGI directory for each virtual host

Here is a typical virtual host configuration for two hosts—www.firsthost.com and www.secondhost.com—both of which are assigned IP address 192.169.100.1:

```
NameVirtualHost 192.169.100.1

<VirtualHost firsthost.com>
ServerAdmin webmaster@firsthost.com
DocumentRoot /home/httpd/html/firsthost/
ServerName www.firsthost.com
ErrorLog logs/firsthost-error-log
TransferLog logs/firsthost-access-log
ScriptAlias /cgi-bin/ /home/httpd/cgi-bin/firsthost/
</VirtualHost>
```

```
<VirtualHost secondhost.com>
ServerAdmin webmaster@secondhost.com
DocumentRoot /home/httpd/html/secondhost/
ServerName www.secondhost.com
ErrorLog logs/secondhost-error-log
TransferLog logs/secondhost-access-log
other options here, e.g., <Directory>
ScriptAlias /cgi-bin/ /home/httpd/cgi-bin/secondhost/
</VirtualHost>
```

NOTE   If the IP address in NameVirtualHost is the only IP address for the host, you should include a VirtualHost entry describing the main configuration.

Necessary Procedures

This section gives important procedures for working with Apache.

Starting and Restarting the Service

To start the Apache Web server, issue the command

```
/etc/rc.d/init.d/httpd start
```

To restart the Apache Web server, issue the command

```
/etc/rc.d/init.d/httpd restart
```

NOTE   If the server is configured for inetd operation, you don't need to—and should not—start or restart it.

Stopping the Service

To stop the Apache Web server, issue the command

```
/etc/rc.d/init.d/httpd stop
```

NOTE   If the server is configured for inetd operation, you can't stop it by using the httpd script; you must reconfigure inetd.

Reloading the Configuration File

To cause Apache to reload its configuration file, issue the command

```
/etc/rc.d/init.d/httpd reload
```

You should instruct Apache to reload its configuration file after saving a revised version of the file. When possible, it's better to reload the configuration file rather than stop and restart the service.

Checking Service Status

To check the status of the Apache Web server, issue the command

```
/etc/rc.d/init.d/httpd status
```

NOTE   If the server is configured for inetd operation, you can't check its status by using the httpd script.

Troubleshooting the Service

To troubleshoot Apache, check the system log (/var/log/messages) and the Apache log files (/var/log/httpd/*) for relevant error messages. To check the virtual host configuration, issue the command /usr/sbin/httpd -S. The server should report the virtual host name and port number of the main server and each configured virtual host.

Exam Essentials

Understand, and be capable of implementing, the following network services: Apache, Samba, NFS, basic Sendmail, POP3/IMAP4 e-mail, DNS, and FTP This section described the Apache Web server. You should be capable of installing and configuring Apache.

Be sufficiently familiar with the function, configuration, and logging of those services so as to be capable of basic troubleshooting This section described the Apache Web server. You should be capable of simple troubleshooting of Apache.

Key Terms and Concepts

Bind-listen-connect-accept process The bind-listen-connect-accept process is a process followed by TCP servers that listen for and process client requests.

Privileged port A privileged port is one numbered 0–1023; only a privileged process can access a privileged port.

Socket A socket is a TCP/IP communications facility that consists of a connection between a pair of ports.

Well-known port A well-known port is a port commonly associated with some TCP/IP service. Well-known ports are listed in /etc/services.

Sample Questions

1. Which of the following is the number of a privileged port?

A. 500

B. 5000

C. 50000

D. 500000

Answer: A. Ports 0–1023 are privileged ports.

2. Which of the following is the Apache directive that specifies the IP address of a virtual host?

A. AddressVirtualHost

B. NameVirtualHost

C. ServerName

D. ServerIP

Answer: B. The NameVirtualHost directive specifies the IP address of a virtual host; the ServerName directive specifies the host name of the main host.

▶ Working with BIND

The Berkeley Internet Name Daemon (BIND) resolves IP addresses to host names and host names to IP addresses. This service is often called Domain Name Service (DNS). The overwhelming majority of DNS servers on the Internet run the same server distributed as part of Red Hat Linux. Many servers have names that resemble the name of the associated program; however, BIND's associated program, /usr/sbin/named, is oddly named.

Critical Information

Red Hat Linux helps you configure either of two sorts of DNS:

- a caching-only DNS server

- a regular DNS server

A caching-only DNS server may improve DNS performance of a host that has a slow-speed connection to the Internet. A caching-only nameserver contacts a regular nameserver to resolve IP addresses and host names. But once an IP address or host name has been resolved, the caching-only nameserver stores the result so that future references to the IP address or host name can be resolved without querying another nameserver.

Installation

Red Hat Linux includes these BIND-related packages:

- `bind`, which provides a regular DNS server

- `bind-utils`, a set of useful utilities for administering BIND

- `caching-nameserver`, which configures BIND to provide a caching-only nameserver

In addition, it includes the `bind-devel` package, which is needed only when doing software development of programs that invoke the BIND application programming interface.

To install BIND, move to the directory that contains the packages and issue the following command:

```
rpm -Uvh bind-*.rpm bind-devel-*.rpm
```

If you want to configure a caching-only nameserver, also issue the following command:

```
rpm -Uvh caching-nameserver-*.rpm
```

Basic BIND Configuration

To establish Domain Name Service (DNS), you must configure the main DNS configuration file, `/etc/named.conf`. In general, you must also configure a set of files known as *zone files*, which generally reside in `/var/named`. A zone file is either

- a *forward zone file*, used to map host names to IP addresses

- a *reverse zone file*, used to map IP addresses to host names
- a hint file, which identifies the root nameservers responsible for answering DNS queries for all registered domains

---

TIP If you require a caching-only nameserver, installation of the `caching-nameserver` package correctly configures BIND. However, you can improve the efficiency of name lookup by modifying the default caching-nameserver configuration to include a `forwarders` statement in `/etc/named.conf`. The `forwarders` statement has the form `forwarders` *IP_address*, where *IP_address* specifies the IP address of a DNS service that will respond to queries not resolvable from the cache. If you like, you can specify the IP addresses of multiple servers—just separate each from the next by a space.

The `/etc/named.conf` file identifies each zone file. If the zone file is a forward zone file, `/etc/named.conf` identifies the domain to which the zone file applies; if the zone file is a reverse zone file, `/etc/named.conf` identifies the network to which the zone file applies. The `/etc/named.conf` file also indicates whether the local DNS is a master DNS or slave DNS for the zone. A master DNS is the primary nameserver for its zone, called the *start of authority* for the zone. A slave DNS obtains information from a master DNS, which it regularly contacts in order to keep its information up-to-date.

Here is a typical `/etc/named.conf` file, the format of which is described by the named man page:

```
options {
        directory "/var/named";
};
zone "." {
        type hint;
        file "named.ca";
};
zone "azusapacific.com."{
```

```
            type master;
            file "named.azusapacific.com";
    };
    zone "0.0.127.in-addr.arpa"{
            type master;
            file "named.local";
    };
    zone "1.168.192.in-addr.arpa"{
            type master;
            file "named.reverse";
    };
```

The contents of a correct named.ca hint file can be obtained via FTP from ftp://ftp.rs.internic.net/domain/named.root. The remaining files must be coded by hand. A forward zone file typically specifies the following:

- the host that is the start of authority (SOA) for the zone

- the e-mail address of the administrator responsible for the zone

- mappings from host names to IP addresses for hosts in the zone

In addition, the zone file may specify secondary nameservers, mail exchange records, and host aliases (called *canonical names* or CNAMEs). Here is a typical forward zone file:

```
@               IN      SOA     azusapacific.com.
                root.azusapacific.com. (
                        200002051 ; serial time
                        43200     ; refresh time
                        3600      ; retry time
                        3600000   ; expire time
                        2419200   ; default_ttl
                )
@               IN      NS      azusapacific.com.
@               IN      MX      10 azusapacific.com.
```

```
localhost         IN    A      127.0.0.1
azusapacific.com. IN    A      192.168.1.1
bill              IN    A      192.168.1.2
toshiba           IN    A      192.168.1.99
router            IN    CNAME  azusapacific.com.
www               IN    CNAME  azusapacific.com.
ftp               IN    CNAME  azusapacific.com.
mail              IN    CNAME  azusapacific.com.
```

Note the unusual use of a period in the e-mail address of the zone administrator (root.azusapacific.com.) and following the domain name (azusapacific.com.). The underlying concept is that all host names, fully qualified or not, end with a dot when specified in the zone file and other DNS configuration files. The format of the file is more fully described in the named man page.

The series of numbers in the SOA record specify:

- a serial number used by slaves to determine when information has changed

- the refresh interval at which slaves should check the serial number, specified in seconds

- the interval at which a slave should retry after a failed refresh, specified in seconds

- the interval at which to discard cached information in refreshes that have failed, specified in seconds

- the default interval for which negative responses should be cached, specified in seconds

Here is a typical reverse zone file:

```
@          IN    SOA    azusapacific.com.
     root.azusapacific.com. (
                     2000032502 ; serial
                     43200 ; refresh
```

```
                                3600 ; retry
                                3600000 ; expire
                                2419200 ; default_ttl
                                )
@           IN      NS          azusapacific.com.
1           IN      PTR         wall.azusapacific.com.
2           IN      PTR         p3.azusapacific.com.
99          IN      PTR         laptop.azusapacific.com.
3           IN      PTR         p2.azusapacific.com.
```

Necessary Procedures

This section gives important procedures for working with BIND.

Starting and Restarting the Service

To start BIND, issue the command

```
/etc/rc.d/init.d/named start
```

To restart BIND, issue the command

```
/etc/rc.d/init.d/named restart
```

Stopping the Service

To stop BIND, issue the command

```
/etc/rc.d/init.d/named stop
```

Checking Service Status

To check the status of BIND, issue the command

```
/etc/rc.d/init.d/named status
```

Forcing a Database Reload

You should instruct BIND to reload its database whenever you change a BIND configuration file. To instruct BIND to reload its database, issue the command

```
/etc/rc.d/init.d/named reload
```

Troubleshooting

By default, BIND logs messages to the system log /var/log/messages. If BIND is not functioning properly, check the log for error messages that point to the problem.

Exam Essentials

Understand, and be capable of implementing, the following network services: Apache, Samba, NFS, basic Sendmail, POP3/IMAP4 e-mail, DNS (BIND), and FTP This section described BIND. You should be capable of installing and configuring BIND.

Be sufficiently familiar with the function, configuration, and logging of those services so as to be capable of basic troubleshooting This section described BIND. You should be capable of simple troubleshooting of BIND.

Key Terms and Concepts

Canonical name A canonical name is a host name alias specified in the Domain Name Service (DNS) configuration.

Forward zone file A forward zone file is a Domain Name Service (DNS) configuration file that maps host names to IP addresses.

Reverse zone file A Domain Name Service (DNS) configuration file that maps IP addresses to host names.

Start of authority   The start of authority (SOA) is the host that has primary responsibility for Domain Name Service (DNS) information pertaining to a zone.

Zone file   A Domain Name Service (DNS) file that maps host names to IP addresses or the reverse.

Sample Questions

1. Which of the following correctly summarizes the function of a reverse zone file?

   A. It maps IP addresses to host names.

   B. It maps IP addresses to NetBIOS host names.

   C. It maps host names to IP addresses.

   D. It maps NetBIOS host names to IP addresses.

   Answer: A. The reverse zone file maps IP addresses to host names; the forward zone file maps host names to IP addresses.

2. Which of the following is the main DNS configuration file?

   A. /etc/bind.conf

   B. /etc/named.conf

   C. /var/named.conf

   D. /var/bind.conf

   Answer: B. The main DNS configuration file, which identifies the zone files, is /etc/named.conf.

Working with FTP

*F*TP is a very widely used service, and the Washington University (St. Louis) FTP server is the most widely used FTP server on the Internet. The server lets users upload and download files and directories.

Critical Information

The FTP daemon is named /usr/sbin/in.ftpd; however, its man page is named ftpd. Three levels of FTP access are provided:

- User access, which is access by users who have a login account on the server host. This level of access accords users the usual access privileges defined by their user ID.

- Guest access, which is access by users who have a special guest account that provides only FTP access. This level of access accords users specially defined access privileges.

- Anonymous access, which is access by users who have no defined account on the server host. This level of access accords users access to only a specified directory and its subdirectories (usually /home/ftp). This restriction is enforced by means of a chrooted environment.

The Washington University FTP server can log all accesses. It also provides capabilities that let clients transfer compressed files or transfer entire directories with a single command.

Installation

The Washington University FTP server is distributed as two packages:

- wu-ftpd, which contains the FTP server

- anonftp, which contains the anonymous FTP server

If you require anonymous FTP service, you should install both packages. However, if you don't require anonymous FTP service, you should install only the wu-ftpd package. Unnecessarily installing anonymous FTP may make your system somewhat more vulnerable to attack by hackers.

Basic Configuration

The FTP service has three basic configuration files:

- /etc/ftpaccess, which specifies global options and user permissions.

- /etc/ftphosts, which specifies client hosts that may, or may not, access the FTP service.

- /etc/ftpusers, which specifies users who *may not* access the FTP service. Typically, the file includes entries for root, bin, daemon, adm, lp, sync, shutdown, halt, mail, news, uucp, operator, games, and nobody.

Here are the contents of a typical ftpaccess file:

```
class    all    real,guest,anonymous    *

email root@localhost

loginfails 5

readme   README*      login
readme   README*      cwd=*

message /welcome.msg              login
message .message                  cwd=*

compress       yes         all
tar            yes         all
chmod          no          guest,anonymous
delete         no          guest,anonymous
overwrite      no          guest,anonymous
rename         no          guest,anonymous

log transfers anonymous,real inbound,outbound

shutdown /etc/shutmsg

passwd-check rfc822 warn
```

Administration

By default, the FTP service is run as an `inetd` service. Thus, it is not necessary to start, restart, or stop the service.

The FTP service places log entries in the system log `/var/log/messages`. If the FTP service is not operating properly, check the contents of the system log for log entries that point to the problem.

A common requirement is for a set of directories to be accessible via anonymous FTP, HTTP, and NFS. The FTP server does not follow symbolic links that point outside the directory tree rooted on the home directory of the `ftp` user, so the directories must be subdirectories of that directory, which is generally `/home/ftp`. To provide access via HTTP, establish symbolic links pointing to the directories. To provide access via NFS, simply export the directories.

Exam Essentials

Understand, and be capable of implementing, the following network services: Apache, Samba, NFS, basic Sendmail, POP3/IMAP4 e-mail, DNS, and FTP This section described FTP. You should be capable of installing and configuring anonymous and authenticated FTP.

Be sufficiently familiar with the function, configuration, and logging of those services so as to be capable of basic troubleshooting This section described FTP. You should be capable of simple troubleshooting of FTP.

Key Term and Concept

FTP   File Transfer Protocol.

Sample Questions

1. Which of the following types of files and directories can be accessed by an anonymous FTP user?

A. Files and directories in the home directory of the user `ftp`

B. Files in any world-readable directory

C. Files in the `/tmp` directory

D. Files readable via the user's account

Answer: A. An anonymous FTP user can access only files and directories in the home directory of the `ftp` user. Symbolic links leading outside the home directory of the user `ftp` are not followed. An anonymous FTP user need not have an associated user account.

2. Which of the following is true of the standard FTP configuration?

A. FTP and anonymous FTP run as distinct services.

B. FTP is run as specified in `/etc/inittab`.

C. FTP runs as an `inetd` service.

D. The FTP daemon runs continuously.

Answer: C. FTP is run under control of the Internet super server, `inetd`.

Working with Mail

Almost every network connected to the Internet and almost every Internet user has access to mail. Mail involves two facilities: mail transfer and mail access. The Red Hat Linux *Mail Transfer Agent (MTA)* is Sendmail, which is the most popular MTA on the Internet. Red Hat Linux provides access to mail via the *Post Office Protocol (POP)* or the *Interim Mail Access Protocol (IMAP)*.

Critical Information

The Sendmail program, which handles mail, is extremely flexible, but it is also relatively large and complex. Its features include the following:

- the ability to decode and handle a wide range of destination address formats
- support for virtual mail domains and user aliases
- extensive security and anti-spam facilities

A user typically composes mail by means of a mail client application. Popular clients include Linux as well as non-Linux programs such as Eudora, Mutt, Netscape Communicator, Microsoft Outlook, Pegasus, and Pine.

After composing a mail message, the user sends the message, which is transmitted by a *Simple Mail Transfer Protocol (SMTP)* server. This can be accomplished in a variety of ways. Some mail clients, including most Linux clients, spawn a Sendmail process to transmit a message; others depend on the availability of a remote SMTP server.

If Sendmail is used, the Sendmail process—which is bound to port 25—uses DNS to obtain the *Mail Exchange (MX)* information that pertains to the destination host, which specifies the mail gateway host through which mail messages for the destination host should be sent. The Sendmail process then uses SMTP to transfer the message to the mail gateway host. The gateway host, in turn, transfers the message to the destination host. The SMTP server of the destination host accepts or refuses the message, based on the server configuration. For example, the server may refuse messages from unresolvable domain names, which may indicate that the message has been sent by a spammer, an unauthorized user who subverts an insecure mail server in order to transmit large volumes of junk mail.

Once a message has been delivered, the recipient can access it while logged in to the destination host. Alternatively, the user can access the message from a remote host, which contacts a POP or IMAP server on the destination host. The IMAP protocol is newer and generally superior to the POP protocol. For example, POP sends passwords across the Internet as clear text; many IMAP implementations encrypt them.

Installation

The Sendmail program is contained in several packages:

- sendmail, which contains the program itself

- sendmail-cf, which contains files needed to revise the sendmail configuration

- sendmail-doc, which contains the sendmail documentation

The optional packages sendmail-cf and sendmail-doc together require only about 2MB of disk space. So, it's usually reasonable to install all three packages. To install Sendmail, move to the directory containing the packages and issue the command

```
rpm -Uvh sendmail-*.rpm
```

The POP3 and IMAP server both reside in the package imap. To install them, move to the directory containing the package and issue the command

```
rpm -Uvh imap-*.rpm
```

Sendmail Configuration

The Sendmail program has several main configuration files:

- /etc/sendmail.cf, which contains the mail configuration directives

- /etc/sendmail.cw, which specifies the hosts on behalf of which the server will accept mail

- /etc/aliases, which specifies user mail aliases

You can revise the Sendmail configuration in any of several ways:

- By using the linuxconf utility's mailconf subsystem. This is generally the simplest and best approach.

- By using the m4 macro processor to generate a revised configuration. The file /usr/doc/sendmail/README.cf explains the procedure.

- By manually editing the /etc/sendmail.cf file, a method recommended only for Sendmail gurus.

IMAP Configuration

You generally do not need to configure IMAP or POP. However, both services are run via inetd, the default configuration of which is not appropriate for running these services. The /etc/inetd.conf file contains lines that reference the POP and IMAP services, but these lines are commented out in the distributed configuration:

```
#pop-2  stream  tcp  nowait root  /usr/sbin/tcpd ipop2d
#pop-3  stream  tcp  nowait root  /usr/sbin/tcpd ipop3d
#imap   stream  tcp  nowait root  /usr/sbin/tcpd imapd
```

To properly configure inetd, simply locate each of these lines, remove the hash mark (#) at the beginning of the line, and save the revised file. Then restart inetd by issuing the command

```
killall -HUP inetd
```

Necessary Procedures

This section gives important procedures for working with Sendmail.

Starting and Restarting the Service

To start Sendmail, issue the command

```
/etc/rc.d/init.d/sendmail start
```

To restart Sendmail, issue the command

```
/etc/rc.d/init.d/sendmail restart
```

Stopping the Service

To stop Sendmail, issue the command

```
/etc/rc.d/init.d/sendmail stop
```

Checking Service Status

To check the status of Sendmail, issue the command

```
/etc/rc.d/init.d/sendmail status
```

Troubleshooting

In addition to log entries posted to the system log (`/var/log/messages`), Sendmail keeps its own log file, `/var/log/maillog`. If mail service is not operating properly, check both log files for clues to the source of the problem.

Exam Essentials

Understand, and be capable of implementing, the following network services: Apache, Samba, NFS, basic Sendmail, POP3/IMAP4 e-mail, DNS, and FTP This section described mail, including Sendmail and POP3/IMAP4. You should be capable of installing and configuring mail.

Be sufficiently familiar with the function, configuration, and logging of those services so as to be capable of basic troubleshooting This section described mail. You should be capable of simple troubleshooting of mail.

Key Terms and Concepts

IMAP Interim Mail Access Protocol.

MTA Mail Transfer Agent.

MX   Mail Exchange.

POP   Post Office Protocol.

SMTP   Simple Mail Transfer Protocol.

Sample Questions

1. What is the port number associated with the SMTP protocol?

   A. 21

   B. 25

   C. 110

   D. 143

   Answer: B. The SMTP protocol is associated with port 25.

2. Which of the following correctly describes the function of an MTA?

   A. Access to stored mail

   B. Encryption of mail

   C. Transfer of mail from host to host

   D. Troubleshooting of mail transmission

   Answer: C. A Mail Transfer Agent (MTA) moves mail from host to host.

Working with NFS

The *Network File System (NFS)* provides shared access to files and directories. In operation, an NFS server designates one or more directories as available to clients. The designated directories are referred to as *shares*, which are said to have been *exported* by the server. Once exported by an NFS server, an NFS share can be mounted by a client system in much the same way that a local file system is mounted. The Linux NFS implementation is functionally similar to NFS implementations available on other Unix systems, and partially implements NFS version 3.0.

Critical Information

An NFS server runs three NFS-related daemons:

- portmap, which forwards client requests to the correct NFS process
- rpc.nfsd, which translates remote file access requests to local file access requests
- rpc.mountd, which mounts and unmounts file systems

A host may be both NFS server and client, in which case it runs all three daemons.

Installation

The NFS facility is contained in these packages:

- knfsd, which contains NFS server files
- knfsd-clients, which contains NFS client files
- portmap, which contains files related to portmap, used by both NFS servers and clients

To install an NFS server, move to the directory containing the packages and issue the command

```
rpm -Uvh knfsd-*.rpm portmap-*.rpm
```

This command installs both the NFS server and client, which is helpful in troubleshooting the server.

To install only an NFS client, move to the directory containing the package and issue the command

```
rpm -Uvh knfsd-clients-*.rpm
```

Server Configuration

The NFS server configuration file is /etc/exports, each line of which is a directive that specifies a share (that is, an exported directory) and the associated access permissions. Here is a line from a typical /etc/ exports file:

```
/exports/database fred.azusapacific.com
↳bob.azusapacific.com
```

The general form of the directive is

```
path host_list
```

where *path* is the absolute path of the shared directory and *host_list* is a list of one or more hosts that can access the share. Each host should be separated from adjacent hosts by one or more spaces.

A host may be specified in any of several ways:

- by using a host name, if the host is part of the local domain

- by using a fully qualified domain name

- by using a host name containing a wildcard (*)

- by using an IP address

- by using a network address, such as 192.168.1.0/255.255.255.0

A wildcard character matches, at most, a single component of the host name. For example, the host name specifier *.azusapacific.com matches www.azusapacific.com, but not www.science.azusapacific .com. A wildcard can match part of a component of a host name. For example, the host specifier dtc*.azusapacific.com matches dtc01 .azusapacific.com, dtc02.azusapacific.com, and so on.

By default, clients are permitted read-only access to a share, notwithstanding information to the contrary in the exports man page. To allow read-write access, follow the host specifier with **(rw)**. For example, here's a typical read-write share:

```
/exports/database fred.azusapacific.com(ro)
↳bob.azusapacific.com(rw)
```

The host fred is permitted read-only access, whereas the host bob is permitted read-write access. Be careful not to insert a space between the host specifier and the permission.

By default, if a client is logged in as root, the client is not given root access to shared files; instead, such requests are mapped to user ID 65535. If you want to permit root access, specify the no_root_squash option. For example:

```
/exports/database bob.azusapacific.com(rw,no_root_
↳squash)
```

The /etc/exports file is easily edited by hand. However, if you prefer, Linuxconf provides a facility for administering NFS shares.

Client Configuration

As explained, a client can treat an exported directory much like a local file system. To mount a shared directory, a special form of the mount command is used. For example:

```
mount -t nfs server:/exports/databases /mnt/database
```

This command mounts the directory /exports/databases exported by the host named server as the local directory /mnt/database. The special syntax *server:* is used to specify the NFS server that provides the share, and the file system type is specified as nfs.

The script /etc/rc.d/init.d/netfs runs at boot time, automatically mounting the NFS directories specified in /etc/fstab. If you want an NFS share to be automatically mounted at boot time, simply include it in the /etc/fstab file. For example:

```
server:/exports/database /mnt/database  nfs
↳defaults  0  2
```

Several mount options let you control the operation of an NFS share:

- hard,intr lets you kill or interrupt requests blocked by an unavailable server.

- nolock disables file locking so that the NFS client can access an NFS server that lacks locking capability.

- rsize=8192 and wsize=8192 allocate read and write (respectively) buffers larger than the default size to significantly improve NFS throughput.

You can use Linuxconf to mount NFS shares or specify NFS shares to be included in /etc/fstab. Start Linuxconf and choose Access NFS Volume ➢ Add from the menu.

TIP   The nfslock service provides file-locking services for NFS clients. If your NFS client needs to lock files, be sure to enable the nfslock service.

Red Hat Linux also provides the autofs service, which you can configure to mount NFS shares on demand. The autofs service is contained in the optional package of the same name. See the man pages auto.master, autofs(5), autofs(8), and automount for more information.

Necessary Procedures

This section describes important procedures for working with NFS.

Starting and Restarting NFS

To start the NFS server, issue the commands

```
/etc/rc.d/init.d/portmap start
/etc/rc.d/init.d/nfs start
```

To restart the NFS server, issue the commands

```
/etc/rc.d/init.d/portmap restart
/etc/rc.d/init.d/nfs restart
```

Stopping the NFS Server

To stop the NFS server, issue the commands

```
/etc/rc.d/init.d/nfs stop
/etc/rc.d/init.d/portmap stop
```

Controlling NFS Server Operation

The exportfs command lets you control operation of the NFS server on the local host:

- exportfs -v lists shared directories and the associated options.
- exportfs -a *share* exports the specified share.
- exportfs -a exports all shares listed in /etc/exports.
- exportfs -u *share* unexports the specified share.
- exportfs -ua unexports all shares.
- exportfs -r refreshes the share list.

In particular, you should issue the command

```
exportfs -r
```

after any modification of the /etc/exports file.

Checking Service Status

To check the status of the NFS server while logged in to the server host, issue the following commands

```
/etc/rc.d/init.d/nfs status
/etc/rc.d/init.d/portmap status
```

To check the status of a remote NFS server, issue the command

```
rpcinfo -p server
```

where *server* is the host name of the NFS server.

To list the shares exported by a server, issue the command

```
showmount -e server
```

where *server* is the host name of the NFS server.

Troubleshooting

The NFS facility logs messages to the system log file /var/log/ messages. If NFS is not operating properly, check the system log for messages that point to the source of the problem.

Exam Essentials

Understand, and be capable of implementing, the following network services: Apache, Samba, NFS, basic Sendmail, POP3/IMAP4 e-mail, DNS, and FTP This section described NFS. You should be capable of installing and configuring NFS.

Be sufficiently familiar with the function, configuration, and logging of those services so as to be capable of basic troubleshooting This section described NFS. You should be capable of simple troubleshooting of NFS.

Key Terms and Concepts

NFS   Network File System.

Share   A share is a file, directory, or printer made available to specified users or hosts.

Sample Questions

1. By default, what access to shares is permitted to NFS clients?

A. none

B. read-only

C. read-write

D. write-only

Answer: B. By default, NFS clients can read, but not write, to a share.

2. Which of the following is the file that identifies NFS shares?

A. /etc/exports

B. /etc/nfs.conf

C. /etc/nfs/nfs.conf

D. /etc/shares

Answer: A. The /etc/exports file lists exported NFS shares.

Working with Samba

Samba is an open-source implementation of the System Message Block (SMB) service used by Microsoft Windows 9x and NT; the SMB service is sometimes known as Common Internet File System (CIFS). Samba is widely used throughout the Unix and Linux communities. Samba originated in the work of Andrew Tridgell, who reverse engineered the SMB protocol. Subsequently, a worldwide team formed to maintain and enhance Samba.

Critical Information

Samba enables Windows clients to access Linux file systems and printers by using the Network Neighborhood facility of the Windows file manager. Unix and Linux clients can also access shared file systems and printers. Samba is popular even in computing environments that lack Windows clients because its authentication mechanisms are superior to those of NFS.

SMB is a high-level protocol built on Microsoft's NetBIOS protocol, which can be run over a TCP/IP network. NetBIOS duplicates several TCP/IP functions. For example, it has its own host name resolution service, Windows Internet Naming Service (WINS).

Samba actually has two associated services:

- smbd, which authenticates clients, authorizes client access to shares, and provides shared access to files and printers.

- nmbd, which provides a browsing facility that lets clients discover servers and their shares. It can also act as a WINS server, resolving NetBIOS host names to IP addresses.

At any time, one SMB server acts as the *browse master* for a network served by SMB. The browse master (or master browser, as it's sometimes called) maintains information on available servers and shares, and responds to client inquiries attempting to discover servers and shares. Eligible SMB servers compete in an *election* that determines which becomes the browse master. A Samba server can be configured to participate in such an election or to override the election, becoming the browse master despite the presence of other candidate servers.

Linux clients can access SMB shares in either of two ways. The smbclient program provides FTP-like access to shared files and printers, and the smbmount command lets you mount a shared file system much as you would a local file system. The standard printtool utility lets you configure access to Samba printers.

Installation

Samba is contained in three packages:

- `samba-common`, which contains files needed by Samba clients and servers
- `samba`, which contains the Samba server
- `samba-client`, which contains the Samba `smbclient`, `smbmount`, and `smbprint` programs and associated files and documentation

Samba is frequently updated; you should consider downloading the latest packages from the Samba Web site, `www.samba.org`, rather than installing packages contained on Red Hat Linux distribution media.

To install a Samba server, move to the directory containing the packages and issue the command

```
rpm -Uvh samba-*.rpm
```

This command installs both the Samba server and the Samba client, which is helpful in troubleshooting the server. To install only the Samba client, move to the directory containing the packages and issue the command

```
rpm -Uvh samba-common-*.rpm samba-client-*.rpm
```

Basic Server Configuration

The main Samba configuration file is `/etc/smb.conf`, which is described in the man page `smb.conf`, in the documentation files residing in `/usr/doc/samba*` and on the Samba Web site, `www.samba.org/docs`. The configuration file contains two types of directives:

- global directives, which configure the server
- service directives, which configure shared files and printers

This section explains the contents of the Samba configuration file. You can use a text editor to configure Samba by revising the contents of the file. If you prefer using a graphical tool to configure Samba, you can use Linuxconf. Also, the `swat` package provides a Web-based interface for configuring Samba.

Samba Global Directives

You should tailor the following directives—and other directives as needed—to your local requirements:

- `workgroup`

- `comment`

- `hosts allow`

The `hosts allow` directive identifies the client hosts permitted to access the server. The local host address, 127.0.0.1, should generally be included in the list of hosts. Several formats are allowed:

- IP address—for example, 192.168.1.0

- IP address and subnet mask—for example, 192.168.1.0/255.255.255.0

- Partial IP address—for example, 192.168. (note the trailing dot)

- Host name—for example, `client.azusapacific.com`

- Domain or subdomain name—for example, `.azusapacific.com` (note the leading dot and lack of a wildcard)

For Windows *9x* and NT clients, you should generally specify `user` as the value of the `security` parameter. If you prefer authorization to be handled on a per-share basis, however, specify the value `share`. Or, if you prefer authorization to be handled by another server—for example, a Windows NT Primary Domain Controller (PDC)—specify the value `server`. If the client participates in an NT domain, specify the value `domain`.

Samba Service Directives

Here is a typical set of service directives that set up a shared directory:

```
[cdrom]
comment = CDROM mounted in /mnt/cdrom
```

```
path = /mnt/cdrom
read only = Yes
browseable = Yes
valid users = fred, bob
```

The directives establish a share known as cdrom, which provides read-only access to the /mnt/cdrom directory of the Samba server. Only the users fred and bob can access the share. If you want to create a publicly available share, omit the valid users directive and specify public = yes. If you want to grant access to all members of a group, specify @*group*, where *group* is the name of the group.

If you want users to be able to write to the share, omit the read only directive and specify writable = yes. If you don't want the share to be visible in a browse list such as the Windows Network Neighborhood, specify browseable = No.

Here is a sample printer share:

```
[printers]
comment = All Printers
path = /var/spool/samba
public = yes
guest ok = yes
admin users = bob
create mask = 0700
print ok = Yes
browseable = Yes
printable = yes
```

Samba lets you conveniently establish a home directory for a user. To do so, use the homes section of the smb.conf file. For example:

```
[homes]
comment = Home Directories
read only = No
create mask = 0750
browseable = No
```

If you want Samba to function as a logon server, you should define a
netlogon share. For example:

```
[netlogon]
comment = Samba Network Logon Service
path = /home/netlogon
guest ok = Yes
browseable = No
locking = No
```

Client Configuration and Use

If a Samba server has been correctly configured, you should be able to
view browseable shares in the Network Neighborhood of a Windows *9x* client, map them to drive letters, and drag and drop files in
the usual manner.

To access a Samba share or a Windows *9x*/NT share from a Linux
host, issue a command of the form

```
smbmount //server/share /mount_point
```

where *server* is the host name of the server, *share* is the name of the
share, and *mount_point* is the local directory that should become
the mount point. The share is mounted with the permissions associated with the user executing the smbmount command. To allow
non-privileged users to mount shares, you can modify the permissions of smbmnt and smbumount to include setuid (mode 4755).
However, you may prefer to install smbclient and instruct users in
its use; this is a less convenient but more secure approach. To access
a share by using smbclient, issue a command of the form

```
smbclient //server/share
```

where *server* is the host name of the server and *share* is the name of
the share.

Advanced Server Configuration

SMB clients on computers running Windows 95 OSR2, Windows 98, and Windows NT with Service Pack 3 and greater use encrypted passwords, which are not compatible with the default configuration of Samba. You can accommodate such clients by any of several means:

- Configure the client host to use plain-text passwords. However, doing so may compromise security.

- Use a Windows NT Primary Domain Controller (PDC) for authentication and authorization, and configure Samba to use encrypted passwords.

- Configure Samba to use encrypted passwords, and maintain a file containing the encrypted passwords.

For information on configuring Samba to use encrypted passwords, see the file ENCRYPTION.txt that resides under /usr/doc/samba*/docs.

Necessary Procedures

This section gives important procedures for working with Samba.

Starting and Restarting Samba

To start the Samba server, issue the command

```
/etc/rc.d/init.d/smb start
```

To restart the Samba server, issue the command

```
/etc/rc.d/init.d/smb restart
```

Stopping Samba

To stop the Samba server, issue the command

```
/etc/rc.d/init.d/smb stop
```

Checking Samba Status

To check the status of the Samba server, issue the command

```
/etc/rc.d/init.d/smb status
```

Troubleshooting the Service

Samba startups and shutdowns are logged in the system log file
/var/log/messages. In addition, Samba logs messages to its own log
files. The location and names of Samba's log files are configured in the
/etc/smb.conf file. However, they generally reside in /var/log/
samba. If Samba is not operating properly, check these log files for
clues to the problem.

Samba also includes several tools for diagnosing and troubleshooting.
After revising the Samba configuration file, you should issue the command testparm.

This command checks the Samba configuration files for errors. To
help ensure reliable operation, you should correct the errors before
starting Samba.

To list the available shares on a server, issue a command of the form

```
smbclient -L server -N
```

where *server* is the host name of the server. For example, to list the
available shares on the local host, issue the command

```
smbclient -L localhost -N
```

If no shares are visible, the WINS server may not be responding. To
investigate, issue a command of the form

```
nmblookup -B server __SAMBA__
```

where *server* is the host name of the server. The command should display the IP address of the specified host. You should also check that SMB clients are properly configured to use WINS. To do so, issue the command

```
nmblookup -d 2 '*'
```

Client hosts on the local network should respond with their IP addresses.

For further information on troubleshooting Samba, see the file DIAGNOSIS.txt that resides under /usr/doc/samba*/docs.

Exam Essentials

Understand, and be capable of implementing, the following network services: Apache, Samba, NFS, basic Sendmail, POP3/IMAP4 e-mail, DNS, and FTP This section described Samba. You should be capable of installing and configuring Samba.

Be sufficiently familiar with the function, configuration, and logging of those services so as to be capable of basic troubleshooting This section described Samba. You should be capable of simple troubleshooting of Samba.

Key Terms and Concepts

Browse master The browse master (or master browser) is the SMB server on a network that provides clients with information about available servers and shares.

Election Election is the process whereby SMB servers contend to determine which server will function as the master browser.

Sample Questions

1. Which of the following could specify a host in the `hosts allow` directive of the Samba configuration file?

    A. `*`

    B. `*.com`

    C. `*.example.com`

    D. `www.example.com`

    Answer: D. The `hosts allow` directive does not allow wildcards, though it does allow abbreviated host names, such as `.com`, which matches all hosts in the `.com` top-level domain.

2. Which of the following commands lists the available Samba shares?

    A. `nmblookup -B` *server*

    B. `nmblookup -d` *server*

    C. `smbclient -L` *server* `-N`

    D. `testparm`

    Answer: C. You can use the `smbclient` command to list available shares.

Chapter

10

Secondary Network Services

RHCE PREPARATION TOPIC COVERED IN THIS CHAPTER:

▶ **Working with Secondary Network Services**
(pages 272 – 283)

- Working with DHCP

- Working with IPX

- Working with LPD

- Working with News

- Working with Squid

- Working with Time Synchronization

In addition to the primary network services covered in Chapter 9, "Primary Network Services," Red Hat Linux supports many additional services. This chapter explains several of the most important and commonly used secondary network services. The Red Hat Inc. study points for the Red Hat Certified Engineer exam require only conceptual familiarity with these secondary network services. This chapter, therefore, focuses on basic concepts related to secondary network services; however, it also includes practical hints intended to help you install, configure, and use the services.

Working with Secondary Network Services

- Working with DHCP
- Working with IPX
- Working with LPD
- Working with News
- Working with Squid
- Working with Time Synchronization

DHCP, IPX, LPD, News, Squid, and Time Synchronization are the most commonly used secondary network services. Most system administrators are probably responsible for one or more of these services. This chapter introduces these secondary network services, focusing on the capabilities and key terms associated with the services.

Critical Information

Each of the following subsections covers one secondary network service. The study points for the RHCE exam require only conceptual familiarity with secondary network services, so the coverage in the following subsections is not comprehensive. If you are responsible for installing, configuring, and administering a secondary network service, you'll probably find it helpful to consult documentation such as man pages, HOWTOs, and package documentation.

Working with DHCP

A *Dynamic Host Configuration Protocol (DHCP)* server can help you manage your network's IP address space. The Red Hat Linux DHCP server is compatible with the older *BOOTP* protocol still used in some Unix shops. DHCP is particularly helpful if your network includes computers that are intermittently connected or that move from location to location, such as laptops.

When a host running a DHCP client boots, it contacts a DHCP server. The DHCP server can assign such host-related information as the following:

- IP address
- Host and domain names
- Network IP address
- Broadcast IP address
- Default gateway IP address
- DNS server IP address
- WINS server IP address

A DHCP server can be configured to provide static or dynamic information, or both. A static configuration provides a client with a fixed IP address based on the Media Access Control (MAC) address assigned to the client's network interface and the subnet address of the client's point-of-network connection. Thus, the combination of host identity and location determines the assigned configuration.

A dynamic configuration arbitrarily assigns IP addresses from one or more ranges. This conserves IP addresses, because only hosts that are active have an associated IP address. However, the IP address associated with a host may be different each time the host boots. A DHCP configuration can be both dynamic and static, providing designated hosts with a static configuration and other hosts with a dynamic configuration.

Installing DHCP

The DHCP server is contained in the dhcp package. To install DHCP, move to the directory containing the package and issue the command

```
rpm -Uvh dhcp-*.rpm
```

DHCP requires the associated network interface to support, and be configured for, broadcast and multicast operation. To determine if a network interface is properly configured, issue the command

```
ifconfig -a
```

The output pertaining to a typical network interface should resemble the following:

```
eth1 Link encap:Ethernet  HWaddr 00:A0:CC:25:8A:EC
        inet addr:192.168.1.1  Bcast:192.168.1.255
↳Mask:255.255.255.0
        UP BROADCAST RUNNING PROMISC MULTICAST  MTU:1500
↳Metric:1
        RX packets:4648466 errors:0 dropped:0 overruns:0
↳frame:0
        TX packets:679303 errors:0 dropped:0 overruns:0
↳carrier:0
        collisions:33062 txqueuelen:100
        Interrupt:11 Base address:0x6000
```

Note the keywords BROADCAST and MULTICAST, which appear in the third line of the output. If these keywords are not present, DHCP will not operate correctly. To resolve the problem, you may need to do any or all of the following:

- Reconfigure the interface by using the ifconfig command.

- Replace the network interface with a card that supports MULTICAST.

Configuring DHCP

The DHCP configuration file is /etc/dhcpd.conf. Here's a typical configuration that includes both dynamic and static information:

```
default-lease-time 64800;
max-lease-time 64800;

option subnet-mask 255.255.255.0;
option broadcast-address 192.168.1.255;
option routers 192.168.1.1;
option domain-name-servers 192.168.1.1;
option domain-name "azusapacific.com";

subnet 192.168.1.0 netmask 255.255.255.0 {

        server-identifier 192.168.1.1;

        host sara {
                hardware ethernet 00:50:04:d2:3f:15;
                fixed-address 192.168.1.33;
                default-lease-time 2592000;
        }

        range 192.168.1.20 192.168.1.29;
}
```

The configuration assigns the IP address 192.168.1.33 to the interface with MAC address 00:50:04:d2:3f:15. Other DHCP clients are assigned an IP address in the range 192.168.1.20 to 192.168.1.29.

Before starting the DHCP service, you must create the file /var/state/dhcp/dhcpd.leases; otherwise, the DHCP server will terminate immediately after it's started. To create the file, issue the following command:

```
touch /var/state/dhcp/dhcpd.leases
```

TIP Some releases of Red Hat Linux require you to place the dhcpd.leases file in /etc.

Once the DHCP service starts, it stores the assignments it makes—called leases—in the dhcpd.leases file, which you can view by using, for example, the less command or a text editor. Here is an example of such leases:

```
more /var/state/dhcp/dhcpd.leases
lease 192.168.1.20 {
        starts 6 2000/02/12 09:20:15;
        ends 2 2000/05/09 13:58:16;
        hardware ethernet 00:e0:98:77:08:40;
        uid 01:00:e0:98:77:08:40;
        client-hostname "OEMComputer";
}
lease 192.168.1.24 {
        starts 0 2000/03/12 18:20:23;
        ends 0 2000/03/12 18:20:23;
        hardware ethernet 00:50:56:be:01:03;
}
lease 192.168.1.23 {
        starts 6 2000/03/11 21:52:29;
        ends 6 2000/03/11 23:52:29;
        hardware ethernet 00:50:56:a0:01:03;
}
```

Leases are assigned for a finite time, specified in /etc/dhcpd.conf, after which they must be renewed by the client.

To start the configured DHCP server, issue the command

```
/etc/rc.d/init.d/dhcpd start
```

DHCP should add a route to host 255.255.255.255; the route is needed to communicate with Microsoft DHCP clients. Check the system log for messages indicating the status of DHCP. You can do this by issuing the command

```
tail /var/log/messages
```

The result should resemble the following:

```
May  9 07:18:45 www dhcpd: Internet Software Consortium
↳DHCPD $Name:
   V2-BETA-1-PATCHLEVEL-6 $
May  9 07:18:45 www dhcpd: Copyright 1995, 1996, 1997,
↳1998 The Internet Software Consortium.
May  9 07:18:45 www dhcpd: All rights reserved.
May  9 07:18:45 www dhcpd: Listening on
↳Socket/eth1/192.168.1.0
May  9 07:18:45 www dhcpd: Sending on
↳Socket/eth1/192.168.1.0
```

Configuring the DHCP Client

The standard Red Hat Linux DHCP client is a program called pump, contained in a package having the same name. The pump package is part of the standard base installation of Red Hat Linux.

To configure a Red Hat Linux host to use DHCP to determine its network configuration, launch Linuxconf and choose Config ➤ Networking ➤ Client Tasks ➤ Basic Host Information. Select the paragraph or tab corresponding to the network interface (adapter) you want to configure. Set the following options:

- Enabled

- Config Mode = DHCP

Select Accept ➤ Quit ➤ Activate Changes to install the new configuration.

You can check the status of pump by issuing the command

```
/sbin/pump -s
```

To force immediate renewal of a lease, issue the command

```
/sbin/pump -i eth0 -R
```

Working with IPX

Red Hat Linux includes the mars-nwe package. This package provides file and printer sharing for Novell networks, which are based on the IPX protocol. The related ipxutils package includes useful IPX utilities. If you're working with an IPX-based network, you should install both packages.

The mars-nwe package lets you mount IPX file systems by using the ncpmount command or by using a mount command specifying file system type ncp. You can also specify IPX file systems in the /etc/fstab file.

TIP The mount command reports the file system type as ncpfs, but you can specify ncp or ncpfs as an argument to the mount command and in the /etc/fstab file.

Working with LPD

You can easily access a Red Hat Linux printer remotely. Of course, you must first configure the server and client systems. To configure the server system, list each client host in /etc/hosts.lpd. If the client host is under the same administrative control as the server, you can list the host in /etc/hosts.equiv, if you prefer. Also, be sure the host name of the client host can be resolved to an IP address; add a line to /etc/hosts if necessary.

To configure the client, add an entry in the following form to the
client's /etc/printcap file:

```
remlp:\
  :lp=:rm=host:rp=printer:sd=dir
```

In this entry, *host* is the host name of the server, *printer* is the name
by which the target printer is listed in the server's /etc/printcap file,
and *dir* is the spool directory to be used on the client. The spool
directory is usually a subdirectory of /var/spool.

Once the server and client are configured, you should be able to
access the server's printer by issuing commands on the client host. For
example, you can print a file by using the lpr command, and you can
check the print queue by using the lpq command.

Working with News

The inn package provides innd and other programs that support the
Network News Transfer Protocol (NNTP) and Internet news. Internet news transmits and receives postings to Internet newsgroups,
which were the dominant method of multiway user-to-user interaction before the advent of the Web. Today, Web forums provide a simpler way of supporting multiway user-to-user interaction. However,
Internet news remains a popular service, even though it's complicated
to work with and requires significant resources. You can use inn to
support local newsgroups or to provide access to Internet newsgroups. To adequately support Internet newsgroups, the host system
must have multiple gigabytes of free hard disk space and a high-speed
Internet connection.

Like e-mail, Internet news has become a means of transmitting spam.
To suppress spam news articles, you can install the cleanfeed package.

Working with Squid

The Squid proxy server is a caching proxy server compatible with FTP,
HTTP, and SSL. It directly handles HTTP and FTP requests and can

forward SSL requests to another server or proxy. It can, for example, be used to

- Reduce bandwidth demands due to multiple requests for popular Web pages

- Control access to external Web sites by means of Access Control Lists (ACLs)

- Accelerate an HTTP server

The proxy works by caching HTTP data requested through it and serving the cached response rather than repeatedly retrieving popular data from a remote server. It intelligently forwards requests for dynamic content to remote servers—so CGI (Common Gateway Interface) pages, for example, are properly handled.

To accelerate an HTTP server, the proxy typically runs on port 80, the usual HTTP port. It then forwards requests not found in its cache to a Web server running on another port or system.

An instance of the proxy can participate in a hierarchy of cache sites known as the Harvest Cache. The motivation behind the Harvest Cache project is a 1993 study showing that NFSNET backbone FTP traffic could be reduced by 44 percent by means of several well-placed caches.

The proxy is contained in the package `squid-2.2.STABLE4-8.i386. rpm`, along with a 1900-line default version of its main configuration file, `/etc/squid/squid.conf`. The default configuration file is adequate for many applications, so Squid is often ready to go immediately following installation. To start the service, issue the command

```
/etc/rc.d/init.d/squid
```

To configure a Web browser to use Squid, set the browser's proxy host to the host name of the system running Squid and set the proxy port to the port on which Squid is running, generally 3128.

Working with Time Synchronization

Red Hat Linux provides two ways to synchronize system time:

- rdate, which synchronizes to the clock of another host

- xntp3, which synchronizes to Coordinated Universal Time (UTC)

The rdate program, contained in the rdate package, is the older and less sophisticated method of synchronizing time. To synchronize the local host's clock to that of another system, issue a command in the form

    rdate -p -s *host*

where *host* is the host name of the remote host. Often, a command such as this is placed in the /etc/rc.d/rc.local file so that it will be executed when the system boots. Once synchronized, the clocks are apt to drift apart; the rdate command makes no provision for continual synchronization.

The xntpd program, which is contained in the xntp3 package, continually synchronizes the system clock to a precise estimate of UTC, based on time data obtained from remote servers. You can configure the xntpd service to run at desired runlevels. Alternatively, you can use the Cron facility to regularly run ntpdate, another program in the xntp3 package; when invoked, ntpdate adjusts the system clock and then terminates. Both xntpd and ntpdate use the *Network Time Protocol (NTP)*, described in RFC 1305. Typically, a host is configured to synchronize with multiple hosts so that synchronization can continue even if a host cannot be contacted.

NTP hosts are arranged in a hierarchy. Servers near the top of the hierarchy—called *stratum* 1 servers—receive time information from a highly accurate, terrestrial source, such as radio signals sent from an atomic clock. Servers in stratum 2 synchronize to one or more stratum 1 servers, and so on.

NTP continually adjusts the system time, usually to millisecond precision. NTP never adjusts the clock backward; if necessary, it slows the clock until real time catches up with the errant clock.

TIP   Take care when choosing NTP servers with which to synchronize. One study found that a significant number of NTP servers were badly configured and, therefore, reported erroneous time values.

Exam Essentials

Be familiar with other network services supported under Red Hat Linux: Squid, innd NNTP server (news), xntpd, etc.   You should be familiar with secondary network services such as DHCP, IPX, LPD, News, Squid, and Time Synchronization. You should be able to install and configure DHCP and be able to configure LPD.

Key Terms and Concepts

BOOTP   BOOTP is a common Unix protocol that lets a server assign an IP address and other network configuration information to a client host.

Dynamic Host Configuration Protocol (DHCP)   Dynamic Host Configuration Protocol (DHCP) is a protocol that lets a server supply a client host with an IP address and other configuration information.

Network News Transfer Protocol (NNTP)   Network News Transport Protocol (NNTP) is a protocol for transmitting Internet newsgroup articles.

Network Time Protocol (NTP)   Network Time Protocol (NTP) is a method of synchronizing system time.

Stratum   A stratum is a set of systems that share a similar logical network distance from a high-precision time base.

Sample Questions

1. Which of the following services can be used to accelerate a Web server?

    A. DHCP

    B. NNTP

    C. NTP

    D. Squid

    Answer: D. Squid can be used to accelerate a Web server, because it can serve cached pages very quickly.

2. Which of the following services can provide a host with network configuration information?

    A. DHCP

    B. NNTP

    C. NTP

    D. Squid

    Answer: A. DHCP can provide a host with its network configuration.

Chapter

11

System and Network Security

RHCE PREPARATION TOPICS COVERED IN THIS
CHAPTER:

Administering System and Network Security
(pages 286 – 294)

Configuring Authentication *(pages 294 – 303)*

- Configuring NIS

- Configuring PAM

- Configuring LDAP

Restricting Access to Services *(pages 303 – 310)*

A stand-alone computer that is kept in a locked office to which only one user has a key is highly resistant to security threats. However, few users are content to relinquish network access in exchange for improved security. And as a system administrator, you're probably responsible for servers, which, by their very nature, must be connected to a network. Protecting networked multiuser systems requires skill and diligence. This chapter explains computer security fundamentals and gives guidance on how to avoid and recover from common security threats.

Administering System and Network Security

This section presents important system and network security fundamentals. It describes perspectives on security, gives suggestions for improving security, and explains how to respond to a security breach.

Critical Information

System security begins with the installation of the system from distribution media known to be authentic. Prudent system administrators are wary of network installations, which present a would-be intruder with an opportunity to introduce malicious software. Prudent Red Hat Linux system administrators monitor the Red Hat Linux mailing lists and other lists that transmit information on security fixes, and promptly install applicable fixes to close publicly known vulnerabilities. They're also cautious about installing software downloaded from untrusted sites. Such software can include vulnerabilities or even malicious code, leading to a security breach.

Protecting the *root* Account

If not properly managed and used, the root account can provide an intruder with the means to breach your security. To avoid a security breach, you should use the root account only when necessary. Don't, for example, continuously leave open a terminal window logged in as root. Likewise, when logged in as root, be aware of whether the current terminal window is a root or non-root session, and use a window associated with a non-root session whenever possible. By default, the root user receives the special command-line prompt #, whereas non-root users receive $ as a command-line prompt.

Be very careful when issuing commands as root. It's altogether too easy to mistype a command and suffer unintended consequences.

Generally, it's best for only one user to know and use the root account of a system. Likewise, it's generally best not to use programs like sudo, which let non-root users temporarily gain root access. By restricting access to the root account, you can ensure that the individual who has access to the root account is aware of the current system configuration and is able to evaluate proposed configuration changes for possible effects on system security.

It's good practice to include only standard system directories such as /bin, /sbin, /usr/bin, and /usr/sbin in the PATH of the root user. In particular, the current directory and home directory should not be included in the PATH. Omitting these directories from the PATH helps to avoid unknowing execution of malicious code planted by an intruder. Similarly, the default PATH of non-root users should omit the current directory and home directory, or place them at the end of the PATH so that ls, for example, will refer to /bin/ls rather than to a Trojan horse planted by an intruder in the user's home directory.

Managing User Accounts and Passwords

When installing a new system, you should enable the shadow passwords facility, which prevents ordinary users from reading the encrypted passwords associated with user accounts. Otherwise, a would-be intruder can use a program such as crack to discover passwords.

By default, PAM is configured to enforce rules that prevent users from choosing passwords that are particularly easy to guess or crack. Generally, you should not relax or disable this facility; rather, you should consider imposing further restrictions on passwords. See the information on the cracklib PAM module in the /usr/doc/pam-*/txts/pam.txt file.

You should also regularly purge unused user accounts, which may present opportunities for breaching security. The contents of the home directories of such accounts should be erased or archived and erased, because they may contain malicious code, files, or directories that are world-writable.

Executing *setuid* and *setgid* Files and Directories

Files can be setuid or setgid. When a user executes a setuid file, the program runs with the effective user ID of the file's owner, rather than that of the user. Similarly, when a user executes a setgid file, the program runs with the effective group ID of the file's group owner, rather than that of the user.

To enable setuid or setgid, issue a command of the form

```
chmod u+s files   # enable setuid
chmod g+s files   # enable setgid
```
To disable setuid or setgid, issue a command of the form

```
chmod u-s files   # disable setuid
chmod g-s files   # disable setgid
```
Directories can also be setgid. The command to enable or disable setgid for a directory is the same as that to enable or disable setgid for a file. When a user creates a file in a non-setgid directory, the group ownership of the file is set to the user's group ID. However,

when a user creates a file in a setgid directory, the group ownership of the file is set to the group owner of the directory.

Red Hat Linux exploits setgid behavior to facilitate sharing of files and directories. Unlike most other Unix-like operating systems, Red Hat Linux assigns each user to a *user private group* that has the same name as the user's account; as the term suggests, the user is the only member of the user's private group. Also, the /etc/profile script distributed with Red Hat Linux assigns ordinary users a default umask of 002 rather than the more common 022. A umask value of 002 yields a default permission of 664, which implies that the members of the group who own the file can read and write newly created files. However, since the user is the only member of the user's private group, write access is not unreasonably extended.

The point of the user private group and unusual umask value is evident when users must share write access to files or directories. Here's a procedure for implementing sharing:

1. Create a group that represents the department, project, or organization whose members need to share write access.

2. Place each affiliated user in the group.

3. Create a directory to hold the shared files and directories.

4. Set the group ownership of the directory to the group created in step 1.

5. Enable setgid for the directory.

When a member of the group creates a file in the directory, the group owner of the new file is set to the group owner of the directory. And, since the user's umask value is 002, the file permissions are set to 664. Members of the group can therefore read, write, and execute the file. However, non-members of the group can only read the file. Of course, the user can issue the chmod command to restrict or loosen access permissions as desired; in particular, the user can change the file's permissions to exclude access by non-members of the group.

Choosing User IDs for Services

As a rule, daemon processes should run using either an ordinary user account or the special user account nobody. They should generally not run as root, because a vulnerability in the process may provide a would-be intruder with the means to execute a command as root. If the process runs as an ordinary user, the intruder may compromise the user account. If, however, the process runs as root, the intruder may compromise the root account, which compromises the entire system.

The /etc/passwd file contains several user accounts that have been created to avoid running a process using the root account. In particular, the nobody account has no associated home directory or shell and, therefore, cannot log in to the system. The httpd process, for example, runs using the nobody account. An intruder who compromises the nobody account can cause significant harm—for example, by killing processes—but far less harm than is possible via a compromised root account.

Improving Network Security

If a computer system is connected to a network, you should consider the following additional security measures in addition to those described in the preceding section.

As a start, you should not run telnet, rcp, rexec, rlogin, or rsh servers; instead, you should install an ssh server. Unlike ssh, the telnet, rcp, rexec, rlogin, and rsh servers send passwords over the network in clear text. Unless you use ssh, someone running a packet sniffer can easily obtain important system passwords and use them to compromise your system. For the same reason, unless you need it, you should not install an ftp server, particularly an anonymous ftp server. If you need the functions provided by ftp, but don't require ftp as such, you may be able to use scp, which is based on ssh.

Next, you should remove unneeded services from /etc/rc.d/rc?.d and /etc/inetd.conf and configure TCP wrappers to protect services that remain in /etc/inetd.conf. By removing an unneeded service from /etc/inetd.conf, you eliminate the possibility that the unneeded service can be used to compromise your system. Generally, it's also a good idea for you to remove `finger`, `netstat`, and `systat`, which can provide a would-be intruder with potentially useful information about your system. On the other hand, you should run `identd`, which can help track an intruder by confirming the identity of the user account used to request a TCP service.

Finally, you should remove any information that identifies your system's hardware and software configuration from `/etc/issue.net`. A would-be intruder could use this information to determine what vulnerabilities might exist.

Detecting and Correcting

Preventing a security breach is better than coping with a security breach. But, it's not always possible to prevent a breach. Therefore, it's necessary to know both how to detect a breach and recover from it.

Detecting a Breach

A good way to detect a real or attempted breach is to regularly review system logs. Unusual log entries or gaps in recorded information may point to a breach. However, keep in mind that a clever intruder may tamper with system logs, erasing evidence of the breach.

The Red Hat Linux RPM facility can help you to detect a breach. You can use it to verify the file size, modification date, permissions, and MD5 checksum of files owned by an RPM package. However, for this approach to be effective, you must protect the RPM database, `/var/lib/rpm`, against tampering. Unless the database is small, it won't fit on a standard floppy disk, but you can copy the files in the RPM database to offline media, such as a ZIP disk. It's often more convenient to copy the files to another host on the local network, but if that host is compromised, the intruder may still tamper with the RPM database. So, it's best to keep an offline copy of the database.

Several applications provide a more sophisticated facility for detecting actual and potential security breaches. Among these are the following:

- AIDE, `www.cs.tut.fi/~rammer/aide.html`, which is licensed under the GNU Public License

- COPS, www.fish.com/cops, which is free and open source

- Gog&Magog, www.multimania.com/cparisel/gog, which is free and open source

- Tripwire, www.tripwiresecurity.com, which is a commercially licensed product that can be freely used under certain circumstances

These applications can detect changes to files in much the same way as the RPM facility, but they can also monitor files that are not part of an RPM package. The COPS application also checks the system configuration for common errors and omissions that can lead to a security breach. The use of such an application is highly recommended.

Recovering from a Breach

The safest way to recover from a breach is to restore a backup that predates the breach. However, the system may quickly be compromised again if the original vulnerability is not found and fixed. Moreover, it's difficult to determine reliably that a given backup does not contain an image that has been compromised; worse yet, restoring a backup entails loss of data that was added or changed after the backup was made.

So, recovering from a breach often involves a "recovery in place" in which you attempt to find and fix the original vulnerability and any Trojan horses, trap doors, or other malicious code left by the intruder. Here are some considerations to keep in mind:

- You should remove the compromised host from the network; otherwise, the intruder may be able to thwart your recovery efforts.

- You should consider the possibility that the intruder has compromised the security of other hosts on your network.

- You should retain copies of log files and other evidence that might be helpful in identifying the intruder or the extent of the breach.

- You should determine the means used to compromise the system so that you can determine the scope of damage and eliminate the vulnerability.

- You should reinstall the operating system from trusted media.

- You should study every file that is owned by root, especially files that are setuid. Ensure that none of these files has been tampered with; if you're unsure, delete and replace the file.

- You should notify administrators of hosts the cracker may have used in breaching your system. You should also contact any security organizations with which you are affiliated.

Exam Essentials

TIP The RHCE study points do not specifically mention basic system and network security. However, you should be familiar with, and able to implement, common security policies and mechanisms.

Key Term and Concept

User private group   A user private group is a group having one member, which is the identically named user account.

Sample Questions

1. The default umask value assigned to ordinary users by Red Hat Linux is which of the following?

   A. 002

   B. 020

   C. 022

   D. 200

   Answer: A. The default value assigns a permission of 664.

2. When a `setuid` executable is loaded, the effective user ID of the process is which of the following?

A. The group ID of the group that owns the executable file

B. `root`

C. The user ID of the user who owns the executable file

D. The user ID of the user who ran the program

Answer: C. The `setuid` permission causes the process to run using the user ID of the file's owner, which may be `root` or another user.

Configuring Authentication

- **Configuring NIS**
- **Configuring PAM**
- **Configuring LDAP**

The preceding section explained security fundamentals. This section goes on to explain authentication mechanisms, the mechanisms used to identify users so that only authorized users can access a system and its resources.

Critical Information

Red Hat Linux supports three specialized authentication mechanisms:

- NIS
- PAM
- LDAP

This section explains each of these mechanisms in turn, beginning with NIS.

Configuring NIS

Red Hat Linux includes an implementation of version 2 of Sun Microsystems's (Sun's) *Network Information Service (NIS)*, formerly known as Yellow Pages (YP). NIS facilitates management of a local area network by letting you centralize information on user accounts, mail aliases, hosts, networks, and so on. A network managed by NIS is called an NIS domain and must include a master server; it can also include slave servers. The databases that contain network information are referred to as *maps*. An element of information contained in a map, such as the name and IP address of a network, is called a *key*.

NIS is not highly secure; for example, a user with access to an NIS server can obtain the complete contents of the server's NIS maps. Sun's newer NIS+ facility is more secure. However, Red Hat Linux supports only NIS+ clients; NIS+ servers are not supported.

The Red Hat Package Manager (RPM) packages related to NIS are

- ypbind, the NIS client

- ypserv, the NIS server

- yp-tools, useful NIS tools and utilities

In addition, NIS requires the portmap service.

The file /etc/nsswitch.conf specifies the NIS configuration. An NIS server stores information about the domain in /var/yp/domain; NIS clients store cached information in /var/yp/binding.

You can easily determine whether a host is managed by NIS. Issue the command

    domainname

If the host is part of an NIS domain, the command will report the name of the domain.

NIS Commands

Table 11.1 summarizes the most important commands and programs used by an NIS client. Table 11.2 summarizes the most important commands and programs used by an NIS server.

TABLE 11.1: NIS Client Programs

Program	Function
ypbind	Finds NIS information and stores it in /var/yp/binding
ypwhich	Returns the name of the NIS server
ypcat	Prints keys in the specified map
yppoll	Prints the version number of the specified map and identifies the server on which the map resides
ypmatch	Prints selected keys of the specified map
yppasswd	Changes NIS passwords

TABLE 11.2: NIS Server Programs

Program	Function
ypserv	The executable name of the NIS daemon
makedbm	Makes a map database from a text file
yppush	Notifies slave servers of map updates
yppasswdd	The daemon that handles NIS password changes

NIS Configuration

The main NIS configuration file is /etc/nsswitch.conf. Each line of the file, other than comment lines, names an NIS map and specifies the sources used to obtain its keys in the order in which they should be searched. Table 11.3 summarizes NIS maps, and Table 11.4 summarizes the keywords used to specify the sources.

TABLE 11.3: NIS Maps

NIS Map	Shared by Default?	Description
aliases	no	Mail aliases
ethers	no	Ethernet addresses
group	yes	User groups
hosts	yes	Host names and IP numbers
netgroup	yes	List of hosts and users
networks	yes	Network names and IP numbers
passwd	yes	User account information
protocols	yes	Network protocols
publickey	no	Keys used by secure_rpc
rpc	yes	RPC call names
services	yes	Network services
shadow	no	Shadow passwords

TABLE 11.4: Sources of NIS Maps

Source	Description
compat	NIS (in a mode compatible with old versions of the standard C library)
db	Local database
dns	DNS
files	Local files
nis	NIS
nisplus	NIS+

Configuring PAM

The Red Hat Linux *Pluggable Authentication Module (PAM)* facility is more commonly known simply as PAM. PAM lets you configure security policies for a variety of programs. Each PAM-aware program has a configuration file that resides in /etc/pam.d. The contents of the file associated with a program determine how the program authorizes access to its functions. By using PAM, you can configure authorization policies without modifying and recompiling programs.

PAM consists of a series of library modules that are dynamically loaded. The configuration file of a PAM-aware program determines the modules, and hence the actions, that are used to verify authorizations. Following is a list of some of the most important PAM modules:

pam_access.so This module restricts the hosts from which a service can be accessed.

pam_console.so This module confers special privileges to users logged on via the console by making them members of the special, dynamic group console. By this means, console users are able to access the floppy drive, sound subsystem, and joystick and can perform privileged operations such as rebooting and shutting down the system.

pam_listfile.so This module consults a specified file to determine authorizations. The FTP service uses this module to deny FTP access to users listed in /etc/ftpusers.

pam_nologin.so This module prevents users other than root from logging in while the /etc/nologin file exists.

pam_securetty.so This module prohibits logging in as root from a tty device other than those listed in /etc/securetty.

pam_time.so This module restricts the times at which a user can access a service by day or by time of day.

PAM Configuration Files

A PAM configuration file specifies a series of modules that should be loaded and executed to authorize access to the related facility. A module generally returns a pass/fail value. The values returned by the series of modules are used to determine whether to grant or deny access.

The directives contained in a PAM configuration file have the following general format:

   `module_type control_flag module_path arguments`

The `module_type` field indicates the type of authorization performed. The types of authorization that can be performed include the following:

account   Indicates that access is restricted by the age of the password, the time of day, the available resources, or the location of the user.

auth   Indicates that the user is to be authenticated, for example, by prompting for a password.

password   Indicates that the user's authentication information may be updated if appropriate, such as when a user changes his or her password.

session   Indicates the tasks that should be performed before or after the user is granted access.

The `control_flag` field indicates how a module's return value affects the overall result. The control flag value can be any of the following:

- `optional`
- `required`
- `requisite`
- `sufficient`

All modules with the control flag values required and requisite must return a pass; otherwise, authorization is denied. Normally, all modules are executed; however, if a module that has the control flag value requisite fails, access is immediately denied. Similarly, if a module that has the control flag value sufficient succeeds, access is immediately granted. A module that has the control flag value optional does not affect the overall result.

The *module_path* field specifies the location of the module to be executed. See the documentation files in /usr/doc/pam-* for a complete list of available modules and a description of their function and operation.

The *arguments* field specifies one of these values:

debug   Indicates that debugging information should be sent to the system log.

no_warn   Indicates that the module should not issue warning messages.

use_first_pass   Indicates that the module should use a previously entered password rather than prompt for one.

try_first_pass   Indicates that the module should use a previously entered password rather than prompt for one. However, if the previously entered password fails, the module will prompt for a new one.

use_mapped_pass   Indicates that the module should use a previously entered response to generate an encrypted or decrypted key used to store or retrieve a password.

Configuring LDAP

The *Lightweight Directory Access Protocol (LDAP)* provides databases that can store arbitrary information. Consequently, LDAP can serve a variety of uses. Among them, LDAP can provide a more secure alternative to NIS when combined with Secure Socket Layer (SSL). For example, LDAP with SSL features encrypted data transfer and

Access Control Lists (ACLs) to specify which users can access information stored in an LDAP database. Unlike NIS, which relies on refresh intervals to inform slave hosts of changes to stored maps, LDAP can push database updates to clients.

LDAP is contained in the package openldap, which provides the following:

slapd   The LDAP daemon that runs on port 389

slurpd   An LDAP daemon that replicates an LDAP database

The main LDAP configuration file is /etc/openldap/slapd.conf. For more information on LDAP, see the files in /usr/doc/openldap-* and the documentation available on the LDAP Web site, www.openldap.org.

Exam Essentials

Understand basic NIS concepts and the components associated with NIS   This study point does not require you to be able to implement NIS. However, you should be familiar with the terms and concepts related to NIS and programs that comprise NIS. You should also be aware that NIS is not considered a highly secure authentication service.

Understand the purpose of the PAM subsystem, and be capable of implementing basic PAM configuration changes   You should be able to install and configure PAM. It's important that you are able to use PAM to restrict access to hosts and facilities by, for example, time of day or by host.

TIP   The RHCE study points do not mention LDAP. However, you should have a basic understanding of LDAP. In particular, you should know that LDAP is considered more secure than NIS and that—like NIS—it uses a database to store authentication information. You should also know the daemons run by LDAP.

Key Terms and Concepts

Key A key is a string of text used by a cryptographic program as an access code.

LDAP Lightweight Directory Access Protocol (LDAP) can be used to centrally store and manage user accounts associated with a network.

Map NIS databases that contain network information are called maps.

NIS Network Information Services (NIS) centrally store and maintain network information, such as user accounts.

PAM Pluggable Authentication Module (PAM) is a Red Hat Linux facility that makes it possible to configure the security-related options of PAM-aware programs.

Sample Questions

1. What is the name of the RPM package that should be installed to implement LDAP?

   A. ldap

   B. ldapis

   C. ldapssl

   D. openldap

   Answer: D. The openldap package contains support for LDAP.

2. Which of the following presents a secure environment for management of network information?

   A. LDAP

   B. LDAP with SSL

   C. NIS

   D. NIS+

Answer: B. NIS is not a highly secure service. Without SSL, LDAP transmits information in clear text.

Restricting Access to Services

In general, a host that is part of a network is subject to more frequent and greater security threats than a stand-alone host. And, in general, larger networks are subject to greater security risks than smaller networks. An Internet host, for example, faces a variety of threats. However, by controlling access to a network host, you can reduce its exposure to security threats.

Critical Information

Red Hat Linux provides three principal mechanisms for controlling access to a host:

Pluggable Authentication Module (PAM) Facility   You can restrict the users allowed to access a host by configuring the Pluggable Authentication Module (PAM) facility. PAM was described in the preceding section.

TCP wrappers   You can restrict the hosts allowed to access a host by configuring *TCP wrappers*. This section describes TCP wrappers.

IPChains firewall   You can restrict access to the ports used by services by configuring an IPChains firewall. Chapter 13, "Routing," describes firewalls.

The *inetd* Service

The TCP wrappers facility operates in conjunction with the inetd service. This subsection explains the inetd service; the following subsection explains how to configure TCP wrappers.

Services can run stand-alone or under the control of inetd, which is sometimes known as the Super Server. Services running under the control of inetd do not consume memory or processor resources while they are idle; therefore, running services under the control of inetd can increase system efficiency. Services that are lightly used and start quickly are good candidates for running under control of inetd. Services that are heavily used operate more efficiently without the overhead imposed by inetd, and services that are slow to start run poorly under control of inetd.

In operation, the inetd daemon monitors the ports of services running under its control. When a client request is received, inetd launches the service, which satisfies the client request.

The inetd configuration file is /etc/inetd.conf. An easy way to improve system security is to disable unnecessary services. For services that run under control of inetd, disabling a service is as simple as commenting out the related line or lines in /etc/inetd.conf.

Here are some sample lines from a typical inetd.conf file:

```
#
# These are standard services.
#
ftp      stream  tcp     nowait  root    /usr/sbin/tcpd
   ↳in.ftpd -l -a
telnet   stream  tcp     nowait  root    /usr/sbin/tcpd
   ↳in.telnetd
```

Notice that several lines begin with a hash mark (#). These are comment lines, which are ignored by the inetd server. The general format of the remaining lines is

```
service socket_type protocol wait_option userid
   ↳program_path arguments
```

where

- *service* is a service listed in /etc/services.

- *socket_type* has the value stream for TCP services and dgram for UDP services (see the man page inetd.conf for other values that are sometimes used).

- *protocol* is tcp or udp.

- *wait_option* is wait for UDP services and nowait otherwise (see the man page inetd.conf for other values that are sometimes used).

- *userid* specifies the user ID under which the service runs (the user ID is usually root).

- *program_path* specifies the path of the executable file. (When TCP wrappers are used, *program_path* specifies the path of the tcpd program, as explained in the next section.) Note that the program names of many TCP services begin with in.

- *arguments* are arguments used by the program.

When you revise the inetd.conf file, you must prompt inetd to reread the file. To do so, issue the command killall -HUP inetd.

TCP Wrappers

The tcpd program can control access to services that run under inetd. To use tcpd to control access to a particular service, specify tcpd as the program that should run when a client request for that service is received. The name of the program that provides the service—and any runtime arguments you want to pass to the program—is specified as arguments of the tcpd command. A service that runs this way is said to run with a TCP wrapper. In the sample inetd.conf file given earlier, telnet and most other services ran with a TCP wrapper.

The tcpd program uses two configuration files: /etc/hosts.allow and /etc/hosts.deny. The /etc/hosts.allow file contains directives that specify services and the hosts allowed to use them; the /etc/hosts.deny file contains similar directives that specify services and the hosts forbidden to use them. When a host attempts to access a service that has a TCP wrapper, the authorization process works like this:

1. If the /etc/hosts.allow file contains a line specifying that the host is allowed to access the service, tcpd authorizes the access.

2. If the /etc/hosts.deny file contains a line specifying that the host is forbidden to access the service, tcpd denies the access.

3. In all other cases, tcpd authorizes the access.

Using the */etc/hosts.allow* File

As explained earlier, if the /etc/hosts.allow file contains a line specifying that a host is allowed to access a service, tcpd authorizes the access. The lines in the file have the general form

> *service*: *host_list*

where *service* identifies a service that goes by the same name used in the /etc/inetd.conf and /etc/services files, and *host_list* specifies one or more hosts that are allowed to access the service. Each host is separated from a following host by a comma.

Hosts can be specified in any of the following several ways:

- By an IP address, such as 192.168.1.1

- As a network address/netmask pair, such as 192.168.1.0/ 255.255.255.0

TIP   You can also specify a range of addresses by specifying an incomplete IP address followed by a dot. For example, 192.168.1. refers to the same range of IP addresses as 192.168.1.0/255.255.255.0.

- By a host name, such as www.azusapacific.com

- By a domain or subdomain name, such as .azusapacific.com (note the leading dot)

- By the keyword LOCAL, which denotes the local host

WARNING   Owing to a quirk in implementation, the keyword LOCAL matches any host name that has no dots. For example, LOCAL will match a host name entered in /etc/hosts without a dot. If you use the keyword LOCAL, be sure that you don't unintentionally give non-local hosts special privileges.

- By the keyword ALL, which denotes all hosts

You can also use the keyword EXCEPT to specify exceptions to a general rule. For example, the directive

in.ftpd: ALL EXCEPT 192.168.1.0/192.168.1.255

specifies that all hosts except those in the range 192.168.1.0 to 192.168.1.255 may access the FTP service.

You can use the keywords ALL and EXCEPT to specify services as well as hosts. For example, the directive

ALL EXCEPT in.telnetd: www.azusapacific.com

specifies that the host www.azusapacific.com may access all services except telnet.

WARNING   The portmap service is configured to use TCP wrappers, even though it's not mentioned in the inetd.conf file. However, you must not use a host or domain name to specify access to the portmap service; use only IP addresses or the keywords ALL and EXCEPT.

Using the */etc/hosts.deny* File

As explained earlier, if the /etc/hosts.deny file contains a line specifying that a host is forbidden to access a service, tcpd refuses the access unless the access is authorized by a line in the /etc/hosts .allow file. The lines in the /etc/hosts.deny file have the same form as those in the /etc/hosts.allow file. If an access is not explicitly authorized by the /etc/hosts.allow file or forbidden by the /etc/hosts.deny file, the access is authorized.

WARNING   The portmap service is configured to use TCP wrappers, even though it is not mentioned in the inetd.conf file. However, you must not use a host or domain name to specify access to the portmap service; use only IP addresses or the keywords ALL and EXCEPT. Note that denying access to all services via the ALL keyword can implicitly deny access to portmap, which will break the Network File System (NFS) and other services that rely on portmap.

Checking TCP Wrappers

The positive/negative logic behind TCP wrappers can easily become confusing. The tcpdchk command can help you determine that you've properly configured TCP wrappers. Issue the command tcpdchk -v. The command will respond by listing the rules you specified:

```
Using network configuration file: /etc/inetd.conf

>>> Rule /etc/hosts.allow line 6:
daemons: ALL
clients: .apu.edu 216.126.187.244 127.0.0.
access:  granted
```

You can inspect the output to determine whether tcpd understands your specifications the same way you do.

Another useful command is tcpdmatch. Issue a command in the form

```
tcpdmatch service host
```

where *service* specifies a service configured to use TCP wrappers, and *host* specifies a real or hypothetical host. The command determines whether your configuration permits the specified host to access the specified service, and reports the result. The following is an example of such a result:

```
tcpdmatch in.ftpd www.example.net
client:  address  192.168.1.1
server:  process  in.ftpd
access:  granted
```

Substituting Services by Using *twist*

The twist directive can be used in the /etc/hosts.allow and /etc/hosts.deny files to substitute an alternative service for the requested service. For example, the /etc/hosts.allow line

```
in.telnetd: .example.net : twist /usr/local/sbin/
↳telnetd
```

substitutes the program /usr/local/sbin/telnetd in place of the usual telnet service for client hosts in the example.net domain.

You can also use a `twist` directive in the `/etc/hosts.deny` file. For example, the directive

```
in.telnetd: .example.net : twist /bin/echo Hosts from
    ↳example.net not welcome
```

displays a customized unwelcome message for client hosts in the `example.net` domain.

Exam Essentials

Understand the role of `inetd`, `inetd.conf`, and `/etc/services`; and be capable of implementing TCP wrappers security measures You should be able to configure services to run under the control of `inetd`. You should also be able to configure TCP wrappers that restrict access to these services.

Be familiar with, and capable of, implementing access restrictions for primary network services You should be able to restrict access to primary network services, by using TCP wrappers and configuration options related to each particular primary network service.

Key Term and Concept

TCP wrappers TCP wrappers are a facility of the `inetd` daemon whereby access to services can be restricted to designated hosts.

Sample Questions

1. Which of the following is the program that accomplishes TCP wrapping?

A. tcp

B. tcpd

C. tcpwrap

D. twist

Answer: B. The tcpd program checks whether a host is allowed to access a service.

2. Assume that hosts in the domain example.com have names of the form *host*.example.com. Which of the following is a correct host specification for use with TCP wrappers?

A. .example.com

B. *.example.com

C. example.com

D. example.*

Answer: A. A domain or subdomain must be specified with a leading dot.

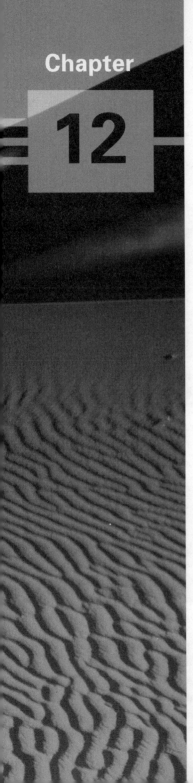

Chapter

12

The X Window System

RHCE PREPARATION TOPICS COVERED IN THIS CHAPTER:

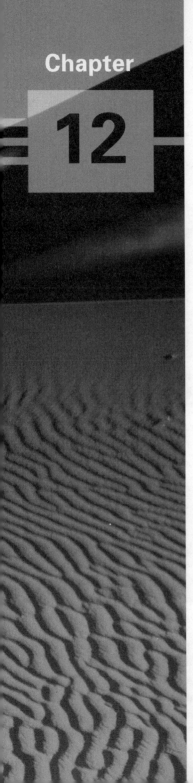▶ Installing and Configuring X *(pages 312 – 326)*

▶ Configuring Window, Desktop, and Display
Managers *(pages 326 – 337)*

▶ Configuring X for Remote Access
(pages 337 – 342)

his chapter explains how to install and configure the X Window system after system installation. Chapter 1, "Installation," explains how to install and configure the X Window system during system installation.

Installing and Configuring X

The X Window system, or X, is the graphical user interface distributed with Red Hat Linux. There is a variety of X implementations; the implementation distributed with Red Hat Linux was produced by The XFree86 Project Inc. Their implementation of X, known as XFree86, is freely redistributable. This section explains basic X operation, installation, and configuration. The following two sections explain how to configure and use more advanced X capabilities, including window and desktop managers and remote X clients.

Critical Information

X includes X servers and X clients; however, in the context of X, the terms have unusual meanings. An *X server* is a video driver for a particular set of video devices. An *X client* is a program or application that uses the graphical user interface provided by an X server. The service that an X server provides is video output.

X servers and clients communicate through the appropriately named X protocol. X is a distributed client/server system: An X client need not run on the same host as the associated X server. For example, an X server can host X clients running on multiple hosts. Similarly, a host can run X clients associated with X servers on several remote hosts.

In addition to servers and clients, X features window managers. A *window manager* works with an X server, providing a standardized graphical appearance and interface behavior to all clients using the server. For example, the window manager draws window title bars and provides an appropriate response when the user clicks a window's close box. The window manager also provides methods of moving, resizing, iconizing, and raising windows.

X also features desktop managers. A *desktop manager* works with a window manager to provide a set of basic capabilities and features needed by most users. For example, a typical desktop manager provides desktop icons, a file manager, a task bar, and so on. The most commonly used Linux desktop managers are KDE and GNOME.

By itself, X is not useful; starting X generally entails starting a window manager and one or more clients. If you launch X without a window manager or clients, all you'll see is a featureless screen.

Important X Directories and Files

The /usr/X11R6/bin directory contains X binaries. For X programs to operate correctly, the /usr/X11R6/bin directory should appear on the program path, stored in the PATH environment variable.

Another important X directory is /etc/X11. This directory and its subdirectories contain the X configuration. The symbolic link /etc/X11/X points to the currently selected X server, which resides in /usr/X11R6/bin.

The /etc/X11 directory also contains the xf86config file, the main X configuration file, which is generally built by using Xconfigurator or XF86Setup.

Necessary Procedures

This section gives procedures for installing and configuring X.

Installing X

To install X, you must install a set of packages that include the following:

- an appropriate X server
- the font server and a set of suitable fonts
- common X code
- an X configuration tool
- libraries
- the xinitrc script

In addition, you'll generally choose to install

- a window manager
- a desktop manager
- one or more X clients

The easiest way to install X is to install it during system installation. This lets you specify the X components that you want to install, rather than the individual packages. Specifying components is more convenient and accurate than specifying individual packages. If you prefer, you can install X after system installation is complete. However, without help, you may find it somewhat cumbersome to identify and install the proper packages. Installing X after system installation is a two-step process:

1. Determine the proper X server.

2. Install the proper packages.

Selecting the X Server

If you like, you can install every X server available on the distribution media, even though a system requires only one. XFree86 includes only 15 servers, and each associated RPM file is only about 1MB in size, so installing unneeded servers won't waste a great deal of disk space. Regardless of the number of servers you install, you must determine which server is appropriate for your system's video device.

Determining the proper X server is sometimes problematical, because there may be none. Although XFree86 is regularly updated, it often lacks support for the latest video hardware. However, some video hardware vendors have begun to distribute XFree86-compatible X servers for their products.

Over 500 video devices are currently supported. Moreover, many video devices that are not fully supported by XFree86 can be run in SVGA, VGA, or monochrome mode by using the appropriate XFree86 server. Of course, the best possible video resolution and color depth may fall short of the full capabilities of the device if this is done.

Table 12.1 summarizes the X servers currently distributed as part of XFree86. Consult the table to determine which server supports your video device.

TABLE 12.1: X Servers

X Server RPM Package Name	Description
XFree86-3Dlabs	Server for devices built around 3Dlabs GLINT and PERMEDIA chipsets, including the GLINT 500TX with IBM RGB526 RAMDAC, the GLINT MX with IBM RGB526 or IBM RGB640 RAMDAC, the PERMEDIA with IBM RGB526 RAMDAC, and the PERMEDIA 2a, 2v, and 2 Classic.
XFree86-8514	Server for the IBM 8514 video cards and compatibles, such as those made by ATI.
XFree86-AGX	Server for the AGX video card.
XFree86-FBDev	Server for the generic frame buffer device.
XFree86-I128	Server for devices such as the Number Nine Imagine 128.
XFree86-Mach32	Server for devices built around the Mach32 chip.
XFree86-Mach64	Server for devices built around the Mach64 chip.

TABLE 12.1: X Servers *(continued)*

X Server RPM Package Name	Description
XFree86-Mach8	Server for devices built around the Mach8 chip.
XFree86-Mono	Generic monochrome server that works with nearly all VGA devices.
XFree86-P9000	Server for devices built around the Weitek P9000 chip.
XFree86-S3	Server for devices built around the S3 chip, including most Number Nine cards, many Diamond Stealth cards, Orchid Fahrenheits, the Miro Crystal 8S, most STB cards, and some motherboards with built-in graphics accelerators, such as IBM Value-Point PCs.
XFree86-S3V	Server for devices built around the S3 ViRGE chip.
XFree86-SVGA	Server for simple frame buffer SVGA devices, including cards built from ET4000 chips, Cirrus Logic chips, Chips and Technologies laptop chips, Trident 8900 and 9000 chips, and Matrox chips. It also works for Diamond Speedstar, Orchid Kelvins, STB Nitros and Horizons, Genoa 8500VL, most Actix boards, and the Spider VLB Plus. It works with many other SVGA devices as well.
XFree86-VGA16	Generic 16-color server that works with nearly all VGA devices.
XFree86-W32	Server for devices built around ET4000/W32 chips, including the Genoa 8900 Phantom 32i, the Hercules Dynamite, the LeadTek WinFast S200, the Sigma Concorde, the STB LightSpeed, the TechWorks Thunderbolt, and the ViewTop PCI.
XFree86-Xvfb	X Virtual Frame Buffer server that runs without display hardware and input devices.

Installing the Packages

Once you know the name of the package that contains the proper X server for your system, you're ready to install X. During installation, you should also install the following additional packages:

- freetype, which contains a library that renders TrueType fonts

- gtk+, which contains a library used by X clients

- X11R6-contrib, which contains many useful X clients

- Xconfigurator, which contains the Red Hat Linux program for configuring X

- XFree86-libs, which contains the main XFree86 libraries

- XFree86, which contains XFree86 common code

- XFree86-75dpi-fonts, which contains the standard Western European fonts for use with X

- XFree86-xfs, which contains the X font server

- xinitrc, which contains a script used to start a window manager

Don't attempt to install the packages one by one. Several of the packages depend on other packages, so installation is likely to fail owing to unsatisfied dependencies. Instead, move to the directory containing the packages and issue a single rpm command that installs all of the packages. The command should have the following form:

```
rpm -Uvh freetype-*.rpm gtk+-*.rpm X11R6-contrib-*.rpm \
    Xconfigurator-*.rpm XFree86-libs-*.rpm XFree86-*.rpm \
    XFree86-75dpi-fonts-*.rpm XFree86-xfs-*.rpm \
    xinitrc-*.rpm XFree86-server-*.rpm
```

where *XFree86-server* is the name of the package containing the proper X server.

You may find the quite extensive XFree86 documentation helpful. The package requires a little over 11MB of disk space. To install it, move to the directory containing the packages and issue the command XFree86-doc-*.rpm.

Configuring X

The main X configuration file is /etc/X11/xf86config. You can manually edit this file; however, most system administrators prefer to configure X by using a tool. Popular tools include the following:

Xconfigurator The Red Hat Linux X configuration tool, which can be used during a text-based installation and after a text-based or graphical installation

XF86Setup The XFree86 X configuration tool

xf86config A text-based X configuration tool

This section explains the use of these tools. In addition, this section describes two other useful tools:

Superprobe A text-based tool that helps you obtain information about your system's video card

xvidtune A text-based tool that helps you tune X to yield the best possible image

Xconfigurator

Most Red Hat Linux administrators seem to prefer Xconfigurator to other X configuration tools. One reason for the preference is familiarity: Xconfigurator is used in the text-based Red Hat installation procedure, so many Red Hat Linux administrators are comfortable using the tool. Xconfigurator supports more cards and monitors than XF86Setup—currently, over 600 cards and 900 monitors.

To launch Xconfigurator, issue the command

```
Xconfigurator
```

Xconfigurator can be used in a special non-interactive "kickstart" mode, in which it probes for information, attempting to configure a card without human intervention. To use kickstart mode, issue the command

```
Xconfigurator --kickstart
```

Alternatively, Xconfigurator can be used in expert mode, in which the user has the ability to override probed values. To use expert mode, issue the command

```
Xconfigurator --expert
```

The following step-by-step explanation assumes that you're using Xconfigurator in ordinary mode—that is, neither kickstart nor expert mode.

Xconfigurator does not support the use of a mouse. Instead, you communicate with the program via the keyboard. The following keys have special meaning:

- Tab, Up, Down, Right, and Left are used to navigate from field to field; the current field is the one that's highlighted.

- The spacebar is used to toggle a radio button or check box.

- Enter is used to click the highlighted button.

To proceed with the configuration, use the navigation keys to highlight the OK button and press Enter to click it. The Choose a Card screen will appear.

You can choose a card from the list and click OK, or you can choose the final entry, Unlisted Card. Xconfigurator will try to determine the proper X server for the selected card. If it cannot, it will display the Pick a Server screen.

Use the navigation keys to highlight the proper server, then click OK. If you're unsure which server to choose, consider choosing SVGA, VGA16, or Mono because these servers support a variety of cards. However, these servers provide limited resolution and color depth; using a generic server may not take full advantage of the capabilities of the system's video device. When you've made your choice, click OK. The Monitor Setup screen will appear. Use the navigation keys to highlight the proper monitor; if you can't find your monitor, choose Custom. Click OK.

WARNING The monitor make and model selection should exactly match those of your monitor. *Don't choose a monitor that's merely similar to, but not identical to, your monitor.* Often, similarly numbered models have quite different operating characteristics. You can permanently damage your monitor by selecting an incorrect monitor. If in doubt, choose Custom and enter the operating parameters directly.

If you chose Custom, the Custom Monitor Setup screen will appear; otherwise, the Screen Configuration screen will appear. Click OK to proceed. The Custom Monitor Setup (continued) screen will appear.

WARNING As the Custom Monitor Setup screen informs you, the horizontal sync rate and vertical refresh rate are critical parameters. Entering an incorrect value for either parameter can permanently damage a monitor. Obtain these values from a reliable source, such as the owner's manual or the manufacturer's Web site. Modern multi-sync monitors are more resistant to damage than older monitors; however, they are not immune. In any case, don't allow a monitor to display a garbled image any longer than necessary; immediately turn off the power and reconfigure the operating parameters.

Select an appropriate *horizontal sync rate* for your monitor. If in doubt of the proper value, choose conservatively in order to avoid damaging the monitor. When you've highlighted the proper sync rate, click OK. A second Custom Monitor Setup (continued) screen will appear. Select an appropriate *vertical refresh rate* for your monitor. If in doubt of the proper value, choose conservatively in order to avoid damaging the monitor. When you've highlighted the proper sync rate, click OK. The Screen Configuration screen will appear.

The screen lets you avoid probing the video card, because probing can sometimes hang a system. Generally, you should select Probe and let

Xconfigurator probe the card; if you experience a problem, you can restart Xconfigurator and skip the probe.

If you select Probe and click OK, a dialog box will confirm your action and ask you to click OK to proceed. If the probe is successful, the Probe to Begin screen will appear. If you select Don't Probe or if the probe fails, you're prompted for the needed information. For example, the Video Memory screen may appear.

Select the amount of video RAM available on your video device and click OK. The ClockChip Configuration screen will appear. Generally, you should select the No ClockChip setting because the X server can probe to determine the ClockChip setting. However, some cards cannot successfully probe; this screen lets you work around this problem. When you've selected the proper ClockChip setting, click OK. If you selected No ClockChip, the Probe for Clocks screen will appear; otherwise, the Select Video Modes screen appears. In the Probe for Clocks screen, click OK to begin the probe. The Select Video Modes screen will appear.

Select one or more desired resolutions and color depths. If you select multiple modes, you can use Ctrl+Alt++ to cycle among them during X operation. However, you must use the + key on the numeric keypad; the ordinary + key will not function for this purpose. When you've selected the desired modes, click OK. The Probe to Begin screen will appear.

Click OK to test your X configuration. If the configuration is a good one, you'll see a small dialog box asking, "Can you see this message?" If you can see the dialog box, click Yes. A second dialog box will ask if you want to configure the system to start X at boot time. Click Yes or No, according to your preference.

If you can't see the small dialog box, Xconfigurator will return you to the configuration procedure after several seconds. You can specify different operating parameters and try again to start X.

TIP Laptops are notoriously difficult to configure for X. One reason is that seemingly identical laptops may contain very different video hardware. For help on configuring Linux laptops, see the Linux Laptop Web page, www.cs.utexas.edu/users/kharker/linux-laptop/.

XF86Setup

The XFree86 Project distributes its own X configuration tool, XF86Setup. Some administrators prefer the tool to Xconfigurator because it allows use of the mouse. To do so, it uses the facilities of the VGA16 server, which is supported by a wide range of video devices.

To use XF86Setup, you should install the following packages in addition to those identified in the preceding subsection:

- glib10, a library of utility functions, some of which are used by the tool

- tcl, a scripting language used by the tool

- tk, a widget set used by tcl

- XFree86-VGA16, the VGA16 server

- XFree86-XF86Setup, the tool itself

To install these packages, move to the directory containing them and issue the command

```
rpm -Uvh glib10-*.rpm tcl-*.rpm tk-*.rpm \
    XFree86-VGA16-*.rpm XFree86-XF86Setup-*.rpm
```

To launch XF86Setup, issue the command XF86Setup.

The XF86Setup introduction screen will appear. The screen provides six buttons across its top:

- The Mouse button lets you configure the mouse.

- The Keyboard button lets you configure the keyboard.

- The Card button lets you configure the video device.

- The Monitor button lets you configure the monitor.

- The Mode Selection button lets you configure the color depths and video resolutions.

- The Other button lets you configure several X options.

To configure the mouse, click the Mouse button. A help screen will appear, explaining various mouse-related options. After you've perused the information, click Dismiss to close the window. The Mouse screen will appear.

Select the desired mouse options. Click Apply to immediately apply the mouse configuration. When the mouse is working properly, click the Keyboard button. The Keyboard screen will appear.

Select the desired keyboard options. Click Apply to immediately apply the keyboard configuration. When the keyboard is working properly, click the Card button. The Card screen will appear.

Select the proper card from the list. If the card is not listed, click the Detailed Setup button to enter the configuration manually. The Detailed Card screen will appear.

Select the proper configuration for the card. If you prefer, you can click the Card List button to return to the Card screen. When the configuration is properly set, click the Monitor button. The Monitor screen will appear.

Enter the horizontal sync rate and vertical refresh rate for the monitor. Or, if you prefer, select the list item that corresponds to the characteristics of the monitor. Click the Mode Selection button. The Mode Selection screen will appear.

Select the mode or modes and the color depth you prefer. Select only values supported by the video device. When you've made your selections, click the Other button. The Other screen will appear.

The Other screen lets you enable and disable several X options. When you've selected the configuration you prefer, click Done. XF86Setup builds the configuration you've specified and stores it in the /etc/ X11/xf86config file.

xf86config

The third X configuration tool, xf86config, is a text-based tool that uses a prompt/reply dialog to configure X. As such, the tool is somewhat cumbersome to use. But it is highly flexible and is contained in the XFree86 package. Thus, xf86config may work where other tools require the installation of additional packages.

The steps in the xf86config dialog resemble those of Xconfigurator and XF86Setup, because all gather essentially the same information. The basic steps are

1. Introduction

2. Mouse configuration

3. Keyboard configuration

4. Monitor configuration

5. Card configuration

6. Server selection

7. Mode selection

8. Configuration file generation

Superprobe

The Superprobe tool can help you determine the type and operating characteristics of a video device. The tool is contained in the XFree86 package. To run Superprobe, issue the command SuperProbe.

The tool may hang some systems. You can type Ctrl+C to interrupt the program before the probe is initiated.

xvidtune

The xvidtune tool can help you fine-tune an X configuration. It lets you interactively adjust video modes and scan rates for optimal performance. The tool is part of the XFree86 package.

WARNING If you improperly specify a scan rate, the xvidtune tool can damage a monitor. Be careful to provide only correct values.

Exam Essentials

Understand X in general and the XFree86 X server in particular, including its configuration file and the primary tools used for editing that file You should know how to install and configure X, both during and after system installation. You should know how to use all the popular tools for configuring X, including Xconfigurator, XF86Setup, xf86config, Superprobe, and xvidtune.

Key Terms and Concepts

Desktop manager A desktop manager is an X client that provides desktop icons, a task bar, a pager, a file manager, or other common desktop functions.

Horizontal sync rate The horizontal sync rate of a monitor is a crucial operating parameter. A monitor can be damaged by operating it at an inappropriate horizontal sync rate.

Vertical refresh rate The vertical refresh rate of a monitor is a crucial operating parameter. A monitor can be damaged by operating it at an inappropriate vertical refresh rate.

Window manager A window manager is an X client that is responsible for many aspects of the visual appearance and behavior of displayed windows, such as title bars and window close boxes.

X client An X client is a program that uses X as its user interface.

X server An X server is a video driver associated with the X Window system.

Sample Questions

1. The component of X responsible for interfacing with the video hardware is which of the following?

A. The client

B. The desktop manager

C. The server

D. The window manager

Answer: C. The server acts as a device driver, providing graphics service on behalf of applications, which are known as clients.

2. Which of the following X servers supports the greatest number of video device types?

A. XFree86-AGX

B. XFree86-S3

C. XFree86-SVGA

D. XFree86-W32

Answer: C. The SVGA server supports many SVGA devices. Only the VGA16 and Mono servers support more.

Configuring Window, Desktop, and Display Managers

A suite of programs cooperates to provide the X environment. These include

- the *window manager*, which draws borders, title bars, menu bars, and window manipulation buttons

- the *desktop manager*, which provides the desktop environment, including the file manager, help system, and virtual desktop

- X clients, which are the applications you run

In addition, if you log in via X, a *display manager* authenticates your identity by using the PAM facility. This section introduces you to window, desktop, and display managers, explaining how to select and configure them.

Critical Information

Red Hat Linux lets you choose one of three X display managers:

- XDM, the display manager distributed by the XFree86 Project

- GDM, the display manager distributed with GNOME

- KDM, the display manager distributed with KDE

If you want to be able to provide a *chooser*, you should configure XDM as the preferred display manager; both GDM and KDM have some peculiarities that limit their ability to work with choosers. For example, GDM doesn't respond to chooser messages and therefore won't appear on the chooser menu. The KDM display manager responds to chooser messages, but sometimes won't provide a chooser.

Desktop Environments

Red Hat Linux lets you choose between two primary desktop environments:

- GNOME

- KDE

By default, the GNOME environment includes the GNOME desktop manager and the Enlightenment window manager. The KDE environment includes the KDE desktop manager and the KWM window manager. This section describes these desktop environments, explains how to choose between them, and explains how to configure them to work with alternative window managers.

Using the GNOME Desktop Manager

The open-source GNOME desktop environment is written using CORBA (Common Object Request Broker Architecture) and the GIMP (GNU Image Manipulation Program) toolkit (GTK+). Development of GNOME has been graciously funded by Red Hat Inc. through RHAD Labs.

GNOME-compliant applications are session aware, meaning that they save their state when you exit GNOME. When you reenter GNOME, session-aware applications reopen documents that were previously open, reposition the cursor to its original position, and generally help you resume work where you left off. GNOME developers plan to eventually offer a capability that resembles Microsoft's Object Linking and Embedding (OLE), through CORBA.

GNOME is often used with the Enlightenment window manager, which was specially designed for use with GNOME. However, it can also be used with other window managers. Several window managers have been revised to work better with GNOME, including Window Maker and IceWM, which are considered GNOME-compliant. Authors of other window managers, including AfterStep and FVWM, are generally working toward GNOME compliance.

GNOME includes many useful features and facilities, such as

- a file manager, GMC, that supports drag-and-drop operations
- desktop icons that represent programs and directories
- a virtual desktop that can exceed the size of the physical screen
- a pager that lets you navigate the virtual desktop
- a panel that provides functions similar to those provided by the Microsoft Windows Taskbar
- launchers that let you launch applications by clicking the mouse
- themes that let you choose a coordinated visual appearance

Using the KDE Desktop Manager

The KDE desktop manager provides features and facilities similar to those provided by GNOME. Unlike GNOME, which uses the separate Enlightenment window manager, KDE has its own window manager, KWM, which is the most popular window manager for use with KDE; however, KDE is also compatible with such window managers as AfterStep, Enlightenment, and WindowMaker.

KDE was written using the Qt toolkit, authored by Troll Tech, a Norwegian software development company. Originally the Qt toolkit had a somewhat restrictive license, which slowed acceptance of KDE by the open-source community. Recently, the Qt license restrictions have been lifted, and KDE has found a much wider following.

Choosing a Window Manager

As explained, the window manager supplies borders, title bars, menu bars, window manipulation buttons, and other visual elements. Some popular window managers include

- AfterStep, which resembles the GUI formerly used by the NeXTStep operating system.

- Enlightenment, the window manager favored by GNOME. Enlightenment is a feature-rich window manager that requires considerable system resources.

- FVWM, a rather old and yet very efficient window manager that can mimic Windows 95 or Motif. FVWM was developed for Linux use and remains popular.

- Sawfish, formerly known as Sawmill, a new and largely GNOME-compliant window manager noted for its low resource requirements in comparison to Enlightenment. In Red Hat Linux 6.2, it's distributed as the `sawmill` and `sawmill-gnome` packages.

- WindowMaker, another window manager that resembles NeXTStep. WindowMaker is both popular and efficient.

If the ~/.Xclients script exists, it determines which window manager is run. If no ~/.Xclients script exists, the /etc/X11/xinit/Xclients script determines which window manager is run.

Starting X

You can set a system to provide a console login or an X login. The /etc/inittab file contains the line:

```
id:n:initdefault:
```

where *n* is the default runlevel. Set *n* to 3 to provide a console login; set *n* to 5 to provide an X login. The X startup process depends on the runlevel you specify.

If you specify runlevel 3, you should start an X session by issuing the command

```
startx
```

X will source the file ~/.xinitrc, if it exists; otherwise, X sources the file /etc/X11/xinit/xinitrc. In turn, this file sources ~/.Xclients if it exists and /etc/X11/xinit/Xclients otherwise. Under Red Hat Linux 6.2, this file also sources all scripts in /etc/X11/xinit/xinitrc.d.

If you specify runlevel 5, X will display a login prompt. When you log in, X will source ~/.xsession, if it exists. The ~/.xsession file can be revised by the user and, therefore, may start an alternative window or desktop manager. If ~/.xsession does not exist, X will source ~/.Xclients if it exists and /etc/X11/xinit/Xclients otherwise.

Using X Clients

When launching an X client, you can specify options that determine the client's appearance. Some of the most useful options are summarized in Table 12.2. For example, to launch an X terminal having green text on a black background, issue the command

```
xterm -foreground green -background black
```

You can control the operation of X by entering a control sequence from the keyboard. Table 12.3 describes several of the most useful control sequences.

TABLE 12.2: Popular Options for X Clients

Option	Description
-background *color* or -bg *color*	Set the color of the window background.
-bordercolor *color*	Set the color of the window border.
-borderwidth *width*	Set the width of the window border (in pixels).
-display [*server*]:*n.m*	Set the display, where *server* is the host, *n* is the display number, and *m* is the screen number. The first display and screen are designated 0.0.
-font *font*	Set the default font used in the window.
-foreground *color* or -fg *color*	Set the color of the window foreground.
-geometry *width*x*height*+x+y	Set the size and location of the window (in pixels), where *width* is the window width, *height* is the window height, x is the horizontal offset of the top left corner of the window, and y is the vertical offset of the top left corner of the window.
-title *string*	Set the window title.

TABLE 12.3: Useful Control Sequences

Control Sequence	Description
Ctrl+Alt++	Switch video mode (must use + key on numeric keypad).
Ctrl+Alt+Backspace	Exit X.
Ctrl+Alt+F*n*	Switch to a text-mode virtual terminal, *n*=1 to 6.
Ctrl+Alt+F7	Switch from text-mode virtual terminal to X.

Necessary Procedures

This section explains how to

- Select the display manager

- Configure XDM to provide a chooser

- Switch desktop managers

- Access a remote X font server

- Use the Xnest program

Selecting the Display Manager

To select the display manager, revise the `/etc/sysconfig/desktop` file as follows:

- For the GDM display manager, specify `GNOME`.

- For the KDM display manager, specify `KDE`.

- For the XDM display manager, specify `AnotherLevel`.

Configuring XDM to Provide a Chooser

To configure XDM to provide a chooser, you must modify the XDM configuration file `/etc/X11/xdm/Xaccess`. You must add one or more `chooser` directives, which have the following general form:

```
client CHOOSER server_list
```

where `client` specifies the client hosts to whom a chooser will be provided and `server_list` specifies the servers that will appear in the chooser.

The client hosts can be specified by using wildcards. Consider the following sample configuration:

```
workstation        CHOOSER server1 server2
*.azusapacific.com CHOOSER server3
*                  CHOOSER server4
```

The first line specifies that the host workstation will be provided a chooser that shows hosts server1 and server2. The second line specifies that all hosts in the azusapacific.com domain will be provided a chooser that shows host server3. The final line specifies that all hosts will be provided a chooser that shows host server4. If the name of a host matches several CHOOSER lines, the line appearing first is used. In the sample configuration, the host workstation.azusapacific.com would be provided a chooser that shows server1 and server2, even though the host name matches lines 2 and 3 as well as line 1.

You can specify the list of servers dynamically by using the keyword BROADCAST. For example, consider the following directive:

    * CHOOSER BROADCAST

The BROADCAST keyword causes the display manager to assemble a list of X servers on the local network by sending a special broadcast message. All servers that respond to the broadcast message will be included in the chooser.

By default, XDM ignores chooser requests. To configure xdm to respond, you must comment or remove the last line in /etc/X11/xdm/ xdm-config:

    DisplayManager.requestPort: 0

NOTE If you prefer to use KDM as a display manager and want it to provide a chooser, you can configure KDM using the same procedure used for XDM. To configure GDM to provide a chooser, you must set Enable=1 in the [xdmcp] section of the /etc/X11/gdm/gdm.conf file and force GDM to reread the file by issuing the command killall gdm.

Switching Desktop Managers

To specify the desired desktop manager, use an X term to invoke the Switchdesk utility by issuing the command

    /usr/bin/switchdesk

The program presents a small dialog box. Select the desired desktop manager and click OK. The following desktop managers are supported:

- GNOME

- KDE

- AnotherLevel, a desktop manager that resembles the desktop manager once used in the NeXTStep operating system

The change does not have an immediate effect. You must exit X and reenter it to load the specified desktop manager.

When Switchdesk is run, it creates two configuration files—which are actually scripts—that reside in the home directory of the running user:

- `.Xclients`, which invokes `.Xclients-default` or a special `.Xclients` file that pertains to a specific host

- `.Xclients-default`, which launches the window and desktop managers

Accessing a Remote X Font Server

By default, each system configured to run Red Hat Linux runs its own copy of the X *font server*, XFS, which provides access to locally stored fonts, including True Type fonts. However, you can reconfigure a system to access a remote X font server, if you prefer.

To do so, modify the `FontPath` directive of the `/etc/X11/xf86config` file of each client system. By default, the directive has this form:

```
FontPath "unix/:-1"
```

To access a remote font server, revise the directive to have the form

```
tcp/server:7100
```

where *server* is the host name or IP address of the host running the font server. You must also modify the `/etc/rc.d/init.d/xfs` file. To do so, change the line

```
daemon xfs -droppriv -daemon -port -1
```

to read

```
daemon xfs -droppriv -daemon -port 7100
```

TIP   By default, an X font server listens on port 7100. However, you can assign another port, if you prefer. To do so, modify the font server configuration file, `/etc/X11/fs/config`, and the font server SysVInit file, `/etc/rc.d/init.d/xfs`.

Using the Xnest Program

Sometimes it's useful to run multiple X servers on a single host that has only a single video adapter. For example, you may want to test a new window while already running a local X server. Xnest provides an X server that runs in a window owned by the currently running X server. You can run multiple instances of Xnest and use each X server it provides just as you would an ordinary X server.

For example, to create a second X server by using Xnest, issue the following command:

```
Xnest :1 &
```

Similarly, to create a third X server by using Xnest, issue the following command:

```
Xnest :2 &
```

To create a second X server and use it to log in to a specified host, issue a command of the form

```
Xnest -query server :1 &
```

where *server* is the host name or IP address of the host you want to log in to. Similarly, you can use Xnest to log in to an arbitrary host or to obtain a chooser:

```
Xnest -broadcast :1 &       # log in to any host on the
                            # local network
Xnest -indirect server :1 & # log in via chooser
                            # provided by server
```

Exam Essentials

Be familiar with the window manager and desktop environment choices available under Red Hat Linux, and know how to select these choices   You should be familiar with the most popular desktop environments used with Red Hat Linux, including GNOME, KDE, and AnotherLevel. You should know how to choose the desktop manager and display manager, how to use Xnest, how to configure X to use a remote font server, and how to configure the display manager to provide a chooser.

Key Terms and Concepts

Chooser   A chooser is a dialog box provided by an X display manager, which lets the user select a login host and possibly other options.

Desktop manager   A desktop manager is an X client that provides desktop icons, a task bar, a pager, a file manager, or other common desktop functions.

Display manager   A display manager is a special X client that provides the means to log in to a system via X.

Font server   A font server provides local or remote access to fonts used to render X glyphs (characters).

Window manager   A window manager is an X client that is responsible for many aspects of the visual appearance and behavior of displayed windows, such as title bars and close boxes.

Sample Questions

1. What is the utility used to specify the desktop manager?

   A. control-panel

   B. switchdesk

C. xdm

D. xinitrc

Answer: B. The switchdesk utility lets you specify the desktop manager.

2. What is the file that specifies the display manager?

A. /etc/X11/prefdm

B. /etc/X11/xdm/default

C. /etc/sysconfig/desktop

D. /usr/bin/prefdm

Answer: C. The file /etc/sysconfig/desktop specifies the current display manager.

Configuring X for Remote Access

One of the most useful features of X is its support for remote clients and *remote logins*. Using this feature, you can run an X client on one host and display the client's user interface on another host. For example, you can run a program on a remote supercomputer, yet control the program and view its output via your own desktop. This section explains the procedure for configuring and using remote clients and servers.

Critical Information

X is a network-based system, which lets you launch remote clients or remotely log in to a host. X implements a simple *host-based security* scheme that prevents unauthorized hosts from accessing an X server. More sophisticated, user-based authentication schemes are also supported.

Necessary Procedures

This section gives procedures for configuring host-based X, launching a remote client, and logging in remotely via X.

Configuring Host-based X Security

Host-based X security is configured via the xhost command. You can view the current security settings by issuing the command xhost, which will report whether access control is currently enabled or disabled and list the hosts on the access list. For example, the following output indicates that access control is currently disabled and that, if access control were enabled, only the hosts dale and roy could connect:

```
access control disabled, clients can connect from
⤷any host
INET:dale
INET:roy
```

You can issue the xhost command to query a local or remote X server. Issuing the command remotely lets you verify that the local host has permission to access the remote server, which is identified by the value of the DISPLAY environment. For example, the following commands check the permission of the local host to access the X server running on the host bigger:

```
export DISPLAY=bigger:0.0
xhost
```

Other forms of the xhost command must be executed locally—that is, on the host running the X server. To enable host-based security, issue the command

```
xhost -
```

To disable host security, so that all hosts can access the local X server, issue the command

```
xhost +
```

To extend permission for a client to access the local X server, issue a command of the form

```
xhost +client
```

where *client* is the IP address or host name of the client. To deny permission for a client to access the local X server, issue a command of the form

    xhost -*client*

where *client* is the IP address or host name of the client. The X server stores the IP addresses of hosts, rather than host names, on the access list. Therefore, DNS must be able to perform a forward and reverse lookup on any host name you specify.

Launching a Remote Client

Launching a remote client is simple and can be accomplished in any of several ways. One way is to use the display argument provided by most X clients. For example, the following command launches the X client xeyes to run using the X server on the host bigger:

    xeyes -display bigger:0.0 &

The general form of the command for launching a remote X client is

    xclient -display *server*[:*m*[.*n*]] [*xclient_args*])

where

- *xclient* and *xclient_args* are the client and its optional arguments.

- *server* is the host name or IP address of the X server.

- *m* is the optional server display number (by default, 0).

- *n* is the optional server screen number (by default, 0). This argument is used in the somewhat unusual situation of a server that has multiple screens associated with a single display.

For example, to use this command form to launch xeyes, you might specify

    xeyes -display biggest:0.0 &

If you plan to launch several X clients, you may find it more convenient to set the DISPLAY environment variable. Subsequently, when you launch an X client, the value of the DISPLAY environment variable determines the X server that is used. For example, the following sequence of commands launches xeyes and xclock to run using the X server on the host bigger; it also launches a second instance of xeyes to run on biggest:

```
export DISPLAY=bigger:0.0
xeyes &
xclock &
xeyes -display biggest:0.0 &
```

If the X server's host authentication feature is active, the client host must be authorized to access the X server. Otherwise, the client program fails with a message such as the following:

```
Xlib: connection to "bigger:0.0" refused by server
Xlib: Client is not authorized to connect to server
Error: Can't open display: bigger:0.0
```

TIP Follow the command to launch an X client with an ampersand (&) if you want the shell to immediately return a new prompt.

Suppose you're currently logged in to the host workstation and you want to run a program—say, xterm—on the host server but receive its output locally, on the host workstation. The following sequence of commands accomplishes that goal:

```
[user@workstation]$ xhost +server
[user@workstation]$ telnet server
(log in dialog omitted)
[user@server]$ export DISPLAY=workstation:0.0
[user@server]$ xterm &
```

Configuring Remote Login

In addition to running X clients remotely, you can remotely log in to a host that is running an X display manager. The display manager displays a dialog box that lets you specify the login username and password. Some display managers provide dialog boxes that let you specify the desired window manager or other options.

To log in to a host running an X display manager, issue a command of the form

```
X -query server
```

where *server* is the host name or IP address of the host running the display manager. To log in to an arbitrary host on the local network, issue the command

```
X -broadcast
```

Some hosts are configured to provide a chooser, a special menu that lets you select the host you want to log in to. To request a chooser, issue a command of the form

```
X -indirect server
```

where *server* is the host name or IP address of the host configured to provide a chooser.

Exam Essentials

Understand and be capable of implementing and using the remote capabilities of X, including remote logins and remote clients   You should know how to launch remote clients and how to log in remotely via X. You should also know how to configure X's host-based security.

Key Terms and Concepts

Host-based security   X provides a facility that lets you restrict the hosts that can access an X server.

Remote login   X lets you remotely log in to a host via the host's display manager.

Sample Questions

1. To disable host-based X security, which of the following commands should you issue?

   A. xhost +

   B. xhost -

   C. xhosts +

   D. xhosts -

   Answer: A. The xhost + command lets any host access the X server.

2. To log in to the X server on the host server, which of the following commands should you issue?

   A. X -broadcast server

   B. X -indirect server

   C. X -query server

   D. X server

   Answer: C. The -query option lets you specify the login host.

Chapter

13

Routing

This chapter explains the use of a Red Hat Linux system as an IP router. It also explains how to configure a firewall that can protect a local area network from unauthorized use.

Configuring Routing

Red Hat Linux is a capable router, as well as server or workstation. The following are among the router-related features of Red Hat Linux:

- Support for WAN protocols such as X.25, frame relay, and PPP

- Support for LAN functions such as IP forwarding, firewalling, and masquerading

- Advanced routing capabilities such as quality of service, policy-based routing, and transparent proxying

Critical Information

Only hosts with multiple network interfaces can perform routing. The most basic routing operation is *forwarding*, which forwards packets received on one network interface to another network interface. *Routing* is the process of forwarding packets based on the packet source and destination addresses and other relevant information. A *route* is the path taken by a packet. A *router* is a host or device that performs routing. A Red Hat Linux host can function as a dedicated router, or it can perform routing in addition to functioning as a server or workstation. Routers are often used in this fashion to join networks and subnetworks.

Red Hat Linux can perform both *static* and *dynamic routing*. In static routing, the rules that govern the paths taken by packets are fixed and can be adjusted only manually. In dynamic routing, the rules are adjusted automatically. Networks that feature dynamic routing can sometimes continue to function when one or more network components fail; the remaining components automatically adjust their routing rules to bypass the failed components. Of course, if the only connection to a given host fails, then it's not possible to access the host. Therefore, dynamically routed networks generally feature hosts and networks having redundant routes; if one route fails, routing rules can be adjusted to use a remaining operational route.

Static Routing

Static routing is simpler to configure and use than dynamic routing. Most small networks of a few score hosts are configured to use static routing. To set up static routing, you must enable IP forwarding and properly configure the routing tables. In addition, the kernel must be configured to support the desired routing options. The standard Red Hat Linux kernel supports the most commonly used routing options. However, you may choose to recompile the kernel to enable additional options or suppress unneeded options.

Configuring static routing requires the `route` command, which is contained in the `net-tools` package automatically installed during the standard installation procedure. You can use the `route` command directly, but many Red Hat Linux system administrators prefer to configure routing by using Linuxconf, which invokes `route` based on information you supply in the dialog boxes.

Conceptually, the routing configuration consists of a table that contains routing rules. Each rule has two or three components:

- A destination IP address, which can refer to a host, subnetwork, or network.

- An interface, which refers to a network adapter.

- An optional gateway IP address, which refers to a host that routes packets to the specified destination. If the gateway IP address is omitted, the destination IP address is assumed to be directly reachable via the specified interface.

NOTE PPP and SLIP devices always act as gateways. You don't need to—and shouldn't—specify a gateway address for a destination reachable via PPP or SLIP.

A Sample Network

Figure 13.1 shows a sample network, which consists of two subnetworks joined to one another and to the Internet by a router. The route commands corresponding to the sample network are

```
route add -net 192.168.1.0 netmask 255.255.255.0 eth0
route add -net 192.168.100.0 netmask 255.255.255.0 eth1
route add -net 1.1.1.0 netmask 255.255.255.0 eth2
route add default gw 10.1.1.2 eth2
```

FIGURE 13.1: A typical network

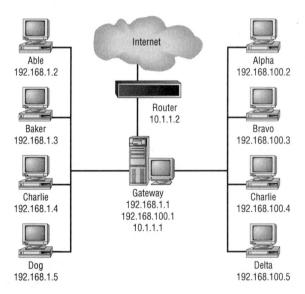

If you issue the route command without arguments, it reports the current routing rules. Here is the output corresponding to the sample network:

```
Kernel IP routing table
Destination   Gateway Genmask         Flags Metric Ref Use Iface
192.168.1.1   *       255.255.255.255 UH    0      0   0   eth0
192.168.100.1 *       255.255.255.255 UH    0      0   0   eth1
10.1.1.1      *       255.255.255.255 UH    0      0   0   eth2
192.168.1.0   *       255.255.255.0   U     0      0   0   eth0
192.168.100.0 *       255.255.255.0   U     0      0   0   eth1
default       router  0.0.0.0         UG    0      0   0   eth2
127.0.0.0     *       255.0.0.0       U     0      0   0   lo
```

The Flags field can contain such values as

- U, which indicates that the network link is up
- H, which indicates that the destination address refers to a host rather than a network
- G, which indicates that the routing rule specifies a gateway

The Metric, Ref, and Use fields are irrelevant except when using dynamic routing.

Kernel Configuration

The Linux kernel provides a variety of network-related options. Table 13.1 summarizes the most important options. Two especially important options optimize Red Hat Linux for use as a router: IP: advanced router and IP: optimize as router not host. If a Linux system is used primarily—or exclusively—as a router, you should specify these options and recompile its kernel.

TABLE 13.1: Kernel Networking Options

Typical Value	Option	Description
Y/N	IP: advanced router	Specify Y if the host is used mostly as a router.
Y	IP: aliasing support	Includes support for assigning multiple IP addresses to a single network interface; commonly used to support multihosting, virtual domains, or virtual hosting.
N	IP: ARP daemon support	Includes support for a user-space ARP daemon that can maintain a table large enough to handle a very large switched network (more than several hundred hosts).
M	IP: autofw masquerade support	Includes support for masquerading of protocols that lack their own protocol helpers.
Y/N	IP: broadcast GRE over IP	Includes support for using Generic Routing Encapsulation (GRE) to construct a broadcast WAN, which operates like an ordinary LAN.
Y	IP: firewall packet netlink device	Includes support that lets you create a character-special file that receives a copy of packets that match specified criteria; used to monitor network traffic and detect possible attacks.
Y	IP: firewalling	Includes kernel support for firewalling and masquerading.
M	IP: GRE tunnels over IP	Includes support for GRE, allowing encapsulation of IPv4 and IPv6 packets over IPv4. This support is more compatible with Cisco routers than that provided by the IP: tunneling option.

TABLE 13.1: Kernel Networking Options *(continued)*

Typical Value	Option	Description
Y	IP: ICMP masquerading	Includes support that enables a firewall to translate ICMP packets originating from the local network and destined for a remote host to appear as though they had originated from the firewall host. Used, for example, to allow hosts that have only private IP addresses to access the Internet.
M	IP: ipmarkfw masquerade support	Includes support for Firewall Mark Forwarding, a facility similar to port forwarding.
N	IP: kernel level autoconfiguration	Enables automatic configuration of the IP addresses of network interfaces and the routing table during kernel boot; used to support diskless hosts that boot via the network.
Y	IP: masquerading	Includes support that enables a firewall to translate UDP and TCP packets originating from the local network and destined for a remote host to appear as though they had originated from the firewall host. Used, for example, to allow hosts that have only private IP addresses to access the Internet.
Y	IP: masquerading special modules support	Includes support for modules that can modify masquerade rules, used by such modules as ipautofw and by port forwarding.
M	IP: masquerading virtual server support	Includes support that lets you build a virtual server that consists of two or more real servers.

TABLE 13.1: Kernel Networking Options *(continued)*

Typical Value	Option	Description
12	IP: masquerading VS table size	Specifies the size of the hash table used to manage active connections; the actual table size is 2^n, where n is the value specified.
N	IP: multicast routing	Includes support for routing multicast IP packets—that is, packets that have multiple destination addresses.
N	IP: Multicasting	Includes support for addressing packets to multiple computers—used, for example, by hosts connected to the MBONE, a high-speed audio-video network.
Y/N	IP: optimize as router not host	Disables support for copy and checksum operations that improve host performance but degrade router performance.
Y	IP: TCP syncookie support	Includes support for cookies that protect against a SYN flood denial-of-service attack.
Y	IP: transparent proxying	Includes support that enables a firewall to redirect packets originating from the local network and destined for a remote host to a local server (a transparent proxy server).
M	IP: tunneling	Includes support for encapsulating packets having one protocol within packets of another protocol.

TABLE 13.1: Kernel Networking Options *(continued)*

Typical Value	Option	Description
M	IPL ipportfw masquerade support	Includes support for port forwarding, which lets you forward packets originating outside the local network and destined for a specified port of the firewall host to a specified port of a host on the local network.
M	IPVS: round-robin scheduling	Specifies that the virtual server will use round-robin scheduling.
M	IPVS: weighted least-connection scheduling	Specifies that the virtual server will use weighted least-connection scheduling.
M	IPVS: weighted round-robin scheduling	Specifies that the virtual server will use weighted round-robin scheduling.
Y	Kernel/User netlink socket	Includes support for communication between the kernel and user processes via character-special files.
Y	Netlink device emulation	A backward compatibility that will soon be removed.
Y	Network firewalls	Includes support for packet filter–based firewalling and masquerading.
Y	Packet socket	Includes support for the packet protocol, used by programs such as tcpdump to communicate directly with network devices.
Y	Routing messages	Includes support for the special file /dev/route, which lets you read network-related information.
Y	Socket filtering	Includes support that lets user programs filter packets, except TCP packets.

TABLE 13.1: Kernel Networking Options *(continued)*

Typical Value	Option	Description
Y	`TCP/IP networking`	Includes support for the TCP/IP protocols.
Y	`Unix domain sockets`	Includes support for Unix domain sockets, which are used even by hosts not connected to a network.

Dynamic Routing

Red Hat Linux provides two daemons that support dynamic routing. If you want dynamic routing, you should install and configure one or the other. The `routed` daemon provides basic dynamic routing via the Routing Information Protocol (RIP). The more sophisticated `gated` daemon supports a variety of routing protocols such as the following:

- RIP and RIP-2

- Intermediate System to Intermediate System (IS-IS)

- Open Shortest Path First (OSPF-2)

- Exterior Gateway Protocol (EGP)

- Border Gateway Protocol (BGP-4)

RIP, IS-IS, and OSPF-2 are *interior routing protocols* suitable for use within a network or autonomous set of networks. RIP is a *distance-vector routing protocol*, one that merely informs its neighbors of its routing table. IS-IS and OSPF-2 are also *link-state routing protocols*, protocols that require each routing host to maintain a map of the network. When the status of a network link changes, broadcast messages notify routers of the change. RIP is suitable for managing LANs; OSPF-2 is suitable for managing very large networks.

EGP and BGP-4 are *exterior routing protocols* suitable for use between autonomous networks. In particular, BGP-4—which is also a distance-vector protocol—is the protocol used on the Internet, and is therefore much used by ISPs. EGP is a rather old protocol that is no longer popular. Table 13.2 summarizes these protocols.

TABLE 13.2: Routing Protocols Supported by Red Hat Linux

Protocol	Interior or Exterior	Type
BGP-4	exterior	distance-vector
EGP	exterior	distance-vector
IS-IS	interior	link-state
OSPF-2	interior	link-state
RIP, RIP-2	interior	distance-vector

Necessary Procedures

This section gives procedures for enabling IP forwarding, specifying routing rules, and disabling dynamic routing.

Enabling IP Forwarding

Unless you enable IP forwarding, a host will not forward IP packets. The likely result is that network operations fail with the message "host unreachable."

You can enable IP forwarding in any of several ways. The simplest is to use Linuxconf (or Netconf). Select Config ➢ Networking ➢ Client Tasks ➢ Routing and Gateways ➢ Defaults from the Linuxconf menu. The Routing Defaults screen appears. To enable IP forwarding, click the Enable Routing button and then click Accept.

If you prefer, you can enable IP forwarding by editing the file /etc/sysctl.conf to include the line

```
net.ipv4.ip_forward=1
```

WARNING In early releases of Red Hat Linux 6.2, Linuxconf does not properly update the /etc/sysctl.conf file. Therefore, under such releases, you cannot use Linuxconf to enable packet forwarding.

Another way to enable IP forwarding is to manipulate the /proc file system. Issue the command

```
echo "1" >/proc/sys/net/ipv4/ip_forward
```

The drawback of this method is that you will have to reissue the command each time you reboot the system.

Using Linuxconf to Specify Routing Rules

To specify routing rules for accessing a network by using Linuxconf, select Config ➤ Networking ➤ Client Tasks ➤ Routing and Gateways ➤ Other Routes to Networks from the Linuxconf menu. The Route to Other Networks screen appears. Specify the destination IP address and (optionally) the network mask of the network. Also specify the IP address of the gateway host on the local network that provides access to the network.

You can similarly specify routing rules for accessing a host. Select Config ➤ Networking ➤ Client Tasks ➤ Routing and Gateways ➤ Other Routes to Hosts from the Linuxconf menu. Unless a host is the only host on its network that you want to access, it's generally more convenient to specify a routing rule for the network than to specify a routing rule for each of the network's hosts.

TIP The file /etc/sysconfig/static-routes holds the network and host routes entered via Linuxconf. You can edit this file directly, if you prefer.

Using the *route* Command to Specify Routing Rules

Rather than use Linuxconf to establish routing rules, you can issue the route command. However, when you reboot the system, you must reestablish routing rules created by using route. Therefore, it's generally much more convenient to use Linuxconf.

To specify a network routing rule by using route, issue a command of the form

```
route add -net ip_address netmask mask_address
↳interface
```

where *ip_address* is the IP address of the network, *mask_address* is the network mask address of the network, and *interface* is the network device by which to access the network. For example, the command

```
route add -net 192.168.1.0 netmask 255.255.255.0 eth0
```

adds a routing rule for the network 192.168.1.0, accessible via interface eth0.

To specify a host routing rule, issue a command of the form

```
route add -host ip_address interface
```

where *ip_address* is the IP address of the host, and *interface* is the network device by which to access the host.

Disabling Dynamic Routing

When using static routing, you should disable the routed daemon. To do so, launch Linuxconf and select Config ➤ Networking ➤ Client Tasks ➤ Routing and Gateways ➤ The Routed Daemon from the Linuxconf menu. The Routed Daemon screen appears. Click the Does Not Export Any Routes (Silent) button and then click Accept.

Exam Essentials

Possess basic familiarity with configuration issues—routing options, IP forwarding, kernel configuration—associated with using Red Hat Linux as a router You should be able to enable/disable IP forwarding, to disable dynamic routing, and to specify routing rules via Linuxconf and the route command. You should also be familiar with, and able to specify, kernel options related to routing.

Key Terms and Concepts

Distance-vector routing protocol A distance-vector protocol is a routing protocol whereby a router informs its neighboring hosts of the contents of its routing table.

Dynamic routing Dynamic routing is a routing technique whereby the contents of routing tables are automatically updated as network conditions change.

Exterior routing protocol An exterior routing protocol is a routing protocol intended for use between autonomous networks.

Forwarding Forwarding is the process whereby packets received on a network interface are routed to the proper outgoing network interface.

Interior routing protocol An interior routing protocol is a routing protocol intended for use within an autonomous network.

Link-state routing protocol A link-state protocol is a routing protocol that maintains a map—or, at least, a partial map—of the network.

Route A route is a path from a source host to a destination host over which packets pass.

Router A router is a system or device that forwards packets along an appropriate route.

Routing   Routing is the process of transporting packets along a route.

Static routing   Static routing is a routing technique whereby changes to routing tables are performed manually.

Sample Questions

1. Which of the following commands could establish a network route?

A. route add -host 192.168.100.0 \
    netmask 255.255.255.0 eth0

B. route add -net 192.168.100.0 \
    netmask 255.255.255.0 eth0

C. route -add host 192.168.100.0 \
    netmask 255.255.255.0 eth0

D. route -add net 192.168.100.0 \
    netmask 255.255.255.0 eth0

Answer: B. The –net argument specifies that the rule is a network rule rather than a host rule. The add flag must be specified as add, not –add.

2. Which of the following disables dynamic routing?

A. echo "0" > /proc/sys/net/ipv4/dynamic_routing

B. Editing /etc/sysconfig/network-scripts

C. The Linuxconf Gated Daemon screen

D. The Linuxconf Routed Daemon screen

Answer: D. The /proc file system does not provide an option for disabling gated, and /etc/sysconfig/network-scripts is a directory, not a file.

3. Which of the following protocols is a popular exterior protocol?

A. BGP-4

B. EGP

C. OSPF-2

D. RIP-2

Answer: A. OSPF-2 and RIP-2 are interior protocols. EGP is no longer popular.

Configuring a Firewall

Chapter 11, "System and Network Security," describes administrative measures intended to protect a system from unauthorized use. In addition to such protective measures—which are implemented at the system level—most system administrators employ additional measures implemented at the network level. One popular measure is the *firewall*, which filters incoming and outgoing packets, allowing only authorized packets to enter and leave a network.

Many sites purchase dedicated hardware units that function as firewalls or firewall/routers. However, Red Hat Linux lets you configure a router that runs on a PC or other platform supported by Red Hat Linux. This section explains basic Linux firewall concepts and how to implement simple firewalls.

Critical Information

A firewall blocks unauthorized packets from entering or leaving a network. Version 2.2 of the Linux kernel includes support for the IPChains facility, which can be used to construct an IP firewall—that is, a firewall that filters TCP/IP packets. Some earlier versions of the Linux kernel supported the ipfwadm facility, a less flexible facility that is now obsolete. Figure 13.2 shows a typical firewall configuration. In the sample configuration, all packets entering and leaving the protected local network must transit the Linux firewall. Based on a set of firewall rules, the firewall blocks suspicious and unauthorized packets.

FIGURE 13.2: A typical firewall

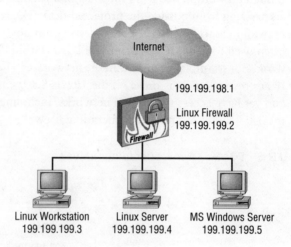

To support a firewall, the Linux kernel must be compiled with the appropriate options:

- Network firewalls
- IP: `firewalling`
- `/proc` file system

The standard Red Hat Linux kernel supports these options. To determine whether a kernel supports the necessary options, check for the file `/proc/net/ip_fwchains`; if this file exists, the options are supported.

TIP Some firewall documentation states that the kernel option IP: always defragment must be configured. This option can now be enabled dynamically by including the line net.ipv4.ip_always_ defrag=1 in the file /etc/sysctl.conf.

Masquerading

Masquerading is closely related to firewalling, and often a Red Hat Linux system is configured to provide both functions. In masquerading, packets leaving a protected network are rewritten to appear as though they originated from the firewall host. Similarly, related packets arriving from outside the protected network are rewritten by the firewall host to specify the actual destination host. Masquerading is often used to conceal the identity of hosts within the protected network. For example, hosts within the network can be assigned private IP addresses—such as those on the 192.168.1.0 Class C network—and yet have access to external networks, including the Internet. Figure 13.3 shows a typical masquerading firewall.

FIGURE 13.3: A masquerading firewall

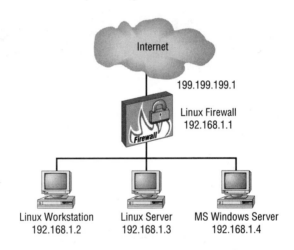

The kernel of a masquerading Linux host should have been compiled with the following options in addition to those required to support firewalling:

- IP: transparent proxy support

- IP: masquerading

- IP: masquerading special modules support

- IP: ipportfw masq support

The standard Red Hat Linux kernel includes these options.

Using the IPChains Facility

The IPChains facility lets you control the progress of IP packets through the Linux kernel. Figure 13.4 shows the kernel packet path.

FIGURE 13.4: The kernel packet path

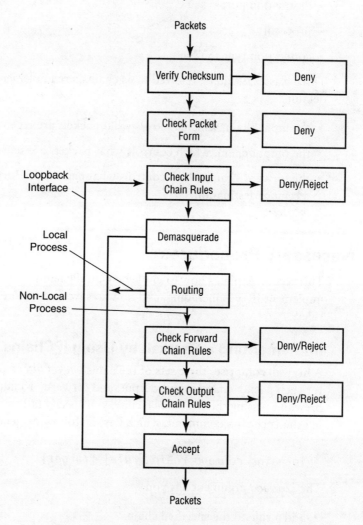

The IPChains facility lets you specify rules that can block, divert, or rewrite IP packets. The rules can distinguish packets based on

- source host or network IP address
- source port
- destination host or network IP address
- destination port
- protocol
- connection type (SYN)

Three classes of filters, referred to as chains, are implemented by default:

- the input chain, which controls what packets are received
- the output chain, which controls what packets are sent
- the forward chain, which controls what packets are forwarded to a remote destination

Necessary Procedures

This section explains how to implement an IPChains firewall, how to implement IP masquerading, and how to save and restore IPChains rules.

Implementing a Firewall by Using IPChains

A firewall comprises three sets of IPChains *packet filter* rules, one set for each packet chain: input, output, and forward. To implement a firewall by using the IPChains facility, you specify filter rules by issuing the ipchains command, which has the following general form:

```
ipchains command chain [rule] [target]
```

The *command* argument lets you

- add a rule to the specified chain

- delete a rule from the specified chain
- delete all rules from the specified chain
- list the rules in the specified chain
- specify a default policy for the specified chain

For example, to list the rules associated with the input chain, issue the command

```
ipchains -L input
```

Similarly, to flush all the rules associated with the output chain, issue the command

```
ipchains -F input
```

Table 13.3 summarizes the values that can be specified for the *command* argument.

TABLE 13.3: IPChains Commands

Command	Description
-A	Appends the specified rule to the end of the specified chain
-D	Deletes the specified rule from the specified chain
-L	Lists rules in the specified chain
-F	Deletes all rules from the specified chain
-P	Sets the default policy of the specified chain to the specified target
-h	Displays command help

Table 13.4 summarizes the values that can be specified for the `target` argument. To specify that the default policy for packets on the input chain is DENY, issue the command

```
ipchains -P input DENY
```

TIP It is generally good practice to set the default policy to DENY. If a packet does not match a rule that specifies some other target, the packet will be denied—that is, discarded. Any omission from the rule set will therefore cause a packet to be discarded; the discarding of packets will likely be noticed and the rule set fixed. If the default policy were ACCEPT, an omission from the rule set would allow inappropriate packets to transit the firewall, possibly leading to a security breach.

TABLE 13.4: IPChains Targets

Target	Description
ACCEPT	Admits the packet.
DENY	Denies the packet without sending an error message to the sender.
REJECT	Denies the packet and sends an error message to the sender.
MASQ	Outgoing packets are rewritten to appear as though they originated from the firewall host. Incoming packets are reverse-masqueraded—that is, rewritten to have the proper destination host.
REDIRECT	Incoming packets are redirected to a port, regardless of the specified packet destination.
RETURN	For a built-in chain, packets are handled by using the default rule for the chain. For a user-defined chain, the packet is sent back to the calling chain.

Table 13.5 summarizes the form of the `rules` argument. Addresses can be specified by using any of several forms. For example, you can specify the source host IP address

```
-s 192.168.1.0
```

or the destination network IP address

```
-d 192.168.1.0/24
```

The /24 specifies that the network mask consists of 24 bits; the associated network address is therefore a Class C network address having a network mask value of 255.255.255.0.

TABLE 13.5: IPChains Rules

Rule	Description
-d *address* [*port*]	Specifies the destination IP address or address and port.
-i *interface*	Specifies the interface at which an input packet was received or to which an output packet is directed.
-j *target*	Specifies the target action.
-p *protocol*	Specifies the protocol (TCP, UDP, ICMP, or ALL).
-s *address* [*port*]	Specifies the source IP address or address and port.
-y	Specifies a TCP SYN packet, used to initiate a connection with a server.

You can specify a port or range of ports with the address. For example, the rule

```
-d 192.168.1.0/24 25
```

specifies a packet, destined for port 25—the SMTP port—of hosts on the 192.168.1.0 network. The more general rule

```
-d 192.168.1.0/24 0:1023
```

specifies a packet destined for any privileged port of a host on the 192.168.1.0 network.

Several special values can be specified in rules. For example, the value any refers to any IP address, as does the value 0/0. Also, you can precede a rule with ! to negate the meaning of the rule. For example, the rule ! -y refers to a packet other than a TCP SYN packet.

You can combine several rules to form a compound rule. For example, the command

```
ipchains -A input -d 192.168.1.0/24 -p UDP -j DENY
```

includes a rule that refers to UDP packets destined for a host on the 192.168.1.0 network; moreover, it specifies that such packets should be discarded. Most IPChains rules include a -j argument that specifies the associated target action.

The ipchains command logs packets if the rule matching the packet includes the -1 flag. The log entries have the source kern (referring to the kernel) and the priority info. So, by default, they're sent to /var/log/messages. For further information on the ipchains command, see its man page.

Implementing Masquerading by Using *ipchains*

Masquerading is a form of Network Address Translation (NAT) that is commonly used to translate private (RFC 1918) IP addresses to the address of the firewall host so that hosts behind the firewall can access exterior networks, including the Internet.

To specify masquerading by using ipchains, add one or more entries specifying the MASQ target to the forward chain. For example, suppose that the 192.168.1.0/24 network is a protected local network and that the interface eth2 is an external interface of the network's firewall host—that is, an interface connected to exterior networks. The command

```
ipchains -A forward -i eth2 -s 192.168.1.0/24 -j MASQ
```

establishes a forwarding rule that masquerades packets originating from the protected network (192.168.1.0/24) appearing on the external interface (eth2).

Special kernel modules support masquerading of commonly used protocols. You should load the necessary modules so that the protocols operate properly. These modules and their associated protocols are

- ip_masq_cuseeme (CUSEEME)

- ip_masq_ftp (FTP)

- ip_masq_irc (IRC)

- ip_masq_quake (Quake)

- ip_masq_raudio (Real Audio)

- ip_masq_vdolive (VDO Live)

Saving and Restoring IPChains Rules

Many system administrators create an /etc/rc.d/rc.firewall script that issues ipchains commands and other commands. Generally, they modify the /etc/rc.d/rc.local script to invoke /etc/rc.d/rc.firewall. This technique for implementing a firewall lets you intersperse comments among the ipchains commands, making it easier to understand and modify the firewall.

However, if you prefer, you can use the ipchains-save and ipchains-restore commands to implement a firewall. The ipchains-save command dumps the current firewall rules to stdout and the ipchains-restore command loads the firewall from stdin. By redirecting stdout to a file, you can cause ipchains-save to dump the current firewall rules to a disk file. The Red Hat Linux 6.2 script /etc/rc.d/init.d/ipchains tests for the existence of a file named /etc/sysconfig/ipchains; if the file exists, the script runs ipchains-restore against the file.

Exam Essentials

Be capable of using ipchains to implement basic firewalling policies
You should be able to use the ipchains command to construct firewall rules. You should also be able to configure IP masquerading and to save and restore IPChains rules.

Key Terms and Concepts

Firewall   A firewall is a system or device that blocks unauthorized traffic from entering or leaving a network.

Masquerading   Masquerading substitutes a specified IP address in place of the IP address found in an IP packet.

Packet filter   A packet filter is a facility for selectively blocking packets that match specified criteria.

Sample Questions

1. The Red Hat Linux firewall facility is implemented by using which of the following commands?

A. The firewall command

B. The ipchains command

C. The ipfwadm command

D. The ipportfw command

Answer: B. The ipfwadm command was supported by some earlier versions of the Linux kernel.

2. To determine whether a Linux kernel supports firewalling, you should check for the existence of which file?

A. /proc/net/ip_always_defrag

B. /proc/net/ip_fwchains

C. /proc/sys/net/ipv4/ip_always_defrag

D. /proc/sys/net/ipv4/ip_fwchains

Answer: B. The existence of ip_fwchains indicates support for firewalling; the ip_always_defrag option should be enabled on systems that provide a firewall.

Index

Note to Reader: In this index, **boldfaced** page numbers refer to primary discussions of the topic; page numbers in *italics* refer to figures.

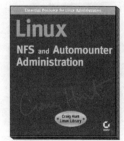